BETWEEN FAITH AND SOCIAL ACTIVISM

Essays in Honour of Fr. George Ehusani

Adonis & Abbey Publishers Ltd
St James House
13 Kensington Square,
London, W8 5HD
United Kingdom

Website: http://www.adonis-abbey.com
E-mail Address: editor@adonis-abbey.com

Nigeria:
Jimmy Carter Street,
Suites C3 – C6 J-Plus Plaza
Asokoro, Abuja, Nigeria
Tel: +234 (0) 7058078841/08052035034

Copyright 2021 © Fr. George Ehusani

British Library Cataloguing-in-Publication Data
A catalogue record for this book is available from the British Library.

ISBN: 9781913976095

The moral right of the author has been asserted.

All rights reserved. No part of this book may be reproduced, stored in a retrieval system or transmitted at any time or by any means without the prior permission of the publisher.

BETWEEN FAITH AND SOCIAL ACTIVISM

Essays in Honour of Fr. George Ehusani

Edited by

Taiwo Abioye
Arua Eke Arua
Anthony Okeregbe,
and Emmanuel Ojeifo

Foreword

Fr. George Ehusani: The Priest as a Social Activist

Jideofor Adibe

It is a privilege to be asked to write a foreword for a book to commemorate the 40th anniversary of the ordination of Fr. George Ehusani, who was my parish priest at the Church of Assumption, Asokoro, Abuja, before he left in early 2013 to concentrate on his Foundation, the Lux Terra Leadership Foundation. When I began worshipping at the parish sometime in 2012 - at the prompting of some acquaintances who talked glowingly of the parish priest as a very brilliant, no-nonsense clergy, I found his way of delivering homilies through power point presentation and question-and-answers of the gospel readings, rather strange. I was more used to a priest delivering his homily after the gospel reading, in a top-down fashion, not homilies being presented as if they were classroom lectures or seminars. However, I quickly realized the model could be an ingenious way of not only encouraging active participation of the parishioners in understanding the gospel readings but also perhaps a subtle way of addressing accusations that Catholic liturgical services could be boring because the parishioners tend to be regarded as depositories while the priest is seen as the sole depositor of biblical wisdom and mysteries.

As I came to know more about Fr Ehusani – from his books, lectures, TV programmes and social engagements - he reminded me more of Liberation Theology - a Christian theological orientation which flowered in Latin America in the 1960s and 1970s, after the Second Vatican Council of 1962-1965. Liberation theologies of various hues have a common thread in evangelisation with social responsibility. In essence, it is a theology which was rooted in priests, especially Catholic clergy in Latin America, consciously taking the side of the poor, the voiceless and the oppressed, while not abandoning their calling as priests. This always raised a fundamental question: how does a priest navigate the trope between liturgy and sacramental ministry on the one hand and commitment to the poor and good governance on the other hand?

In an article in *The New York Times* of May 9, 1971, about Camilo Torres, the Colombian priest who was killed in the mountains of Bucaramanga by Government troops, on February. 15, 1966, four months after joining the guerrillas of the Army of National Liberation,

Maurice Zeitlin, a distinguished Professor of Sociology, wrote: "In the innards of the Roman Catholic Church, an institution which above all has been the rampart of the existing order in Latin America, there has appeared a movement of new priests preaching the gospel of socialist revolution in the language of Christianity."

While the Colombia or the Latin America of the 1960s and 1970s is markedly different from Nigeria of today, there are similarities - the increasing pauperization and alienation of the citizens as well as poor governance by the elite and political class have led to a concomitant radicalization of socially conscious priests. Fidel Castro, the Cuban revolutionary, lawyer and politician who led Cuba from 1959 to 2008 summed this phenomenon as, "the Communists in Latin America have become theologians and the theologians Communists".

Unlike Camilo Torres who discovered Marxism late in his calling as a priest and eventually joined armed revolutionary struggle, Fr. Ehusani is not a Marxist and is unlikely to be involved in an armed agitation. But he belongs to a generation of African priests and theologians who are socially conscious, who insist that Jesus Christ came to transform the whole person – including his or her spiritual, socio-economic and political circumstances, and who refuse to be content with merely preparing poor oppressed souls for heaven.

Radicalized socially conscious priests are as much committed to their priestly vocation as they are to fighting the wider societal structures that they believe impede the work of evangelization. Some will go even further to say that before liberating the souls of the masses, the stomachs of those masses must first be liberated from the rumblings of hunger and that it is a sacred duty to speak the truth to the powers that are responsible for such conditions of the masses.

Born in Okene, Kogi State in 1957, George Ehusani was ordained a priest on August 15, 1981 in Okene, at the age of 23. He later studied at the Holy Apostles' College, Cromwell, Connecticut, USA, where he obtained a Master of Arts degree in Theology, in 1988, and capped it with a Doctor of Ministry from Howard University School of Divinity, Washington DC in 1990. He became the Deputy Secretary General of the Catholic Secretariat of Nigeria (CSN), Lagos, in 1994, and in 2000, became the substantive Secretary-General of the Secretariat, succeeding the irrepressible Fr. (now Bishop) Matthew Hassan Kukah. Fr. Ehusani was appointed Parish Priest of the Church of the Assumption, Asokoro,

Abuja in 2008, where he served until 2013. He had earlier in 2009, established the Lux Terra Leadership Foundation as a training and human development centre for leaders in the Church and the wider Nigerian society. In 1991 Fr. Ehusani staged a memorable one-man protest to call attention to the deplorable condition of service of civil servants, especially schoolteachers in Kogi State.

Fr. Ehusani still serves on the Board of a number of local and international organisations, including being on the Editorial Board of The Guardian Newspapers and being a Member of the Board of Trustees of the Centre for Values in Leadership, and the Nigerian Sodium Study Data and Safety Management Board. He is also a Fellow of the Nigerian Psychological Association.

The crucial questions which essays in this volume seek to answer are: how does Fr. George Ehusani balance his priestly vocation with his social activist passions as a teacher, defender of the voiceless, writer, social commentator, TV personality and musician? And what are the philosophical underpinnings of both his priestly vocation and social activism? I believe the contributions in this book are honest attempts to answer the above questions, as each author sees it, by critically interrogating his engagements in the various tropes he uses to pursue his passions.

Professor Jideofor Adibe

Dept of Political Science, Nasarawa State University, Keffi;
Publisher, Adonis & Abbey Publishers Ltd.

Preface

Between Faith and Social Activism: Essays in Honour of Rev. Fr. George Ehusani is a collection of peer-reviewed papers written in honour of the Reverend Father George Omaku Ehusani on the occasion of the 40th anniversary of his priestly ordination. Fr. George Ehusani is currently the Executive Director, Lux Terra Leadership Foundation, Abuja, a multi-resource and training organisation whose purpose is to expose current and future leaders in both the Church and society to the dynamics of purposeful, visionary, transformative and inspiring servant-leadership. Fr. Ehusani is a theologian, teacher, speaker, poet, composer/musician, human rights activist, social commentator and writer. As his profile shows, Fr. Ehusani has impacted scores of people; young and old, Christian and non-christian who have come in contact with him or have had the privilege of interacting with his numerous essays, books, poems, homilies, reflections and songs on the radio, television, and the internet. Fr. Ehusani has bequeathed an enduring legacy of spiritual uprightness, sacrifice, justice, humility, fair play, honesty, dedication, selfless service and commitment to humanity as a unique creation of God. For this reason, the editors of this book among other academics, priests, and professionals mooted the idea of a collection of essays in honour of Fr. George Ehusani. This collection of essays captures the purview of Fr. Ehusani's prophetic calling, his passion to serve God and man and his radical approach to issues.

Chapter One is titled *"Imagery and Didactics: A Priest's Civic Engagement from the Pulpit."* In this chapter, Taiwo Abioye investigates Ehusani's priestly civic engagements from the pulpit using imagery and didacticism in his sociopolitical writings. The chapter reveals how the church cannot be separated from the people and should be seen as a tool for social emancipation. Using vivid lexical and metaphorical imagery, it foregrounds the insights drawn from the ensuing exploration of the concept of didactic indexation from the platform of Ehusani's priestly Calling. It teaches moral lessons as it warns the country and its leaders of impending danger, exposes the rot in the entire system and admonishes the Nigerian elite to turn away from corruption, from utter insensitivity to and negligence of the people. It concludes that pertinent moral lessons are taught through Ehusani's civic engagements from the pulpit.

Chapter Two features "A Philosophical Appraisal of George Ehusani's African Christian Humanism". Anselm Kole Jimoh and

Stephen Ogbeiye George argue that Ehusani's African Christian humanism (ACH) is an anti-secular, anti-materialist humanism, premised on traditional African and Christian understanding of the dignity and values of the human person that is incessantly accosted with modern forces of dehumanisation. The authors explicate this notion of humanism, critically reviewing the depersonalisation and dehumanisation of the human person occasioned by secularised humanism. Then, they examine Ehusani's thesis of Ọzọvẹhẹ, and finally, conclude that Ehusani's ACH clearly articulates an imperative vision towards the restoration of the eroding dignity and value of the human person. This is in line with Ehusani's call for an alteration in perspective, where he proposes a new vision of reality that is holistic, functional, and humane, an African Christian humanistic value system, that will reprioritise our developmental efforts.

In Chapter Three, "Beyond Aesthetic Appeal to Healing Sounds: An Existentialist Reflection on George Ehusani's Liturgical Music", Anthony Okeregbe presents a new dimension to music, liturgical music and music therapy. The chapter re-establishes the role liturgical music plays in fostering mindfulness, healing and spiritual wellness through a phenomenological analysis of selected songs in Ehusani's musical collection. Ehusani's use of music is seen as therapeutic in a special sense of being a Jungian-logotherapy influenced technique that uses positive affirmations through music or songs to nurture the soul, mind and emotions.

Chapter Four's focus is on "An Expository Analysis of the Human Person and Human Dignity in George Ehusani's Christian Humanism". In this chapter, Phillip Edema argues that challenges signify a negative anthropology of human nature; and thus, have serious moral implications for the dignity of the human person, which affects to a large extent the progress and socio-political development of any society and by extension, leads to a dysfunctional world. Using George Ehusani's Christian humanism – a notion that is hinged upon African traditional heritage in arguing for a holistic, functional and humane community, he suggests an instructive framework for the task of restoring the meaning and wholeness of the human person, community and the entire cosmos. This is because such notion recognises that the life of the human person having been endowed by God, is neither replaceable nor reducible; and that the dignified life of the human person so endowed is itself the basis for coming to terms with the meaning of the entirety of creation.

Chapter Five is titled "From Pastoral Caregiving to Secondary Traumatic Stress: A Discussion of the Potential Risk Factors among Catholic Priests". In this chapter, Richard Ehusani sets out to examine secondary traumatic stress and highlight the potential risk factors for developing secondary traumatic stress among priests. The factors discussed indicate a personal, social, and spiritual cost associated with priestly ministry. The prophetic calling, coupled with the veil of confidentiality under which they work is a burden because they take on trauma and cannot talk about it, while helping others navigate their stress, fear, anger, sadness, and trauma. The paper suggests the need to provide adequate mental health support for priests, the need for specialized training of priests and seminarians in working with trauma as the mental wellbeing of the individual priests and parishioners would mean well for the church, the community and the society.

Chapter Six: Analysing one of the poems in his poetry collection *Flames of Truth*, titled: "Prophetic Imagination," William Orbih in this chapter, "A Critical Look at Father Ehusani's Prophetic Imagination", provides answers to the question: 'What is the exact content of George Ehusani's prophetic imagination?' In other words, what is, as Thomistic philosophy will ask, the efficient and final cause of Ehusani's prophetic imagination? It argues that in the poem "Prophetic Imagination," Ehusani provides us a glimpse into his holistic self and explains his many involvements in the church, in civil society, governance, etc. He concludes by saying that this prophetic imagination is shaped by the richness of the long humanistic tradition of his Christian faith.

In Chapter Seven, "Re-Imagining Leadership to Reclaim the Failing Promise of Nigeria", Pat Utomi examines leadership deficit, poverty indices, religious and social impact, and stunted economic growth as the bane of the Nigerian society. He interrogates good leadership in the 20th century and models of economic development, and observes that Nigeria lags behind in this wise. He concludes by pointing out ways by which the Christian Church and other faith groups can rebuild the future of Nigeria.

Chapter Eight is entitled "Peacebuilding and the Imperative of Ongoing Interfaith Dialogue and Conflict Management". In this chapter, Anthony Azuwike focuses on the fact that Nigeria, a classic example of a multi-ethnic, multi-religious, multi-cultural nation, has known its fair share of conflict, often occasioned by an admixture of social, cultural and extremist religious factors of bias and intolerance. Unfortunately, this ethno-religious affiliation often interferes with the social and political life of the nation, thus consistently raising the question of the place of religion in the national constitutional order. This makes it imperative that every possible avenue must be explored in sustaining interfaith dialogue at all levels. Such will ensure that conflict is mitigated, and in the event of conflict, society is not caught off-guard as it will leverage the peace and understanding already built in time of peace in managing the conflicts that may arise. The paper suggests how the country can engage in a robust interfaith dialogue that will build peace, mitigate and manage conflict.

In Chapter Nine, "The Representation of Social Activism in George Ehusani's Writings", Abiodun Jombadi examines subjective stances and ideological leanings in George Ehusani's selected writings. The qualitative analytical approach brings to the fore the wider social, psycho-spiritual and political context within which the texts are constructed. van Dijk's socio-cognitive approach of critical discourse analysis unravels the ways ideologies are typically expressed and reproduced in the samples and also showcases the way identities are socially and emotionally constructed and social actors are represented.

David Igbokwe in Chapter Ten, "Psychospiritual Healing as Panacea for the Societal and Psychological Distress in Nigeria", argues that the social and psychological distress experienced for decades by many Nigerians can best be addressed by a psychospiritual healing that integrates and uses harmony restoration as a tool to ensure complete harmony and wholesomeness in individual citizens. The author recommends psychospiritual healing of depressed and traumatized Nigerians, following the example of Father Ehusani and the Psychospiritual Institute of the Lux Terra Leadership Foundation. The government must also assist in this regard by ensuring the psychological and general well-being of all Nigerians, towards meeting Goal Three of the United Nations (2015) Sustainable Development Goals (SDGs), namely, good health and well-being.

Chapter Eleven. In this chapter, "A Digital Priest in a Digital Society: Exploring the Persona of Rev. Fr. George Ehusani", Justine Dyikuk posits that modern culture, with its trappings of advances in Information and Communications Technology (ICT) and irresistible smartphones' Internet-based communication has made ministry challenging. It is within this popular culture that the Catholic priest is called to ministry; to navigate between faith and culture in his society. He investigates Fr. Ehusani's efforts in combining his vocation as a priest with his engagement with the print and electronic media, commitment to the Word and Sacraments, being media-savvy and willingness to be relevant digitally as factors that keep him afloat in a digital society. It recommends mentoring the young in media and ministry and further documentation of useful resources as helpful tips for remaining relevant to contemporary times.

Rex Emmanuel Odoemenam in "Truth in the Lens of Trilogy: George Ehusani's Poesies" reviews Ehusani's Truth Trilogy: *Fragments of Truth* (1997), *Petals of Truth* (1998), and *Flames of Truth* (2006).

Editors

Table of Content

Foreword
Jideofor Adibe
.... iv

Preface
.... vii

Contributors
.... xv

A Profile of Father George Omaku Ehusani
.... xiv

Chapter One: Imagery and Didactics: A Priest's Civic Engagements from the Pulpit
Taiwo Abioye
.... 23

Chapter Two: A Philosophical Appraisal of George Ehusani's African Christian Humanism
Anselm Kole Jimoh and Stephen Ogbeiye
.... 47

Chapter Three: Beyond Aesthetic Appeal to Healing Sounds: An Existential Reflection on George Ehusani's Liturgical Music
Anthony Okeregbe
.... 67

Chapter Four: An Expository Analysis of the Human Person and Human Dignity in George Ehusani's Christian Humanism
Philip Edema
.... 89

Chapter Five: From Pastoral Caregiving to Secondary Traumatic Stress: A Discussion of the Potential Risk Factors among Catholic Priests
Richard Ehusani
.... 111

Chapter Six: A Critical Look at George Ehusani's Prophetic Imagination
William Ikhianosimhe Orbih
....123

Chapter Seven: Re-Imagining Leadership to Reclaim the Failing Promise of Nigeria
Pat Utomi
....143

Chapter Eight: Peacebuilding and the Imperative of Ongoing Interfaith Dialogue and Conflict Management
Anthony Azuwike
....159

Chapter Nine: A Critical Analysis of Social Activism in George Ehusani's Writings
Abiodun Jombadi
....181

Chapter Ten: Psychospiritual Healing as Panacea to the Societal and Psychological Distress in Nigeria
David O. Igbokwe
....201

Chapter Eleven: A Digital Priest in a Digital Society: Exploring the Persona of Rev. Fr. George Ehusani
Justine John Dyikuk
....221

Chapter Twelve: Truth in the Lens of Trilogy: George Ehusani's Poesies
Rex Emmanuel Odoemenam
....235

Chapter Thirteen: Rev. Fr. George Ehusani: The Torch Bearer
Andrew E. Zamani
....245

Afterword: Fr. George Ehusani: A Tribute
....255

Index
....258

Contributors

Taiwo ABIOYE is a Professor of English, Visiting Professor at Veritas University, Abuja and Research Professor at Lux Terra Leadership Foundation, Abuja. Her teaching and research focus on interdisciplinary knowledge, and its discourses include Stylistics, Applied Linguistics, Women Issues and English Literacy. She has published widely in these areas, including several on Fr. George Ehusani and his literary output. One such publication is *Language and Ideology in George Ehusani's Writings* (2011) and reprinted as *Language and the Moral Imperative in George Ehusani's Writings* (2019). She is a member of the Nigerian Academy of Letters. tbunmiabioye@gmail.com

Anselm Kole JIMOH is a Catholic priest of the Diocese of Auchi, Edo State. An Associate Professor of Philosophy and currently the Head of Department of Philosophy at SS. Peter and Paul Catholic Major Seminary, Bodija, Ibadan, Oyo State. He specialised in Epistemology, with special interest in African Epistemology. Some of his publications include *Certitude and Doubt: A Study Guide in Epistemology* (2013, Revised 2nd Edition in 2017), "An African Theory of Knowledge" (Palgrave Macmillan, 2017), "Reconstructing a Fractured Indigenous Knowledge System" (Synthesis Philosophica 33 (1), 2018), and "Justice and the Othered Minority: Lessons from African Communalism" (Springer, 2019).

Stephen OGBEIYE is a Catholic priest of the diocese of Uromi, Edo State, with a Licentiate in Philosophy from the Pontifical Urbaniana University, Rome (2019). He is a lecturer in the Department of Philosophy, SS Peter and Paul Catholic Major Seminary, Bodija, Ibadan. jimohanselm@gmail.com

Anthony OKEREGBE is a Senior Lecturer in Philosophy, Department of Philosophy and affiliate, Institute of African and Diaspora Studies, University of Lagos. A University of Edinburg Catalyst Fellow 2019, his teaching and research focus is on Existential Philosophy and Contemporary African Philosophy. He is a faculty member of Lux Terra Leadership Foundation, Abuja, Nigeria and Visiting Member, Editorial Board of *The Guardian*, Lagos. He is published widely in books and journals, including *Rev. Fr. George Ehusani in Conversation, Vol. 2: The Passion to Serve Humanity* (2011). tonyokeregbe@yahoo.co.uk

Philip Akporduado EDEMA is a Senior Lecturer at Department of Philosophy and Religious Studies, Augustine University, IIara-Epe, Lagos, Nigeria. His teaching, competence and research interests cover applied ethics, metaphysics, Karol Wojtyla's personalism, philosophical anthropology, socio-political philosophy, African philosophy, Logic and philosophy of peace studies. He has published several papers in reputable outlets that include *A Complementarity Reflection on Human Interest and Common Good in Africa: Nigeria's Ghana-Must-Go & South Africa's Xenophobic Attack Examples. (Brill Leiden, 2020).* philip.edema@augustineuniversity.edu.ng

Richard EHUSANI is a Catholic priest from the Diocese of Lokoja, Nigeria. He was ordained priest in 2007 after his formation at the Seminary of Saints Peter and Paul, Bodija, Ibadan. He holds a Bachelor of Arts degree in Philosophy (University of Ibadan, 2002); a Bachelor of Theology (Pontifical Urbaniana University, Rome, 2006); a Master of Arts degree in Theology (Creighton University, Omaha - Nebraska, USA, 2017); a Master of Science degree in Psychology (California Southern University, Costa Mesa - California, USA, 2018); and a Doctor of Philosophy in Psychology (Walden University, Minneapolis – Minnesota, USA, 2021). He is a member of the American Psychological Association and a lifetime member of the Golden Key International Honor Society. He has been recently appointed to the Faculty team of the Psycho-Spiritual Institute of Lux Terra Leadership Foundation, with campuses in Nairobi, Kenya, and Abuja, Nigeria. richardehusani@yahoo.com

William ORBIH is a priest of the Catholic Archdiocese of Abuja and currently a Ph.D. student of theology at the University of Notre Dame, Indiana, USA. He has done prior studies in the areas of philosophy, theology, religious studies and peace studies. His present fields of scholarly interest include African literary studies, History of Christian Theology and World Religion. worbih@nd.edu

Pat UTOMI is a professor of Political Economy and a member of Faculty of the Pan Atlantic University who has garnered an avalanche of accolades worldwide. He is a distinguished scholar, a renowned author, pioneering civil society leader and founder of the *Centre for Values in Leadership*. He is also a member of the Board of Trustees of the Lux Terra Leadership Foundation, established by Rev. Fr. George Ehusani. Utomi's concern for the leadership deficit in Nigeria and his desire to turn things around propelled him, at some point, to run for the office of the President of Nigeria. The wellbeing of Nigeria and Nigerians continues to be his abiding passion. putomi@lbs.edu.ng

Anthony AZUWIKE is a Catholic priest ordained in 2001 for the Diocese of Issele-Uku, Nigeria. He holds a Bachelor of Arts degree in Philosophy from the University of Ibadan, Nigeria (1997), Bachelor of Theology from Pontifical Urban University, Rome (2001), Masters degree in Education (Leadership and Administration) from Christian Brothers University, Memphis in Tennessee, USA (2008), Bachelor of Laws (LLB) from the University of Southampton, England (2014), Master of Laws (LLM), (2016) and Doctor of Juridical Science degree (SJD) (2017), both from Emory University School of Law, Atlanta, USA. He was called to the Nigerian Bar in 2018. He is currently pioneering efforts towards establishing the Justice Chike Idigbe Faculty of Law at Veritas University (Nigeria's Catholic University), Abuja. frokechukwu@yahoo.com

Abiodun JOMBADI lectures at the Department of Linguistics, African & European Languages, Kwara State University, Malete, Nigeria. His research interest focuses on (critical) discourse analysis, pragmatics, computer-mediated discourse and syntax. He has published scholarly articles in *New Horizons in Nigerian Languages* (LAP LAMBERT), *International Journal of Novel Research in Education and Learning* (IJNREL), *Springboard Journal* (Unilorin Press), *The Achievers' Journal* (ICI), *LASU Journal of Humanities* (LJH), etc. He is the author of *Practical Spoken English* (Artitude) and *Basic Studies in English* (Olad). He is a co-editor of *International Journal of Entrepreneurship Innovation & Management* (IJEIM), an international open access journal. jombadi_abraham@yahoo.co.uk

David IGBOKWE is a Licenced Clinical Psychologist. He is a Senior Lecturer in Psychology at Baze University Abuja and Visiting Senior Lecturer at Nile University of Nigeria, Abuja. He previously taught at Covenant University for more than a decade and has published widely in high impact local and international outlets. He has served as a Stress Counsellor with the World Health Organisation (WHO), Nigeria Country Office, Abuja. davidigbokwe@yahoo.com

Justine John DYIKUK is an author, journalist and researcher. He holds a Bachelor of Philosophy from the Pontifical Urbanian University, Rome and a Bachelor of Theology from the University of Jos. He bagged a Diploma in Pastoral/Communication Studies from the Catholic Institute of West Africa, Port Harcourt and a Master of Arts in Pastoral/Communication Studies from the University of Calabar. He is the Editor-in-Chief of Bauchi Caritas Catholic Newspaper and Director of Communications, Bauchi Diocese where he blogs and freelances. He is currently a lecturer in the Department of Mass Communication, University of Jos, Nigeria. justinejohndyikuk@gmail.com.

Rex Emmanuel ODOEMENAM is a poet, novelist and playwright. He is the author of "Far Together: Seventh Gulp", "Weeping Shadows" and many other creative works published on various platforms. He is the founder of Confluence of Future Arts and lives quietly in the city of Abuja. orexemma@gmail.com

Andrew ZAMANI is the immediate past President of the Nigerian Psychological Association and Professor of Clinical Psychology at the Nasarawa State University, Keffi, Nigeria. He is the current Director of the Institute of Governance and Development Studies at the same University and member, Executive Committee of the Pan African Psychology Union and the World Association of Cultural Psychiatry. His research interests cover psychological stress, trauma, as well as culture and mental illness. zamandeza@gmail.com

Hyacinth Eme Ichoku is a Catholic priest and a Professor of Development Microeconomics with primary interest in Health Economics. Until his appointment as the Vice-Chancellor of Veritas University Abuja in 2018, he was a Professor in the Department of Economics at the University of Nigeria, Nsukka (UNN), where he taught Microeconomics, Econometrics and Public Finance for many years.

A Profile of Father George Omaku Ehusani

Fr. Emmanuel Ojeifo

Rev. Fr. George Ehusani is a priest of the Catholic Diocese of Lokoja, Nigeria. He is the Founder and Executive Director of Lux Terra Leadership Foundation – an institute committed to the professional training and ethical formation of present and future leaders of the Church and Society in Nigeria. He is also the Founder and Faculty Member of the Psycho-Spiritual Institute (PSI) with campuses in Nairobi, Kenya, and Abuja, Nigeria. The Institute which was established to promote the integration of Psychotherapy and Christian Spirituality in English speaking African countries, is affiliated to the Catholic University of Eastern Africa (CUEA), for the award of master's degree in Psycho-Spiritual Therapy. The Abuja campus of the Institute in partnership with Nasarawa State University, runs short training programmes on Psycho-Trauma Healing to equip a wide range of professionals and volunteers with basic skills to support trauma victims.

Fr. Ehusani was born on December 6, 1957 in Okene, Kogi State. He was raised a Catholic by his parents, although his grandmother who was a pioneer Catholic in Okene, played an influential role in his religious upbringing. It was the heroic life of Christian witnessing of his grandmother as well as his admiration for Rev. Fr. Alexius Makozi, his cousin who later became his bishop, that influenced his decision to become a priest. From his youth, George distinguished himself in peer leadership such that at the age of 16 he became President of the Young Catholic Students both in his secondary school and in the Diocese of Lokoja.

He graduated from Secondary School in 1975 and applied for admission to the major seminary under the Diocese of Lokoja. He was admitted and in October of the same year, he resumed his priestly formation at Saints Peter and Paul Catholic Major Seminary Bodija, Ibadan, for his studies in Philosophy. On completing his studies in Philosophy in 1978, he was sent to Saint Augustine's Major Seminary, Jos, where he had his theological formation. George was ordained a priest on August 15, 1981 in Okene, by Most Reverend Alexius Makozi, Bishop of Lokoja Diocese. He was 23 years old. His first posting as a priest was to his home parish of Christ the King Okene where he served as Assistant Parish Priest. In 1984, he was posted to the Teacher Training College in Ogori/Magongo as a Teacher and Chaplain. After a few years of teaching and pastoral ministry at the College in the then Ogori and Magongo parish, Fr. Ehusani proceeded to the United States of America for advanced studies. He studied first at the Holy Apostles' College, Cromwell, Connecticut, where he obtained a Master of Arts degree in Theology, in 1988, and thereafter at Howard University School of Divinity, Washington DC, where he obtained a Doctor of Ministry degree in 1990. His doctoral dissertation titled "'Ozovehe:' An African Christian Humanism won the award of the best dissertation of the year at the Howard University Divinity School.

On his return to Lokoja Diocese, Father Ehusani was appointed Editor of *The Light* – the monthly Catholic Newspaper of Lokoja Diocese. At this time, Father Ehusani's passion for social justice and equity had become quite visible. It is on record that he staged a one-man protest during the heyday of the military regime to call attention to the poor condition of service of civil servants, especially schoolteachers in Kogi State. In 1994, he became Deputy Secretary General of the Catholic Secretariat of Nigeria (CSN), Lagos, and together with Father Hassan Kukah, the Secretary General, were widely seen as the leading moral voice of the Catholic Church in the politics of the nation under the military regimes of Generals Ibrahim Babangida and Sani Abacha.

During this time, Father Ehusani was reckoned nationally for his fiery Newspaper articles that were published almost on a weekly basis, where he challenged the military rulers of the day to quit the stage. He was also a key player in the civil society campaign for a return to democracy that eventually happened in 1999.

In the year 2000, Father Ehusani took over from Fr. Matthew Hassan Kukah (now Bishop) as Secretary General until February 2007. During his time as Secretary General, Fr. Ehusani played a key role in the construction and relocation of the Catholic Secretariat of Nigeria from Lagos to Abuja, the Federal Capital Territory.

At the end of his service at the Catholic Secretariat of Nigeria, he took a sabbatical year from 2007 to 2008 and spent it working at *Misereor*, the Social Development department of the German Catholic Bishops Conference. On his return to Nigeria in 2008, Father Ehusani was appointed by Archbishop John Onaiyekan (now Cardinal) as Parish Priest of Church of the Assumption, Asokoro, Abuja, where he served until February 2013.

In 2009, Father Ehusani established the Lux Terra Leadership Foundation, as a training outfit and human development resource centre for leaders in the Church and society in Nigeria. For several years before then, he served as a Faculty Member of the Haggai Institute for Advanced Leadership Training, whose leading campuses are located in Hawaii and in Singapore. He continues to serve on the Board of a number of local and international organisations, including the Editorial Board of *The Guardian* Newspapers, the Board of Trustees of the Centre for Values in Leadership, and the Nigerian Sodium Study Data and Safety Management Board. He is also a Fellow of the Nigerian Psychological Association.

A theologian, teacher, poet, human rights defender, social commentator as well as an amateur musician, George Ehusani has published numerous books and journal articles, and given several Conference papers, covering a wide range of issues, from the Dynamics of Justice and Peace to the Challenge of Leadership, and from Christian Anthropology to the Imperative of Psycho-Spiritual Integration. He runs two weekly programmes on national television, namely: "Reflections with Father George Ehusani," and "Sunday Homilies."

Father Ehusani is a pioneer in the deployment and use of contemporary digital interactive media for homily delivery. His innovative method of preaching which employs the use of PowerPoint and question and answer format in line with the Socratic dialectic method of knowledge production and delivery, is a sharp departure from the traditional approach to homily delivery in the Catholic Church. However, it has played a key role in his effort to open up the treasury of God's word for the spiritual nourishment and doctrinal edification of the People of God.

Father George Ehusani is recognised in Nigeria as a prominent moral voice and regular advocate for equity, and the justice that makes for peace, unity, dialogue and human solidarity, using both the traditional electronic and print media outlets, as well as social media platforms. His leadership formation programmes, his pioneering psycho-trauma healing training workshops, his justice and peace advocacy, as well as his inter-religious dialogue initiatives, have over the years been widely acknowledged, such that he is the recipient of numerous awards, including the prestigious Konrad Adenauer Stiftung Prize for International Development, which was conferred in 2017.

Father George Ehusani has gathered a wide readership and followership, not only in Nigeria, but also in the international community. Millions of people watch his TV programmes on African Independent Television and Lumen Christi Television, as well as via his online platforms.

Among his published book titles are the following: *An Afro-Christian Vision – Ozovehe: Towards a More Humanized World* (American University Press, Maryland, USA, 1991); *The Politics of Population Control* (Ahmadu Bello University Press, 1992); *The Social Gospel* (Ambassador's Publication, 1993); *A Prophetic Church* (Pauline Publications, 1996); *Fragments of Truth* (Poetry) (Kraftgroit Books, Ibadan, 1997); *Petals of Truth* (Poetry) (Kraftgroit Books, 1998); *Nigeria: Years Eaten By the Locust* (Kraftgroit Books, 2002); *Gospel Reflections for our Time* (Pauline Publications Ibadan, 2004); *Flames of Truth* (Poetry) (Kraftgroit Books, 2006); *Conversation with Fr. George Ehusani* vol. 1 (Lux Terra Leadership Foundation, 2011); *Conversation with Fr. George Ehusani* vol. 2 (Lux Terra Leadership Foundation, 2011); *A Word for the Day* (Lux Terra Leadership Foundation, 2020).

CHAPTER ONE

Imagery and Didactics: A Priest's Civic Engagements from the Pulpit

Taiwo Abioye

1. Introduction

Reverend Father George Ehusani means many things to many people. He is a priest, teacher/lecturer, poet, speaker, songwriter, musician, social commentator and writer. He served as Deputy Secretary-General and, later, Secretary-General of the Catholic Secretariat of Nigeria from 1994 to 2007. Between 2007 and 2008, he spent his sabbatical year at the Development Agency of the German Bishops Conference. And from 2008 to 2013, he served as Parish Priest of the Catholic Church of the Assumption, Asokoro, Abuja. He is the Executive Director of Lux Terra Leadership Foundation, an outfit for the training of future leaders of the Church and society in Nigeria. In 2012, he established the Psycho-Spiritual Institute (PSI), with its first study centre in Nairobi, Kenya, to train experts in psycho-spiritual therapy for English-speaking African countries. The Institute, an affiliate of the Catholic University of East Africa, Nairobi awards a Master's degree in Psycho Spiritual Therapy ("Ehusani: Priest, gentleman and scholar " at 35...*https://guardian.ng/opinion/ehusani-priest-gentleman-and-scholar-at-35/*).

Jegede (2019, pp. 7) describes Ehusani (in the foreword he wrote in *Language and the Moral Imperative in George Ehusani's Writings*) as "... a remarkable, greatly talented, versatile, enigmatic, yet simple, easy-going, but very focused and firm Nigerian and reverend gentleman, Father Omaku George Ehusani...a theologian, teacher, speaker, poet, musician, human rights activist, social commentator and writer of numerous journals and newspaper articles."

Ojeifo (2016) also has this to say about him:

> Father Ehusani has spent his life touching other people's lives positively and helping thousands of young people to discover the meaning and purpose of their lives. His power-packed homilies, wise counsels and spiritual guidance have transformed the lives of many people. As a human rights activist and fiery writer, Father Ehusani is one of the most gripping clinical analysts of the Nigerian condition. His book, *Nigeria: Years Eaten by the Locust*, chronicles the many provocative essays and biting satires that he published in several Nigerian newspapers at the height of the most brutal military regime in Nigeria

2. Exploration of Related Literature

Rev. Fr. George Ehusani sees himself as:

> ... a priest who has a prophetic calling to discern evil and to denounce it, in order to save the people as individuals and as a corporate entity of the unwholesome consequences of such evil. I recognize that as Scripture says, I shall be held responsible if I remain silent and refuse to speak out as I watch in broad daylight a band of misguided professional politicians and a gang of shameless sycophants... (Ehusani, 2006).

We are thus not surprised that:

> *A Prophetic Church* (1996, 2003) is a wake-up call for a refocusing of Christian values and a definite commitment towards the realization of the prophetic Church. In true Juvenalian tradition, Ehusani presents a forceful and compelling argument for truth, social transformation, love, trust, justice and equity. He advocates an end to mere pontification and, in typical Ehusanian style, calls for mass action against societal ills (Abioye, 2019, p. 19).

In the same book, Ehusani advocates that the Church's social teaching must be seen as a tool for social emancipation, presenting the Church, the prophetic Church, as the conscience of a nation. He agonizes over the fact that majority of Nigerians "eke out a miserable existence on the edge of human society" (p. 21) while "there is no social security of any form for poor people. There are no social benefits of any kind for our numerous unemployed people..." (p. 21).

He further argues that:

> The Nigerian environment itself is utterly distressed. Public property and utilities are treated with carelessness, apathy and neglect. The roads are death traps…Virtually all public institutions are in the same state of distress as the roads. Hospitals lie fallow and overgrown with weeds due to disuse. This is not because Nigerians are no longer sick. It is because there is no money to run the hospitals, to buy drugs, and to pay the doctors and nurses sufficiently… (p. 22).
>
> Side by side with this state of near-destitution of the majority, however, is the affluence and conspicuous consumption of a few super-rich Nigerians whose wealth and privilege have multiplied to about the same degree as the misery of the masses (p. 23).
>
> What is wrong today is not only the manifestation of gross social inequalities but the fact that dubious values now form the predominant aspiration of people in the society… A person's character no longer means much to many in our society. It is not who you are, but what you have that matters these days. And it does not seem to matter how you acquired what you have (p. 25).

He concludes in the same book that the case with Nigeria "is clearly a case of impoverishment, not poverty" (my emphasis, p. 19). Thus, for Ehusani, his "constituency", the Church, cannot be separated from the people. The people need the Church for social relevance and social change. Even though Ehusani wrote this book in 1996, it is instructive that it is still topical and relevant in 2021. This makes it possible and exciting to investigate his priestly civic engagements from the platform of the pulpit.

A lot has been written about Fr. George Ehusani in the print and electronic media and in scholarly publications. For instance, Abioye investigated "stylistic devices, pragmatic functions, and resourcefulness of rhetorical questions" (Abioye, 2008); and "Language, metaphor and ideology in George Ehusani's Writings" (Abioye, 2011, 2019). Fr. Ehusani has written scores of books and articles and presented many homilies (sermons or messages). They include, among others, the yearly *New Year Prayers;* an anthology of poems: *Fragments of Truth, Flames of Truth, Petals of Truth, (The Truth Trilogy)* and "Reflections". He equally has many videos on YouTube and a collection of songs/gospel CDs. Therefore, this chapter examines how, as a priest, Ehusani has used imagery and didactics in his civic engagements over the last 40 years since his ordination. For this purpose, two books and 11 articles, in which imagery and didactics are intertwined, are analysed to highlight the messages of his civic engagements.

3. Imagery

Image and imagery are used interchangeably in this paper. Llorens (2003) explains that demarcating "image" and "imagery" conceptually is not easy. Imagery seems to be everywhere and nowhere in particular. It is often conflated with other commonly used terminology (figurative language, symbol, metaphor, etc.); the boundaries are fuzzy. Llorens (2003, p. 2) further argues that "image and imagery are among the most widely used and poorly understood terms in poetic theory, occurring in so many different contexts that it may well be impossible to provide any rational, systematic account of their usage". *The Princeton Encyclopaedia of Poetry and Poetics* (2012) further defines imagery as referring to "images produced in mind by language, whose words may refer either to experiences which could produce physical perceptions, if the reader were to have those experiences or to the sense impressions themselves" (p. 560).

According to Abrams (1999), "Imagery" (that is, "images" taken collectively) is used to signify all the objects and qualities of sense perception referred to in a poem or other work[s] of literature, whether by literal description, by allusion, or in the vehicles (the secondary references) of its similes and metaphor. In illustrating the usage of imagery, he also avers that "imagery is used, more narrowly, to signify only specific descriptions of visible objects and scenes, especially if the description is vivid and particularised... Commonly, in recent usage, imagery signifies figurative language, especially the vehicles of metaphors and simile" (p. 121).

Abrams (1999) further explains and describes imagery. According to him, the term "image" should not be taken to imply a visual reproduction of the object referred to. Some readers experience visual images and some do not; and among those who do, the explicitness and details of the pictures vary greatly. Also, "imagery" in this usage includes not only visual sense qualities, but also qualities that are auditory, tactile (touch), thermal (heat and cold), olfactory (smell), gustatory (taste), and kinesthetic (sensations of movement).

To Eyoh, imagery is a "mental picture created through words and the imaginative faculty, manifesting itself in various figures of speech. The mental and imaginative faculties, as well as feeling, are central to the study and efficacy of imagery in a work of art" (2012, p. 1). The concept of imagery is a traditional element of poetry, prose and drama, constituting an essential stylistic tool in the hands of writers. Imagery has also been described as a fundamental and omnipresent constituent of the mental life of human beings, cognitive of prerequisite symbolization and thought (Eyo, 1997; Yeibo, 2012). The study of the poetic function thus offers a window into the cognitive semiotics of the magnetic mind (Brandt & Brandt, 2005, p. 117).

In this chapter, imagery refers to the use of figurative language that evokes the five senses of hearing/sound (auditory), touch (tactile), taste (gustatory), sight (visual), smells, fragrances and odour (olfactory). Many African poets/writers draw images from their local environment to pass across their messages, and J. P. Clark epitomizes this in some of his poems, such as "Night Rain", "Abiku", "Streamside Exchange", "Ibadan" and "Fulani Cattle". His writings depict the African landscape from the deserts of Northern Nigeria to the riverine Niger-Delta region, emphasizing, ironically, the poverty in the oil-rich but materially poor Niger-Delta and his rich Ijaw culture, legends and folktales. Wole Soyinka, Nobel Laureate in Literature, uses powerful imagery to depict the Yoruba pantheon of gods such as Ogun and Sango and dense and proverbial language portraying his colourful Yoruba culture. Thus, in their endeavour to express their ideas effectively, African writers choose a language that enables them to see, hear, taste, touch or smell what they are saying. So, when readers experience what the writers are expressing, the message is better understood (Chege, 2016). Thus, the analysis of the extant works of George Ehusani exemplifies and textualizes the concept of imagery and didactics drawing from the preceding explorations.

4. Didactics

On didactic literature, Abrams (1999) gives a detailed background meaning and usage(s) of the term. As a prominent figure in the classificatory paradigms of literary terms, his view is apposite in this work. According to him,

> ... The adjective "didactic," which means "intended to give instruction," is applied to works of literature that are designed to expound a branch of knowledge, or else to embody, in imaginative or

fictional form, a moral, religious, or philosophical doctrine or theme. Such works are commonly distinguished from essentially imaginative works (sometimes called "mimetic" or "representational") in which the materials are organized and rendered... (p. 65).

Didacticism is a valuable tool in the hand of an African writer for passing their message across to their readers. This is crucial because, in most African settings, the essence of storytelling is for moral values. In some other instances, stories – verbal or written – are used for making critical comments on sociopolitical and moral/ethical issues in society. For instance, if a married person exhibits societally unethical attitudes in a marriage, people have ways of making jest of such a person with the sole aim of correcting the behaviour. Awuzie's understanding of this fact informed the explanation given below:

> One of the most fascinating debates over the years in the criticism of African literature is the argument that it is a literature of didacticism. This is because, like Chinese literature and some indigenous Indian literatures, African literature aims at informing and correcting some of the ills facing the African society. Even though African literature has been said to have borrowed so much from European literary culture, especially in the areas of form and language, didacticism cannot be said to be one of those concepts that African literature inherited from the European literary culture. It is important to note, therefore, that didacticism in African literature is rather a concept that has its root in African oral tradition and [it] is employed in the written African literature (2012, p. 159).

Dada (2019) counters the accusation by western critics that African literature is monolithic, lacking in aesthetic beauty. In his view, the deployment of didactic elements in African literature is appropriate. Many western critics, standing on their altar of hegemonic prescriptivism, denigrate the didacticism of African literature. Of course, they use their cultural standards to measure Africa's. This has led to fierce contentions between western critics and their African counterparts. Theories like postmodernism and deconstruction were developed as counter-reactions, illustrating the need for culture-informed perspectives. Therefore, Dada continues:

> The African writer employs African oral traditional form in his writing which, as a matter of fact, includes didacticism. This is because when a

story is to be told in a traditional African society, a lot of traditional African oral "ingredients", such as proverbs, songs, symbols, etc. come into play but these are not usually left loose as individual concepts; they are usually tied together with another of African oral form, *didacticism*, [italics, mine] (p. 60).

The relevance of morality in African writing is corroborated by Okonkwo (2015) in an essay entitled *The African writer as a teacher*. He submits that the African writer imbues his work with themes that address the socio-political, religious and economic necessities of the African society. "The African writer", he continues, "confers relevance and truth on his/her work by sourcing data from an authentic African experience and also makes teaching Africans" ethics and morality collectively woven in didacticism (p. 161). Awuzie also adds:

Didacticism takes different forms and can easily be contained in a story irrespective of the nature of the problem the writer aims at correcting through his story and irrespective of the kind of European form the writer imports to tell his story... what a European critic may call "realism"—a literary ideology popularised by the French writer, Emile Zola, in his essay, "The Experimental Novel"—an African critic may see as didactic (p. 162).

Evolving studies have shown that the African concept of didacticism is all-encompassing (Akporobaro, 2005). This is because of the belief that African stories would have nothing to teach, educate or inform the reader if the narratives do not pick from the realities of the African society or if it does not draw from its environment (Okonkwo, 2015). While investigating Fr. George Ehusani's writings, this chapter would foreground the insights drawn from the ensuing exploration of the concept of didactic indexation.

5. Civic Engagement

Civic engagement, according to Adler (2005), is a widely used term with little consensus on a specific and consistent definition; the literature offers a range of meanings that encompass individual and collective civil and political participation. "Throughout psychology, education, and political science literature" (p. 7), Adler continues:

Civic engagement is referred to as community service, activism, volunteerism, social action, and political participation. One common factor among most definitions is that civic engagement is performed by a citizen and, his or her actions, whether individual or collective, interact with society, and more often address the problems or concerns of the public (2005, p. 7).

Civic engagement has been described by Ehrlich (2000) as working to make a difference in the civic life of communities and developing the combination of knowledge, skills, values, and motivations to make that difference. It means promoting the quality of life in a community through both political and non-political processes. Civic values and attitudes have been adjudged as some of the most commonly assessed areas of civic learning (Keen, 2009). Civic values include dispositions such as respect for freedom and dignity, empathy, open-mindedness, tolerance, justice, promoting equality, integrity and responsibility to a larger good (National Task Force, 2012). Other conceptualizations have included involvement in programmes to clean up the environment, interest in influencing political policy and decision making (Lott & Eagan, 2011). Amnå (2012, p. 14) also asserts that "the term civic engagement is often used to indicate the social, civic, and political dimensions of engaged citizenship".

Civic engagement, in the view of Flanagan and Wray-Lake (2011, p. 37), refers to:

> ...involvement in one's community, nation, or world. Among adolescents, these actions take a vast array of forms – being active in community-based organization, volunteering to provide a service to a group in need, engaging in extracurricular activities that benefit the school community, challenging unjust practices such as unequal funding of schools...working with fellow citizens to build intergroup understanding and promote civil rights, and staying informed about issues that affect the public and [expressing] one's view on government views.

According to Adler (2005), civic engagement used to be a sociopolitical engagement undertaken by young people. He explains, however, that the turn of events has changed that procedural method, emphasizing that it is no longer an exclusive reserve of the young people. It implies that young and older people are now involved in it. In his words:

> Civic engagement refers to the ways in which citizens participate in the life of a community in order to improve conditions for others or to help shape the community's future. This term has been used to date primarily in the context of younger people. But in the past few years, a new movement has emerged to promote greater civic engagement by older adults (p. 5).

To effectively and successfully carry out civic engagements, specific methodologies and frameworks have to be adopted. Fr. George Ehusani uses the medium of writing to incorporate most of the scholarly outlined skills and frameworks, as seen in the subsequent analysis of his extant works. Among other skills and methodologies, the following approaches are suggested as bases for implementing civic engagements:

> Critical inquiry, analysis, and reasoning; Seeking, engaging, and being informed by multiple perspectives; Written, oral, and multi-media communication; Deliberation and bridge-building across differences; Collaborative decision making; *writing, proficiency in English, and oral presentation skills* [italics mine]; Collective decision-making skills include a "distinct set of skills and behaviours which are necessary for a democracy"; including the ability to express an opinion, hearing others' opinions, and working towards a consensus for the collective; Critical thinking or cognitive skills; civic skills, are necessary for describing, analyzing, synthesizing, and constructing opinions and positions on issues with civic relevance. (Kirlin, 2003; National Task Force, 2012).

6. Textualizing Imagery, Didactism and Civic Engagement in George Ehusani's Writings

As noted in the review of related literature, writing is one of the skills through which citizens in a community engage adequately with the happenings in the society. In 'Why we must fear the Almajiri revenge' (2020), Ehusani highlights some of the problems of the Almajiri system in Nigeria, using northern Nigeria as a launching pad. The system is not strange to Nigeria; thus, Ehusani uses the narration of a child whose father kept in the care of a Mallam, teaching in an Almajiri school. Ehusani beams light on parental irresponsibility and its attendant effects on society at large, affirming that it is the height of failure on the father's part to have dumped a child in a school without the requisite schooling arrangement.

As if that is not enough, in the story, we realize, rather painfully, that the father did not regularly check on the welfare and academic progress of the child. Instead, the father visited the school with an economic entitlement expectation. For four years, a father abandoned his child in a school without a formal plan. He only returned to scoop the hoped-for accrued economic gains and profits, thereby equating the child to a landed property whose value would have appreciated over some time. Even if we should accept the commodification of the child, should not the man, from time to time, check the location of the said property – to know if government or developers – have encroached on it? It is clear that Ehusani has used his text to respond to the notion that "No devoted and patriotic writer can escape this task of social crusading, re-ordering, re-orientation, re-educating, re-engineering and re-shaping that must be done in the society" (Asika & Okoye, 2015, p. 15).

As a result of utter parental neglect, Almajiri children have been made victims of 'psychological trauma' and deprived of parental love and care. The painful death of the child was avoidable if the parents had been checking on him in the school. Perhaps, the child would have confided in them some of the challenges they were facing. Then, the father would have made an adequate arrangement either by changing his school or providing better accommodation to avert the death of the promising child. Ehusani deploys the child's death in 'Why we must fear the Almajiri revenge' to reflect on the strange predicaments inherent in running Almajiri schools in northern Nigeria. More than anything else, the children kept in Almajiri schools are deprived of and completely denied parental care, love, and the natural bonding between children and their parents. The absence of these could constitute psychological, sociological and ontological disorders in these "wretched of the earth" (Fanon, 2004). One of the consequences of the foregoing is that the children become gullible willing tools for terrorist-related activities.

George Ehusani's *Why we must fear the Almajiri revenge* could, therefore, be likened to an exclusive military intelligence to forestall the palpable danger around us. Furthermore, using the imagery of painful and avoidable death due to neglect, we are warned about what will likely happen to our country if we continue to neglect our civic responsibilities. Using the lexical and metaphorical imagery of the child abandoned by the parents, Ehusani forcefully projects the image of a dirty, hungry, tattered-looking and utterly neglected child that should have been under the shelter, care and protection of his parents for all to see. That child symbolizes Nigeria: neglected, abandoned and left to die by our leaders. Goaded by one of the civic engagement methodologies – the ability to express an opinion - Ehusani foreshadows the substantial and consequential threat the Almajiri system portends to the Nigerian society. The government should urgently reform the system; otherwise, it would require no terrestrial prophecy or rocket science for us to know that the children would become thorns in our flesh. Not just reform and restructure the almajiri system, but the entire Nigerian project requires urgent action before getting to the point of no return. This potential threat is avoidable.

'End of a bad dream' (1998) presents the Nigerian civil society in an inebriated state, oblivious of what is happening to the country. This projects unto our psyche the image of the proverbial ostrich burying its head in the sand and leaving its body exposed. Even though Ehusani wrote this article 22 years ago, the situation in the country is more or less the same. *Nigeria, Years Eaten by the Locust* (2002, 2019) is a collection of articles written during the military dictatorship years in Nigeria. It documents Nigeria's woes and presents the way forward. Ehusani concludes that these years, as the title suggests, have been eaten by the locust: a complete waste of energy and resources. This implies that the pangs inflicted on the people by the powerful imagery of a swarm of locusts on the tree called Nigeria (which invariably will consume it) represent oppression, waste, social vices, devastation, criminality and profligacy. He uses his outstanding proficiency in English to describe, analyze, synthesize, and construct opinions and positions on issues with civic relevance in Nigerian society.

In *A call to radical discipleship* (2019), Ehusani advocates for fundamental and progressive followership, emphasizing that the problem with Nigeria is not only with the leaders but with the followers as well. In his typical call for the truth in all things (Abioye, 2019, pp. 71-72), he argues that:

> The truth must be taught and preached, no matter how bitter it may be; that political deceit, even when adorned in gold, is sin; that dishonesty in business, even when justified by the laws of economics is sin; and that civic lying, even when it is the order of the day, is sin…ignite our Christian candle to fight back the forces of darkness and decay, whether as responsible parents or respectful children, devoted teachers

or diligent students, God-fearing doctors or dedicated nurses, dutiful administrators or faithful labourers.

Nigerian democratic transition: One more opportunity for real change (2015) and *Nigerian youth: Sowing the whirlwind* (2002, 2019) epitomize what is evolving now as the "*Soro Soke*" agitation that climaxed on October 20, 2020, with the senseless killing of unarmed protesters after about two years of outcry against Nigeria's ills on the social media. The senseless killing was preceded by about two weeks of peaceful protest, online activism, and civil demonstration properly coordinated and well-managed by Nigerian youths who asked the government to put an end to police brutality and scrap the Special Anti-Robbery Squad (SARS), a notorious and controversial arm of the Police allegedly involved in extortion, unlawful arrests and detention, kidnapping, rape, extra-judicial killings, etc. The protest also advocated for good governance, among other things. It was tagged: *#ENDSARS*. Things, however, took a tragic turn when uniformed men allegedly started shooting sporadically into the crowd of the protesters. This unrest culminated in the death of several protesters, with scores wounded. Ehusani, in the texts mentioned above, subtly called for social change, a paradigmatic shift in the *status quo antebellum*. Police brutality and wanton extortions are not exceptions. Following the notion that a writer is a prophet, perhaps the teachings of Ehusani could be likened to a prophecy come true in Nigeria. It had never envisaged that the Nigerian youth – home and abroad – against tribal and religious creeds could successfully stage such a historic protest together.

Nigerian Youth: Sowing the Whirlwind (2002, 2019) uses the powerful imagery of the whirlwind, described as "an extremely strong wind that moves quickly with a circular movement" (Ehusani 2019, p. 43), carrying all kinds of debris and causing a lot of damage. It is like a tornado, which is a natural disaster. This article warns, just like *Why we must fear the Almajiri revenge*, that failure to reckon with the youth in the country's affairs is a disaster waiting to happen. Ehusani gives his reasons:

> And so the youth, as victims of primary violence inflicted by a culpable elite adult class, have unwittingly become instruments and weapons for the rape of society and have become veritable tools for scuttling their own future, a future without focus, without direction and without hope. Long denied a culture of peaceful demonstration under the repressive and regimented command military, and with no identifiable place in the national order, our youth find relevance and release in

thuggery, in armed banditry, in disruptive social upheavals, in transferred aggression and in sundry forms of secondary violence [...my emphasis] (p. 198).

Continuing, Ehusani frowns at the Nigerian leadership class for her utter insensitivity to and negligence of the growing population without commensurate economic long term plans. To him, part of the overwhelming social vices and malaise in the society is attributable to the Nigerian nation, which he describes as a nation that:

> ...breeds a restless and disoriented youth population, breeds a lawless society. A nation that marginalizes her young discounts her vitality. A nation that teaches the wrong moral lessons learns nothing edifying. A nation that neglects her youth condemns herself to inertia and retrogression. A nation that destroys youth aspirations destroys her future. But a nation that effectively mobilizes and cultivates her youth invests in a just and egalitarian society, and plants the seeds of peace, stability and prosperity (*Why we must fear the Almajiri revenge* p. 199).

The imagery created above gives the impression of a careless and unserious nation that is not interested in the future of its youths. The didactic or moral lesson here is that Nigeria is not paying enough attention to the future of children and youths, which can be very costly in the next couple of years. In other words, "a writer ought not to be like the proverbial man who was busy pursuing a rat while his house was on fire. A writer in a society is the moral conscience of his society, and his art should gear towards social issues and social rehabilitation" (Asika & Okoye, 2015, p. 12). Ehusani wonders whether he is in a trance given the avalanche of societal ups and downs. As a committed social critic and civic engagement agent, he willingly offers himself for a psychological examination to possibly ascertain the state of things in the country because the situation beats his imagination:

> Perhaps I need to be schooled in the dynamics of duplicity and compromise. Perhaps I need to take lessons in the dynamics of settlement and realism. Perhaps someday, I shall be able to live comfortably, eat well, and laugh in the midst of these abnormalities. But when that day comes, and when the internal transformation takes place, shall I still answer my name? Shall I still be the same person? Ah,

my story must sound lunatic. Yet how sane is life in Nigeria? When the entire society seems lunatic? (Ehusani, 2019, p. 110).

Rhetorically, Ehusani has appropriated the image of deconstructive binaries of the triumph of mediocrity, "where compromise is king, where corruption is clothed in purple and adorned with gold" (p. 75), to announce how corruption has eaten deep into the fabric of the Nigerian society. These images are powerfully extraordinary. They force anyone who reads them to think critically. They are deployed to depict the monumental nature of corruption in the country. Achebe advises the committed writer to play their role "as a cultural nationalist, as a teacher, a social critic, an actor rather than a reactor, and as a literary critic" (1964, p. 76). Ehusani has harkened to that call, and he has actually been strengthened by his priestly calling.

Before our very eyes (2002, 2019), Ehusani makes an uncommon critical evaluation of an era in Nigeria when the constitutionally enshrined democratic right of expression has been significantly suppressed. The tone of the barrage of rhetorical questions he uses illustrates a state of mortgaged freedom of speech of co-stakeholders in society. It appears as if some of the social critics, for fear of the unknown and the level of suppression witnessed, have to look for safe havens outside the shores of Nigeria. Bewildered by the turn of events, he wonders, "have they all gone in the company of Achebe and co who have left" (p. 46) out of frustration?

Again, Ehusani establishes himself as a member of the society, enmeshed in its sociopolitical sensibilities. As Ker (2016, p. 49) explains, "The writer is a member of a society and his sensibility is conditioned by social and political happenings around him. These issues will therefore perforce be present in his work". Given the role of a writer as conscience of the society, Ehusani deploys powerful images and metaphors to drive home his point. He uses these figures of speech in questioning the silence, equivalent to that of the graveyard, of the people and encourage them to speak up when such civic engagement is needed most.

The rot in our judicial system is also exposed, using figurative signification. The clause "justice is castrated" typifies the forceful elevation of corruption and the triumph of injustice. In other words, justice is traded in favour of the highest bidder. The perversion of justice, Ehusani implies, is forced on the judge via the unleashing of maximum force in "judges are rendered impotent" (2002 p. 82). Barrenness is to a woman what impotence is to a man. Essentially, the concept of impotence primarily belongs to and operates in the human biological reproductive system. It symbolizes the inability to produce and function in the procreation genealogy, implying a failure to perpetuate the family name. The conspicuous inversion in judges being rendered impotent, as textualized in the piece, testifies to the grave damage done to the Nigerian judiciary and judicial administration/processes. The ideational signification of the image of *impotence* highlights the absence of one of the hallmarks of the judiciary in the world – *Independence*. Using powerful images, he alerts the society to the chaotic moment when "law stands in the dock and crime climbs the bench" (p. 30) and the fourth estate of democracy – the media – is stifled with little or no hope in sight. These metaphors are contextualizations of the palpable strangulation of the masses' voice and inalienable right of expression.

Like a pantheon of faith, Ehusani encourages the people who are already in a state of despair to locate their solace in God through 'Keeping hope alive' (2002, 2019). As a keen observer, he notices that given the prevailing ugly situation in the country, the people are weary and hapless. The only leeway is the belief in the all-powerful God capable of changing conditions from bad to good. And that informed his incorporation of the biblical allusion to indicate his point. The excerpt, "where our ancestors threaten to drive us to a state of despondency" (p. 45), is illustrative. By this, he signifies that, at a point of blurred hope, the only way out is to "seek solace in the hand of God who is the ultimate miracle worker…and supreme Agent of change" (p. 45). This is textualized in the following:

> Where our circumstances threaten to drive us to a state of apathy and despondency, we can seek solace in the hands of our Creator, who is the ultimate miracle worker. Where the exigencies of our times threaten us with despair, we can seek refuge in God, who is the supreme agent of change. And why not? Did he not cause Ezekiel to put back flesh on dry bones and raise from the valley of dry bones a huge and an immense army? Did he not transform the shame of the crucifixion to the glory of the resurrection? (Ehusani 2002, p. 154).

This Refuge Provider, Miracle Worker and Fortune-Giver, Ehusani confirms, can turn situations around for good. After all, "Did he not cause Ezekiel to put back flesh on dry bones and raise from the valley of dry bones a huge and an immense army?" (p. 154) – an uncommon miracle that defies all known clinical experimentations. Through these visible images and metaphors, Ehusani rekindles the people's hope in God, using metaphorical allusion to the crucifixion and resurrection of Jesus Christ as a pretext.

In *Bye-bye to the motherland* (2002), Ehusani, again, wears his garb of critical civic engagement. The image of a child bidding his motherland goodbye comes to mind, evoking mental and psychological distance between mother and child. This piece beams a searchlight on the series of abnormalities prevalent in Nigerian society. It is a unique experience and an aberration where the Nigerian security agents intimidate, harass and cajole Nigerians at the points of entry into the country and exit from the same with reckless abandon. When some citizens who live in saner climes are treated with disdain and assaulted without provocation, the resolution has always been, "Never Again!". The excerpt below paints a metaphoric image:

> ...Indeed, what place has the man or woman of principles in a land of duplicity, where compromise is king? What chances of survival have saints and scholars at a time when corruption is clothed in purple and adorned with gold? (Ehusani, 2002, pp. 32-3).

A similar incident occurred in Abuja, the Nigerian Federal Capital Territory, when a Nigerian who lives in Sweden but was held back by the Covid-19 lockdown, was subjected to harassment and exploitation through multiple charges and unwarranted delays for him to be tested for Covid-19 in compliance with the international travel protocol. This incident, in 2020, accentuates the frustration of Ehusani's narrative written 20 years before. Things have not changed.

There is a unique approach to justify the interpolation of didacticism in African writing in Ehusani's songs, poems, homilies, articles, reflections, conversations and sociopolitical discourses. He teaches all who care to listen and learn didactical, political, religious and moral lessons. Besides, he imports this technique to embellish his writings and significantly confirm the continued presence and relevance of didacticism in Nigerian/African writing. Ehusani invites us to the irony of life and twist of fate in 'A peculiar tragedy' (2002). This follows Abioye's contention in *Language and the Moral Imperative in George Ehusani's writings* (2019, p. 56) that "Themes are central to the understanding of our everyday communication since we must know what a message or text is about for us to understand it; the writer's intention, which is also called intended meaning, is bound to be understood in the context of the underlying theme(s)". It is a complete twist of fate that a tree with green leaves falls. The one with forlorn leaves remains alive. Sani Abacha, a former military Head of State of Nigeria, had thrown some people in jail on trumped-up charges of a *coup d'etat*, a treasonable offence punishable by death. Against all sordid prison experiences, the Abacha prisoners were still alive while the man who threw them into prison, with access to all the best medical attention, died.

The disappointment suffered by the political associates of Abacha holds a canonical didactic lesson to humankind on not being desperate and certain about worldly things. Those who ranted, boasted and metaphorically transferred their belief and glory of God to the man – Abacha – were summarily proved wrong due to his sudden death. God, once again, used the incident to manifest His power and wield His authority over the affairs of man. Ehusani makes a mockery of the folly of men, when, out of greed, selfishness and egotism they downplay the place of God in the human ontology.

'Truth as ingredient for peace' (2002, 2019) foregrounds the importance of peace for a healthy, purposeful and prosperous society. Ehusani unravels an underlying deception in expecting peace where all possible tropes of peace have nosedived. He attributes the absence of peaceful strategies to the theory of demand and supply where ingredients of peace, like goods, are in short supply. He also accuses the leaders who play pranks with the people through double standard dealings of hypocrisy. With his emphasis on truth, he argues in 'How God will save Nigeria' (2002) that:

> We suspect that some of our countrymen and women are manipulating the logic of "only God can save Nigeria", to a ridiculous extent that is tantamount to magic…to promote a feeling of utter helplessness in the face of an otherwise contrived evil, and justify the now widespread disposition of indifference, inertia, inaction and apathy in the people of Nigeria. Once again, religion is being utilized to keep the people quiet while sustaining the status quo of injustice, oppression, human degradation and abuse. This is the type of religion that was identified as the opium of the people, one that lends itself to manipulation by oppressive forces in society to sustain the structures of injustice… (my emphasis; p. 97).

He insists that "It is true that only God can save Nigeria. Yet God will not save Nigeria without Nigerians! God does not impose Himself on anyone. The Christian God that we worship does not save human beings against their will" (Ehusani 2019 p. 56). In seven different sentences within the same article, he repeats (for emphasis) that God will not save Nigeria if Nigerians continue business as usual. And he concludes:

> Those who are calling for prayer must be ready to face squarely the truth of our national existence, and where necessary summon the moral courage and political will to redress the long-standing injustices that have bred so much resentment in the land…They must not only live the truth but courageously proclaim the truth in season and out of season (2002, p. 98).

Asika and Okoye (2015), appraising the duties of writing using literary works, observe that "Writers and literary artists have embraced the genres of literature to preach, shout, satirize and mock to purge their societies of all the cankerworms that militate against positive and developmental inclination" (p. 5). In the same vein, Ehusani has successfully toed the vista in his chronicling of the ills of the society, which is seen in:

> What kind of stability and prosperity can emerge in a land where virtually all the ingredients of peace, such as truth, justice, openness and dialogue are in very short supply? What is the point in going to Church or frequenting the mosque when our lives are not touched? What is the point in offering you sacrifices of peace when we have blood in our hands? What is the point in being religious and having no regard for human life? What is the point in dancing around your altar when our hearts are pulsating with hate? (*A New Year Prayer for Peace, 2019b*).

Given Ehusani's sermon-like piece, he has distinguished himself in his writings as a passionate and objective leader and critic. He is forthright in all his engagements. Even as an ordained Catholic priest, his spear of social criticism does not absolve his Catholic family. The phrase and image in "…offering you sacrifices of peace" 'A New Year Prayer for Peace, 2019b' are ecclesiastical of the Roman Catholic faith. Yet, he uses a texture of purgation of possible impurity and moral burden in the Church. In this way, he is passing moral and religious didactic messages to the faithful. He also questions other miscellaneous undoings that abound and flourish in the Nigerian society thus:

> The authorities do often canvass dialogue, but what kind of dialogue can the birds in the cage or the animals in the pen have with their captors? Do the authorities understand that dialogue begins only when each party involved in a dispute recognizes the right of the other to hold a different opinion? In the circumstances where the right of one party to oppose, to dissent, or to differ is permanently suppressed, are we not then canvassing the dialogue of the deaf? The authorities in our land do say that reconciliation is a priority project for them, and that is why they set up the National Reconciliation Committee, but do they understand that truth is a "*conditio sine qua non*" for genuine reconciliation that is aimed at achieving lasting peace?... But in point of truth don't we need a measure of interference if we must come to terms with our degenerate national conditioning? (Nigeria: Years Eaten By the Locust, 2019, pp. 144-145).

Experience abounds in Nigeria where those who sabotage peace in secret are the same people who proffer solutions for the same in the open. Ehusani also implores the political class to note that opinion would not constantly be singularized in all policy-making and government implementation. He advises them to give room for dissenting voices as they serve as an avenue to bring the leaders to consciousness in power intoxication cases. Ehusani concludes that government, politicians, and groups should tolerate people's opposing views if we must overcome the challenged leadership in the land.

7. Conclusion

This chapter has attempted to investigate imagery, didacticism, and civic engagement tropes in George Ehusani's sociopolitical significative writings. Through the exploration, we come into direct experimentation with his stylistic deployment of imagery, symbolism, didactic elements and practicable civic engagements with the Nigerian society. He has essentially demonstrated an uncommon patriotic role by daring successive governments in his bid to challenge the *status quo antebellum* in the general interest of the poor masses. He identifies leadership and followership failure at all levels; a lack of a sense of ownership and lack of proper structures and opportunities as the bane of Nigerian society.

He has made judicious use of his exalted position as a Priest of the Catholic Church to hold successive governments accountable to the people by way of just policies as well the efficient execution of projects and programmes aimed at the advancement of the common good of all.

To a reasonable extent, he has effectively fulfilled his civic responsibilities. He questioned certain abnormal occurrences in society and proffered possible solutions. His writings exposed the masses and their shortcomings to make them abstain from them and prevent reoccurrence. It is puzzling and painful that since 2002, when some of these articles were published, our circumstances have not changed.

An interrogation of his civic engagements has revealed the use of powerful lexical choices to create vivid metaphorical imagery such as locusts, fire, whirlwind, *almajiri,* shipwreck, opaque vision, bedraggled Nigerian, malodorous gas, the angel of the night, hunger, thirst, etc.; metaphors, which is another form of imagery which serves in activating readers' imaginations; and rhetorical questions. The themes of faith (in the power of God to turn things around: divine intervention), hope (in the Nigerian project), love (for fellow humans), forgiveness (of one another), restoration (of human dignity in Nigeria), are predominant in his writings, which are objective, didactic and address the realities of contemporary society. In his collection of papers, songs, storytelling, reflections, and homilies, Fr. Ehusani projects the multifaceted profile of a social crusader, activist, poet, writer, and Priest who, through his civic engagements, gives moral direction, focus, and support to his people from the pulpit. Indeed, he sees writing as a religious and socio-political commitment to his people and the Nigerian project. This commitment he considers second to his sacred responsibilities as a priest.

References

Abioye, T. (2008). Resourcefulness of rhetorical questions in Ehusani's 'A new year prayer for peace'. *Ibadan Journal of English Studies,* 5, 296-309.

Abioye, T. (2011 & 2019). *Language and the moral imperative in George Ehusani's writings.* Ibadan: Kraft Books.

Abrams, M. H. (1999). *Glossary of literary terms, 7th edition.* New York: Cornell University Press.

Achebe, C. (1964). The role of the writer in a new nation. *Nigeria Magazine,* June 1981, 39-57.

Adler, R. P. & Goggin, J. (2005). "What do we mean by 'civic engagement'?" *Journal of Transformative Education* 3 (3), July, 236-253. DOI: 10.1177/1541344605276792.

Akporobaro, F. B. O. (2005). *Introduction to African oral literature.* Lagos: Princeton Publishing Company.

Asika, I. E. & Okoye, C. (2015). The writer as a dreamer: Utopia and the ideals of utopianism in Ngozi Chuma-Udeh's *The presidential handshake. Global Journal of Human-Social Science: Arts & Humanities - Psychology* 15 (2). Retrieved 10 September 2020 from file:///C:/Users/user/Desktop/Image%20and%20D%20ACTICS/ 4-The-Writer-as-a-Dreamer-Utopia.pdf

Awuzie, S. (2015). Didacticism and the third generation of African writers: Chukwuma Ibezute's *The temporal gods and goddesses. The Cathedral in Tydskrif vir Letterkunde*, 52 (2). file:///C:/Users/user/Desktop/Image%20and%20D%20ACTICS/ 11AwuzieWEB03.pdf

Ayeomoni, N. (2003). The role of stylistics in literary studies. In Oyeleye, L. & Olateju, M. (Eds.), *Readings in language and literature* (Pp177-189). Ile-Ife: OAU Press.

Brandt L. & P. A. Brandt. (2005). Cognitive poetics and imagery. *European Journal of English Studies.*file:///C:/Users/user/Desktop/Image%20and%20D%20ACTICS/Cognitive_poetics_and_imagery.pdf

Chege, P. K. (2016). *Imagery in African poetry.* Unpublished BA Dissertation. Kenya. University of Kenya.

Chinweizu, J. M. (1980). *Towards the decolonization of African literature.* Enugu: Fourth Dimension Publishers.

Dada, P. O. (1996). The tradition of the African novel. In S. O. Asein & A. O. Ashaolu (Eds.), *Modern essays on African literature: Studies in the African Novel,* 1 (pp. 27-36). Ibadan: Ibadan University Press.

Darthone, O. R. (1976). *African literature in the twentieth century.* London: Heinemann.

Eagleton, T. (1996). *Literary theory: An introduction,* 2nd edition. Minneapolis: The University of Minnesota Press.

Eghagha, H. (2017). Little stories in a big world. Monday, October 2. Retrieved from .https://www.thenewsnigeria.com.ng/2017/11/21/the-little-stories-a-testimony/

Ehusani, G. (1997). *Fragments of truth.* Ibadan: Kraft Books.

Ehusani, G. (1998a). *Petals of truth.* Ibadan: Kraft Books.

Ehusani, G. (1998b). End of a bad dream. *TELL,* July 13, p. 34.

Ehusani, G. (2006a). Dancing on the brink of Disaster: An Open Letter to President Olusegun Obasanjo. Retrieved from www.georgeehusani.org

Ehusani, G. (2006b). *Flames of truth*. Ibadan: Kraft Books.

Ehusani, G. (2011). *Father George Ehusani in conversation: Young people and the hunger for meaning*. Ibadan: Kraft Books.

Ehusani, G. (2015). Nigerian democratic transition: One more opportunity for real change. Keynote Address delivered at Lux Terra Leadership Foundation, Abuja. 05 March. Retrieved from *https://guardian.ng/news/buhari-tasked-on-governance-oronsaye-report/*

Ehusani, G. (2017). More on little stories in a big world. Retrieved 12 October 2020. from https://guardian.ng/opinion/more-on-little-stories-in-a-big-world/

Ehusani, G. (2019a). Before our very eyes. *In Nigeria:Years eaten by the locust*. Ibadan: Kraft Books.

Ehusani, G. (2019b). *A New Year Prayer for Peace*. Retrieved from https://www.thebridgenewsng.com/2019/01/03/a-new-year-prayer-for-peace-by-rev-fr-george-ehusani/

Ehusani, G. (2020). Why we must fear the Almajiri revenge. Retrieved from https://www.sunnewsonline.com/why-we-must-fear-the-almajiri-revenge/05/8/2020.

Eyoh, L. (1997). *J. P. Clark-Bekederemo's Poetry: A study in stylistic criticism*. Unpublished Ph.D Thesis, University of Port-Harcourt.

Flanagan, C. & Wray-Lake, L. (2011). Civic and political engagement. In Bradford, B. & Mitchell J. P. (Eds), *Encyclopedia of adolescence*, 2 (pp. 35-43). San Diego: Academic Press.

Frye, N. (1957). *Anatomy of criticism: Four essays*. Oxford: Princeton University Press.

Frye, N. (1986). The archetypes of literature. In Kaplan, C. (Ed.), *Criticism: The major statements* (pp. 501-531). New York: St Martin's Press.

Halliday, M.A.K. (1971). *Linguistics and literary style: An inquiry into the language of William Golding's The inheritors*. London & New York: Edward Arnold

Hope, C. E. (2013). *Towards an understanding of civic engagement and civic commitment among Black early adolescents*. Unpublished PhD Thesis, University of Michigan.

Jegede, O. (2019). Foreword. *Language and the moral imperative in George Ehusani's writings*. Ibadan: Kraft Books.

Lloren, D. (2003). The analysis of poetic imagery. *Jornades de Foment de la Investigació*. Universtat Jaumefile:///C:/Users/user/Desktop/Image%20and%20D%20ACTICS/forum_2003_3.pdf.

Ojeifo, E. (2016). Ehusani: Priest, gentleman and scholar at 35. Retrieved from https://guardian.ng/opinion/ehusani-priest-gentleman-and-scholar-at-35/. October 19, 2020.

Preminger, A. & Brogan, T. V. F. (Eds.) (1993). *The Princeton encyclopaedia of poetry and poetics*. Princeton, New Jersey: Princeton University Press.

Robert, D. R. & Kevin, H. (2003). Civic learning and engagement: A review of the literature on civic learning, assessment and instruments Fourth printing. Research Institute for Studies in Education(RISE): Iowa State University.

Storey, J. (1997). *Cultural theory and popular culture: An introduction*, 5th edition. London: University of Sunderland.

Yeibo, E. (2012). Figurative language and stylistic function in J. P. Clark-Bekederemo's poetry. *Journal of Language Teaching and Research*, 3 (1), 180 -187. file:///C:/Users/user/Desktop/Image%20 and %20D%20ACTICS/23.pdf

CHAPTER TWO

A Philosophical Appraisal of George Ehusani's African Christian Humanism

Anselm Kole Jimoh and Stephen Ogbeiye

1. Introduction

This paper presents a critical analysis and appraisal of George Ehusani's African Christian humanism (ACH) as a contribution towards the restoration of our ailing human values and upholding the dignity of the human person. Consistent with his ardent advocacy for justice, fair play, and respect for human rights and dignity, Ehusani, in his work, *An Afro-Christian Vision "Ọzọvẹhẹ!" Towards a More Humanised World*, condemns the secular and materialistic humanism that characterises the prevailing notion of development in the modern world. He argues that secular humanism, through the ambiguity of modern Western technological civilisation, instrumentalises the human person, and devalues human dignity. Therefore, he proposes an ACH premised on the traditional African and Christian understanding of the dignity and value of the human person. According to him, this would provide us an authentic, holistic and functional vision of the human person.

In this paper, we employ the phenomenological approach to carefully articulate Ehusani's ACH and the hermeneutic approach to explore and critically analyse ACH towards restoring the eroding value and dignity of the human person. Thus, we first of all explicate the notion of humanism. Secondly, we examine how modern secular humanism depersonalises and dehumanises the human person under the veil of technological civilisation. Thirdly, we examine Ehusani's ACH, and conclude that it is a carefully thought out, and well-articulated theory aimed at enabling us restore the value and dignity of the human person being eroded by secular humanism.

What is Humanism?

Over the centuries, advocates of humanism have tried to define and redefine humanism by granting it greater substance with the progression of time. While the Greek and Roman classical writers tried to distinguish what is human from the bestial, as well as, the divine, medieval advocates of humanism focused on the spiritual attributes of the human person to the point of belittling her natural condition. In reaction to this, the Renaissance scholars of humanism recognised the intrinsic value of human life and the enormity of its potential (Ogunmodede, 2010, p. 20). By the start of the twentieth century, scholars tried to give a generalised view of human life. They created an integrated perspective of humanity where personal limitations and provincial interests are lifted for the purpose of giving a universal goal and method in apprehending the notion of humanity (Lamont, 1997, p. 11). However, the idea of a universal goal and method seems unachievable given that the entire notion of humanism aggregates the social, cultural, and religious aspects of the human person.

Although the term 'humanism' is often misconstrued as ingrained in English language, its etymology indicates that it has Italian roots in the concept of *umanisti* which means 'a student of human affairs or human nature.' According to Francis Ogunmodede (2010, p. 21), "*umanisti* is associated with the Latin *humanitas* because the former is a derivative of *studia humanitatis*; a 15th century course of classical studies that consisted of grammar, poetry, rhetoric, history, and moral philosophy." *Humanitas* was a commitment to the ideal that dignified the development of human virtue to its fullest extent in all its forms. It includes; understanding, benevolence, compassion and mercy, which are associated with the modern word – humanity. It is also applied to fortitude, judgement, prudence, eloquence and love of honour, which are more assertive characteristics of someone who is necessarily a participant in active life. Taking a lead from this etymology, Robert Grudin (2020) posits that humanism is the Renaissance movement that is centrally focussed on the ideal of *humanitas*. In an earlier version, he described humanism as:

> [A] realistic social criticism ... utopian hypothesis, [of] painstaking reassessment of history ... bold reshaping of the future... the comprehensive reform of culture, the transfiguration of what humanists termed the passive and ignorant society of the "dark" ages

into a new order that would reflect and encourage the grandest human potentialities. (Grudin, 1988, p. 723)

We can infer from its etymology that humanism is any man-centred philosophy that "recognises the value or dignity of man and makes him the measure of all things or somehow takes human nature, its limits, or its interests as its theme" (Ogunmodede, 2010, pp. 18-19).

More critical studies indicate that the meaning of humanism fluctuates according to the various intellectual movements that identify with it. Thus, it seems futile to provide a generally accepted definition of the concept. However, scholars agree that its simplest and most basic concern is the human person as a being. For instance, Corliss Lamont avers that the primary connotation of humanism is 'human being-ism' which implies a "devotion to the interests of human beings, wherever they live and whatever their status" (1997, p. 17). It is about the need for the human person to find significance in life and existence (Lamont, 1997, p. 3); a search that is majorly determined by the individual's nature and relationship with the environment. Consequently, to properly understand humanism, we need to first understand human nature in relation to his/her environment since this constitutes the fundamental issue of the discourse in humanism.

Concerning human nature, Aristotle (2019, p. 12), like ancient thinkers, posits that to be human, one has to exercise the characteristics of thinking and living. For him, 'to think' represents the human ability to reason, while 'to live' represents the human propensity to fulfil her bodily capacities and desires. He argues that the nature of an entity is the measure by which the entity functions appropriately, and to function appropriately is to advance one's specific end or ends. In short, for Aristotle, the nature of the human person consists in thinking and living (see Younkins 2003). This claim is premised on the idea that the ability to know and understand is a natural capacity that human beings exercise in their search for the truth and pursuit for moral excellence. Humans always try to instantiate their ideals through their actions; they function towards the attainment of the purpose of life, which is earthly happiness or flourishing – *eudaimonia*. This is explicated in the idea of 'the good,' which Aristotle defines as "an activity of the rational soul in accordance with virtue." For him, the good resides in the function of a thing, for the natural function of a thing is determined by the thing's natural end.

Based on Aristotle's theorisation, 'the good' of the human person is achieved through the human exercise of reason and acquisition of virtue. Since "the good of each species is teleologically immanent to that species," Aristotle argues that 'the good,' which is proper to human beings consists in "the activities in which the life functions specific to human beings are most fully realised." Therefore, he avers that human beings should employ their natural abilities to their fullest potential in the attainment of 'the good' by taking pride in being excellent at what they do (see Younkins 2003).

In line with Aristotelian analysis, Thomas Aquinas explains that the human person is a paradox; the only species whose composition straddles the matter-spirit divide because the human nature derives from the unity of the soul which is spirit, and the body which is matter. Even though both the soul and body are distinct parts of the same entity, Aquinas argues that they are not exclusively distinct entities as such, but are distinct as two parts of the same wholly one entity – the human person (see Klima, 2002). Commenting on the complexity of the human nature, Ogunmodede argues that the human person is both mysterious and fascinating and that rationality constitutes her most distinctive aspect. Human rationality differentiates human beings from other animals and living organisms by bestowing on them the ability to reflect and think. Freedom as the ability to make a choice between alternatives is predicated on the individual's ability to provide reasonable justification for his beliefs. This ability makes human beings *homo-libertatis* – the attribute of freedom. Freedom is an essential characteristic of the existential condition of the human person (Ogunmodede, 2010, p. 12). In addition to the attributes of rationality and freedom, human beings are also spiritual, social, and political. These attributes provide the avenues through which they make sense of, and add significance to their life and experiences (Lamont, 1997, p. 3). The essence of the attributes and capacities of the human person manifests in 'the good' that proceeds from the authentic activation of these attributes and capacities.

Despite the rigorous attempts in contemporary scholarship to clarify what 'the good' is, and how to attain it, it remains an increasingly complex issue, especially in more recent times (Lamont, 1997, p. 8). This complexity is responsible for the divergent positions that have dogged a satisfactory and generally accepted definition of humanism. The problem is partly, also due to the relationship between humanism and other equally vague concepts like culture, freedom, civilisation, development, etc., that are themselves tied to the nature of the human person.

Given the historical trajectory of humanism, it is not surprising that it has been variously designated in the course of its conceptual development. According to Edward Chenney,

> It may be reasonable balance of life that the early Humanists discovered in the Greeks; it may be merely the study of the humanities or polite letters; it may be the freedom from religiosity and the vivid interests in all sides of life of a Queen Elizabeth or a Benjamin Franklin; it may be the responsiveness to all human passions of a Shakespeare or a Goethe; or it may be a philosophy of which man is the centre and sanction. It is in the last sense, elusive as it is, that Humanism has had perhaps its greatest significance since the sixteenth century. (1937, p. 541)

Cheyney's apposite description of the scenario provides the permissibility to skip any specific definition of the concept. However, the sense in which it conceived as "freedom from religiosity and the vivid interests in all sides of life" is of interest to this paper. In this sense, humanism is an attempt to exclude God from the affairs of humans. It entrenches extreme materialistic and secularistic philosophies within its understanding of the human attainment of 'the good.' We can trace these philosophies to the scholars of the European Renaissance. As Lamont argues, even when we claim that contemporary philosophical conception of humanism transcends its renaissance idea, we cannot deny that it includes the enduring values of the latter (1997, p. 12). George Ehusani's idea of African Christian Humanism (ACH) is a reaction to this sense of humanism.

Humanism is a plainspoken unambiguous view of the universe, human nature, and its problems. Thus, Lamont describes it as "a philosophy of joyous service for the greater good of all humanity in this natural world and advocating the methods of reason, science, and democracy" (1997, p. 13). In its twentieth century understanding, humanism is a heterogeneous approach to human life with the homogeneous emphasis on the autonomy and dignity of the human person, coupled with the value of humane relationships. The heterogeneity is manifested in the varied amount of value placed on human beings and human culture as against the value placed on

God/gods and religion. This includes the level of affirmation that is given to human reasoning when applied to evidence as against theological speculations and revelations (Copson, 2015, p. 2). Since humanism accommodates and affirms the various aspects of human nature, it may be considered as a creed for those who want to live a happy and useful life, with emphasis on the adjudicating role of reason in determining what is true, good and beautiful. In fact, humanism is a commitment to free human emotions from 'irrational restrictions.' Lamont expresses this thus:

> Humanism is a many-faceted philosophy, congenial to this modern age, yet fully aware of the lessons of history and the richness of the philosophic tradition. Its task is to organise into a consistent and intelligible whole the chief elements of philosophic truth and to make that synthesis a powerful force and reality in the minds and actions of living persons. (1997, p. 13)

Concomitant with the above description, Lamont outlines: the belief in naturalistic metaphysics that considers the supernatural as myth; the belief that human beings are products of natural evolution; the human potentiality to solve their own problems; human freedom to choose and act within the limits that shape our destiny; the attainment of the good life through a harmonious combination of personal satisfactions and continuous self-development; etc., as some of the basic principles that embody the modern understanding of humanism. In tune with these principles, humanism is denoted as: scientific humanism, secular humanism, and/or naturalistic humanism. Any of these denotations depend on what aspect of humanism is emphasised.

It is to this end that Barbara Smoker describes humanism as an attitude to life that rests on the belief that "this life is the only life we can expect to have, [therefore], it is especially important to make this life a good one" (2005, p. 29). Accordingly, humanists claim that "human happiness is its own justification and requires no sanction or support from supernatural sources; that … the supernatural … does not exist" (Lamont, 1991, p. 15). If we use our intelligence and cooperate liberally with one another as human beings, humanists claim that we can build a citadel of peace and beauty here on earth. According to Smoker (2005, p. 30), "Humanism stands for the open mind in the open society." This understanding of humanism is conspicuously anti-God and against anything supernatural, and it creates the platform for the objectification of the human person. It also emphasises that our best and only hope is our human ability to reason and the efforts we make to improve the welfare of all humankind. After all, for humanists, the mundane world is our only home, therefore, we should not seek happiness and fulfilment elsewhere, like in the supernatural.

3. Secular Humanism and the Degradation of the Human Person

According to Ehusani, there is an increasing secularistic and naturalistic understanding of humanism. And given that human creativity and ingenuity is at its highest level, it seems humanism is a paradox. On the positive note, there have been technological, agricultural, economical, as well as medical breakthroughs which have advanced the quality of human life. However, the decline in respect for human life, visible in the increased rate of abortion, euthanasia, deterioration in our ecological system, the ever looming threat of war, expresses the negative dimension of humanism (Ehusani, 1991, p. 1). What this implies is the realisation that human intelligence, though important for human survival, can also be an imminent threat to it. This places humanity and humanism at a dilemma of either controlling human intelligence or being controlled and possibly enslaved by it (Ehusani, 1991, p. 12). Subsequently, we are left with fresh moral concerns about the potency of human intelligence and the destruction that could proceed from its unguided application (Ehusani, 1991, p. 9).

Secular humanism opens up the horizon of inquiry because it encourages humanists and scholars in the various disciplines to research into the nature and complexities of the human person and existence, which contribute vastly to our knowledge (Mondin, 1985, p. 7). The search to enhance human welfare through the realisation of her cravings for a life that is full and complete (Ukpokolo, 2011, p. 16), yields great results in the areas of technological, scientific, social and cultural development. However, the wonderful and humanly beneficial discoveries came with a corresponding degradation of the dignity and value of the human person. The attempt to achieve and/or satisfy the human ultimate craving for happiness outside the framework of the supernatural succeeded to enthrone practices that are counterproductive to the dignity and value of the human person. This negativity that came with the attempt to implement the positive and noble ideals of secular humanism is what the Christian notion of humanism and the African practice of humanism oppose. Ehusani's epochal effort in unifying both notions of humanism in his analysis of ACH under the theme, *Ozovehe*, not only raises the contradiction inherent in the practice of secular humanism but also espouses the need for a retrace of our steps from the destructive tendencies and attendant consequences of secularising the notion of humanism.

According to Ehusani:

> the ambiguity of modern western technological civilisation [is such] that one could say with some justification that the twentieth century has seen the emergence of the machine, and the disappearance of the person (1991, p. 1).

He premised this conclusion on his claim that:

> True, human creativity and ingenuity have been put to optimum use in the last few centuries, giving rise to the modern western technological civilisation, which we may refer to as the most glamorous civilisation in the history of humankind. With the tremendous breakthroughs in medical care, in communication, in agriculture and in economics, ours can be called "the best of times." But with the rate of homicide in our cities, the rate of suicide and drug addiction especially among our youth, the wide spread practice of abortion and euthanasia, the rate of deterioration in our ecological system, and the ever looming threat of nuclear holocaust through war or accidental detonation, ours could also be described as "the worst of times". (Ehusani, 1991, p. 1)

He argued that industrialisation brought about the degradation of the human person as an *imago Dei* – image of God. The exaggerated materialism and secularism that came with industrialisation, as the legacy of the West, relegated and subsumed the idea of the human person as the image of God. This legacy earned the West its technological, economic and political ascendency but not without the sore aspect that it is leading the world to oblivion (Ehusani, 1991, p. 2). It deifies the human person as an end itself, and thereby separates him/her from his/her original divine source – God. This, for Ehusani, is "the paradox of our age" (1991, p. 5); an ugly reality that must not be allowed to fester.

The phenomenal technological advancement of the twentieth century has been further developed in a superlative form in our current twenty-first century such that our world has become a global village with the amazing possibilities available that come with the use of smart phones. Today, the world is moving faster than ever with researches in the potential of artificial intelligence (AI) and fifth generation (5G) telecommunications network. These supersonic advancements in technology further strengthen anti-supernatural and materialist ideologies and enhance the claims/attempt of secular humanism to deify the human person. Consequent upon the latter is the decline in the dignity and value of the human person. The 1945 use of the atomic bomb in Hiroshima and Nagasaki is an eye-opener to the reality of the frightening possibility of the harm technology can bring to the human race and life on earth (Ehusani, 1991, p. 7). The infamous 9/11 attacks on the World Trade Centre (WTC) ushered in a wave of unprecedented terror attacks by Al Qaeda, ISIS, Boko Haram, etc. What about the now widespread public and legal practice of homosexuality, the glorification and idolisation of nudity? These are some of the indices that point to the human decline.

The value for human life and the dignity of the human person have fast been eroded with unbridled appetite for wealth, power and control; both at global, international, national and local levels. Given the capitalistic nature of modern day economy, most of the few who have the capital and control the means of production, have exploited wage workers by maximising their wealth through corrupt and unethical means. In many African countries, with Nigeria as a specific example, public office holders, politicians and their appointees, corruptly enrich themselves from the nation's commonwealth. They systematically impoverish the majority of the citizens to the point that the latter beg for a share of what is stolen from them. Consequently, we see in "modern civilisation the cohabitation of abject poverty side by side with stinking wealth; the phenomenon of starvation on the one hand, and what is cynically referred to as '*affluenza*' on the other" (Ehusani, 1991, p. 10). Homicides, suicides, attempts in reproductive technology and genetic engineering to clone human beings, create babes – In *Vitro Fertilisation, Artificial Insemination, Surrogate Motherhood, Embryo Transfer*, and with "the abuses that go with these reproductive procedures, the technological society seeks to remove the 'mystique' surrounding human generation" (Ehusani, 1991, p. 9). Practices like these corrode the dignity, and devalue the uniqueness of the human person because they make the human person an object of scientific study, which though not wrong or unethical, reduce the human person to a thing – a means to an end.

4. *Ozo vẹhẹ*: Ehusani's Idea of African Christian Humanism (ACH)

Ehusani argues that we are getting to the apogee of the degradation of the human person brought about by technological development. The outcome to this is visible in the subtle but no less vicious denigration of humanity displayed in the advertisement and entertainment industries, which among other things, litter our sight and sensibility with obscenity (Ehusani 1991, pp. 11-12). Against the revolutionary, politically motivating, and morally inspiring music of the likes of Fela Anikulapo Kuti, Commander Ebenezer Obey, Christy Essien-Igbokwe, Onyeka Onwenu, Majek Fashek, Sunny Okosun and many of their contemporaries, what we hear these days are vulgar lyrics that barely make sense. They do not convey any moral or political message; just deafening sound-beats, cheaply sold to the emotions of the young generation by mostly nude female and erotic dancers/dancing. These are clear representations of the decadence that has enveloped modern-day because of the secularisation of humanistic ideals. According to Ehusani,

> A critical evaluation of the various trends in the contemporary human society reveals that though our train has gathered a rare momentum, it is derailing. We are headed for destruction, and with our technological powers we are not only taking the whole human community with us, we are also going down the abyss with the plants and the animals, the seas and the rivers. Indeed, the entire ecosystem goes with us on this suicidal ride. (1991, p. 241)

If we are going to salvage human dignity and restore the value of the human person, we need to radically break with the pervasive worldviews rooted in secular humanism that emphasise technology over and above the human person. It is in this wise that Ehusani's ACH presents us with a viable option.

ACH, which Ehusani labels as "An Afro-Christian Vision: *Ozọvẹhẹ!*" is inspired by his belief in the human person as it has been nurtured in him by the traditional African heritage. He describes ACH as "a contemporary reflection on Christian Humanism, using the African traditional humanistic heritage as a *text*" (Ehusani, 1991, p. 1). The latter is richly encapsulated in the names, proverbs, songs, folklores, visual art and customs of the African people. These collections have philosophical themes and wisdom that presage the sacredness and dignity of the human person. They also characterise the human person's superiority over material goods as richly expressed in the Ebira name *Ozovehe* - "the human person is life."

Ozovehe expresses the love of the traditional African for children, family, harmony, wholesome personal relationships, community, hospitality, and certainly characterises the African as humanistic (Ehusani, 1991, p. 2). Unfortunately, according to Ehusani, in today's world, "Africans are poised to abandon whatever remains of this humanism in favour of the accumulation of goods and techniques" because they want to 'catch up' with the West (1991, p. 2); it is a sad development that ACH seeks to address. To better appreciate ACH, let us briefly analyse the notions of Christian and African Humanism.

Christian humanism promotes the self-fulfilment of humanity within the framework of Christian principles. Thus, it is the view that humanist principles like; universal human dignity, individual freedom, rational inquiry, conscience, and the importance of happiness, are consistent with, and are essential components of the teachings of Jesus Christ. Since Jesus Christ became incarnate for the redemption of humanity, Christianity teaches that we should follow the example given by his life (Zimmerman, 2017, p. 5). Even though the basic ideas of Christian humanism were mooted in the patristic era, they came to maturity in the late 15th century. The use of the term 'Christian' to denote humanism is largely to differentiate its foundation for humanist principles, against secularism and materialism that constitute the foundation of modern-day humanism. Christian humanism is grounded on God and the supernatural (Copson, 2015, pp. 2-3). According to Charles Nauert, it is the "connection between their scholarly efforts and their longing for spiritual and institutional renewal in the specific characteristic that distinguishes 'Christian humanists' as a group from other humanists who just happened to be religious" (2006, pp. 179-180).

On the other hand, African humanism "represents the several types of humanist doctrines that have emerged in modern and contemporary periods in Africa" (Ogunmodede, 2010, p. 59). As a cultural activity and heritage it is traceable to ancient Africa, with its finest form of expression in Kemetism or Egyptologism (Ogunmodede, 2010, p. 59). Kemetism is the "philosophy of the Ancient Blacks who developed the civilisation of the Nile Valley of Egypt" (Ogunmodede, 2010, p. 62). It explains the challenges of the universe and provides the earliest account of "human thinking about the nature of the universe, human relations, good and evil, beauty, order and harmony, ethical behaviour, the source of things" in ancient Egypt (Asante, 2000, p. viii). It embodies humanaistic ideals (Ogunmodede, 2010, p. 63) that espouse a holistic humanism – one that lacks the religiosity and secularity of contemporary Western humanist movements. Kemetism previewed Christian humanism in the sense that the latter places emphasis on the holistic nature and role of human the person, as well as the spiritual dimension in contemporary humanism.

ACH refutes the secular humanist view that the human person is an absolutely free being who has no need of religion or God. According to Ukpokolo, secular humanism is "one of the most organised, challenging, and clearly non-theistic philosophies in contemporary times" (2011, p. 3). Based on the false assumption that the human person is nothing more than the material aspect, secular humanists promote a naturalistic approach to the understanding of human nature. They consider life as a singular organisation of matter and argue that human thoughts and actions are guided by a body of principles and values which constitute the framework for engaging the human condition. The question is: Are these claims definitive and reliable? For instance, is the human life not more than just the material? Given that human nature itself is a composition of body and spirit, it goes beyond just the material to include the spiritual, and the spiritual is not and cannot be subjugated to the material (Ukpokolo, 2011, p. 14).

With science came the maturation of secular humanism and a number of positive impacts occasioned by several discoveries that are beneficial to the human race. However, science equally brought in a new dawn in the reduction of the dignity and value of human life. This counter proposition is evident in Ehusani's analysis of how secular humanism has degraded the human person. According to him, the reality of the diversity of human nature points to the limitation of secular humanism. All the efforts to satisfy the natural longing for infinite happiness and fulfilment by wealth and material acquisitions in humans have failed because they cannot be satisfied by material or physical things. The progress in science and technology notwithstanding, we continue to seek for absolute and infinite life.

Christian humanism unlike secular humanism, examines the human being from a more comprehensive point of view that incorporates both the material and spiritual aspects. Ehusani (1991, pp. 42-43) draws from sacred scripture as he summarised the Hebrew or Old Testament belief on the human person in six key points: (i) The human being was created last, and therefore, is the most important of the creatures of God. (ii) The human being is to rule over the earth. (iii) The human being is created directly by God, and thus, has a personal relationship with God which other creatures do not enjoy. (iv) The human being has in her the breath or spirit of Yahweh. (v) Human beings are created social – male and female God created them. And (vi), the human person was created in the image of God – *imago Dei*. According to him, these form the foundation of the Christian teaching on the human person.

In Christian projection, the dignity of the human person is derived from God who created and dignified the human being by sharing with her His own image and likeness. Catholic theologians, for instance, and most Christian thinkers uphold the dignity of the human person. They maintain a healthy balance between human spirituality and materiality, and between the fulfilments of human life here on earth and its supernatural destiny (Ehusani, 1991, p. 53). Aquinas, for instance, explained that the soul and body correspond respectively to the form and matter of the human substance; while the body is the material/physical, the soul is the spiritual and also the principle of life whence the material derives its actions and motivating force (Aquinas, 1965, p. 45). Neither the body nor the soul alone can constitute the human person, they are inseparably related in the human being.

The human being is at the centre of the universe in traditional African cosmology and the universe itself is created and sustained by God (Ehusani, 1991, p. 208). Thus, the traditional African understands life as a sacred gift that originates from God's infinite sacredness. This understanding is noticeable in the central role of the divine in the social and private affairs of African people and cultures. According to Aderibigbe,

> The central place of religion ... has become so evident in any meaningful understanding of African life in all its ramifications – social, economic, and political... Consequently, Africans have evolved and sustained religiously conscious communities, either as devotees of

traditional religion, or as followers of the two 'converting religions' – Christianity and Islam". (Aderibigbe, 2015, p. 7)

It is unthinkable for the traditional African to imagine that anything exists outside of the creative power of God. The traditional African does not consider human existence as a product of chance; therefore, the African does not take existence for granted (Ehusani, 1991, p. 214). Human life derives from God. In fact, religion and religious beliefs permeate the very fibre of life for the African. Hence, John Mite describes the African as "notoriously religious" (1970, p. 1) and posits that "the physical and the spiritual are but two dimensions of one and the same universe, whether it is viewed in terms of time or space, ... human life is a religious experience in that universe" (see Ehusani, 1991, p. 87). In tandem with the robust African communalistic ontology, the human person is perceived from a broader perspective that encompasses both the material/physical and the spiritual/supernatural.

Ehusani's ACH harmonises Christian values with African ideals with the hope of creating a more comprehensive and bias-free understanding of the existential human reality. Prior to the advent of Christianity, African religions promoted beliefs that are founded on human values. Therefore, for Ehusani (1991, p. 207), to harmonise Christian values with African ideals requires more than just to Christianise Africans; it also requires that we Africanise the Christian tradition. If truth is the same everywhere and whatever is true does not need affirmation to make it correct; to simply Christianise Africans would imply a rejection of African religions and values as inferior or false. On the other hand, to Africanise the Christian tradition would demonstrate a recognition of the true values inherent in it and the indigenisation of those values.

According to Fidelis Aghamelu (2009, p. 35), it is in the nature of human beings as *homo socius*, to necessarily live in a community of people where they can fulfil their dreams and desires in life, hence, the reciprocal relationship between the person and the society. This is a shared belief in African ontology and the Christian religion. "The African values community living not only because it is good for kinsmen to do so, but because life is his or her ultimate concern and that life can only grow in relationship" (Ehusani, 1991, p. 221). The sense of family and kinship, "wholesome human relations," "community fellow-feeling" – connection with every member of the society, are cardinal for the traditional African. Except for reasons of grave offence against humanity, traditional

Africans address one another as brothers or sisters. To say, 'he is my brother,' for the African is a communitarian expression that goes beyond a biological bond to include members of the extend family, and in some cases, anyone from one's immediate or remote African community. The extended family is an institution in which everybody is somebody for the African (Ehusani, 1991, p. 222).

The communitarian idea is equally visible in Christian thought where humanity is considered as one large family of God's children. The Fathers of the Second Vatican Council emphasised the dignity of the human person by tracing it to the creative work of God. "God," they said, "did no create man a solitary being. From the beginning 'male and female' he created them. This partnership of man and woman constitutes the first form of communion between persons" (*Gaudium et spes*, 1975, n. 12).

The dignity of the human person accentuates the equality of all irrespective of the essential and accidental qualities. Sex, tribe, colour, race, religion and/or social status are not, and should never be the basis by which we determine human dignity. Ehusani reasons that there is a possible rapport and symbiotic relationship between the African and Christian understanding of human dignity which is aptly expressed in the name *Ozovehe*. Thus, he tries to synthesise both traditions as an Afro-Christian vision aimed at a more humanised world. Given the African's sense of communion, the traditional African rarely gives attention to unnecessary division and unhealthy competition. In this regard, Ehusani asserts that "the division among Christians, giving rise to some mutually exclusive and often antagonistic group and sects is a scandal to the Africans, whose traditional religion constituted the greatest symbol of unity" (1991, p. 224). For the traditional African, what unifies us is more important than what separates us. Therefore, the African value for human life is a challenge to the over-zealous Christian or Muslim crusader to reject the irrationality of religious fanaticism. The latter often results in violence and brutality against the human person. The negative impact of divisions that results from religious beliefs is very visible today in Nigeria where the polity is divided along religious lines. Nigerians, as Africans, need to recover the traditional African understanding of the sacredness of the human person and her irreplaceable place in the world, to create a society and establish institutions that will promote peace, justice, and harmony.

For Ehusani, a dialogue between faith and culture is a good starting point toward the harmonisation between African traditional practices and the Christian tradition. The faith/culture dialogue is an interrelation between a given religion and the cultural practices of a people. According to him, Jesus Christ was born a Jew, into a Jewish culture to implement a universal mission. He lived among the people and accomplished his universal mission without becoming a cultureless universal man. Therefore, Jesus' incarnation and mission present a perfect picture that faith/culture dialogue is not out of place. "There has never been a universal culture. Neither is it desirable to have one" (Ehusani, 1991, p. 204). Faith/culture dialogue is not a hegemony that would pose the danger of one culture and/or tradition overriding the other.

ACH is a call to Christianise the African heritage as well as Africanise the Christian tradition because both traditions share the belief in mutual respect for the dignity of the human person. Pope Paul VI once said (while addressing the Church in Africa), "we have no other desire than to foster what you already are: Christians and Africans." A statement of this sort acknowledges the dignity of the human person and expresses the oneness of our common identity as children of God. As Ehusani argues, the African Christian understands and relates with her Christian faith easily because her African culture and values provide her with a solid foundation upon which to rest her Christian faith. We can plausibly claim that African humanism is a religious humanism. In this regard, Ehusani insists that the African spiritual worldview enriches Christianity and "the African Christian challenges the Church to enter deeply into the culture and embrace not only the languages, the names, the proverbs and the songs, but also ... the thought patterns, attitudes and philosophical dispositions of the Africans" (1991, p. 209). The plausibility of this position is in the logical harmony in the reasoning and philosophy of the African; from the material world to the metaphysical reality of the divinity of God, who is the source of all in being.

5. Conclusion: *Ọzọ vẹ hẹ* and the Restoration of Human Dignity in the Modern Age

The convictions, beliefs, principles, and proposals of secular humanism present a besmirch conception of the human person and so it is anti-human (Ukpokolo, 2011, p. 17). Despite the technological development that secular humanism brings to the human race, its limited perspective of the human person distorts a holistic and authentic vision of humanism. An advancement in science and technology that does not support and protect the dignity and value of the human person is not a positive development of the human race. Humanity requires a proper and comprehensive study of the human person that does not give precedence to one aspect against the other. In this way, we would attain and sustain the true dignity of the human being. Thus, ACH does not just provide an alternative conception to secular humanism, based on its inconsistency with the African tradition and the Christian faith, it rejects secular humanism. Ehusani's ACH is predicated on the fact that "human beings have been deceived by technological science. After liberating them from the authority of God, technological science promised them unending joy, peace, and immortality; but it has failed to deliver any of these goods, leaving them more confused and disoriented" (Ehusani, 1991, p. 241). It proposes the restoration of meaning and wholeness in the human community and the world; an alternative axiology for humanity that is in search of meaning. It requires that the African Christian employs his/her understanding of the divine origin of the human person, supernatural end, and transcendence "to save humanity from … total degradation and fragmentation [which is] bound to result from a warped anthropology and a dysfunctional world-view" (Ehusani 1991, p. 219) championed by secular humanism. For Ehusani (1991, p. 221), the African Christian challenges Westernised Christianity to "recover from the secularism of the modern scientific worldview and rediscover the traditional biblical vision of sacredness and wholeness." Therefore, we submit that Ehusani's ACH is a carefully reasoned and coherently articulated proposal envisioned to restore the fast-eroding value and dignity of the human person.

References

Aderibigbe, I. S. (2015). Religious traditions in Africa: An overview of origins, basic beliefs and Practices. In I. S. Aderibigbe & C. M. J. Medine, *Contemporary perspectives on religions in Africa and the African diaspora* (pp. 7-29). New York: Palgrave Macmillan. Doi: https://doi.org/10.1057.9781137498052_2.

Aghamelu, F. C. (2009). The human person and social order: A moral perspective. *Nnamdi Azikiwe Journal of Philosophy* 2 (1), 35-49.

Alao, O. F. (2005). Misconceptions about African culture and civilization. In S. A. Ajayi, *African culture and civilization* (pp. 12-21). Ibadan: Atlantis books, Ibadan.

Aquinas, T. (1988). *On being and essence: A translation and interpretation* by Joseph Bobik. Indiana: University of Notre Dame Press.

Aristotle. (2019). *Nichomachean ethics* (2nd Revised Edition), edited by R. Crisp. Cambridge: Cambridge University Press.

Asante, M. K. (2000). *The Egyptian philosophers: Ancient African voices from Imhotep to Akhenaten.* Chicago: African American Images.

Copson, A. (2015). What is humanism? In A. Copson and A. C. Grayling, *The Wiley Blackwell handbook of humanism* (pp. 1-33). New Hersey: John Wiley and Sons Ltd., https://doi.org/10.1002/9781118 793305.

Cheyney, E. P. (1937). Humanism. In *Encyclopaedia of the social sciences* vol. IV. New York: Macmillan.

Daugherty, M. (2014). Kemetism: Ancient religions in our modern world. www.anthropologhy.msu.ed. Retrieved 19/11/2020.

Ehusani, G. O. (1991) *An Afro-Christian vision "Ọzọvẹhẹ!": Towards a more humanised world.* New York: University Press of America. *Gaudium et spes*: Pastoral Constitution on the Church in the Modern World. In A. Flannery O.P. *Vatican Council II: The conciliar and post conciliar documents* (pp. 794-879). Mumbai: St. Pauls.

Grudin, R. (2020). Humanism. www.britannica.com/topic/humanism. Retrieved 3/11/2020.

Grudin, R. (1988). Humanism. In P. W. Goetz, *The new Catholic encyclopaedia Britannica* vol. 20. Chicago: Encyclopaedia Britannica Inc.

Klima, G. (2002). Man = body + soul: Aquinas's arithmetic of human nature. In B. Davies *Thomas Aquinas: Contemporary philosophical perspectives* (pp. 163- 182). New York: Oxford University Press.

Mite, J. (1970). *African concepts of God.* London: Heinemann Press.

Mondin, B. (1985). *Philosophical anthropology.* Rome: Urbaniana university Press.

Ogunmodede, F. (2010). Man and humanism: An historico- existential reflection on man in Africa. An inaugural lecture delivered at Seminary of All Saints, Uhiele- Ekpoma, Edo State.

Nauert, C. G. (2006). Rethinking 'Christian Humanism'. In A. Mazzocco, *Interpretations of renaissance humanism* vol. 143 (pp. 155-180). Brill.

Doi: https://doi.org/10.1163/9789047410249_010.

Plato. (2017). *The republic*. Translated by Benjamin Jowett. Oxford: University Press.

Smoker, B. (2005). *Humanism*. 1st Nigerian Edition. Ibadan: Gadfly Publishers.

Ukpokolo, I. (2011). The anti-humanity of secular humanism: An African interrogation of the secular humanist metaphysics of the human person. *Orita: Ibadan Journal of Religious Studies* 43 (2).

Younkins, E. W. (2003). Aristotle, human flourishing, and the limited state. In *Le Quélsécois Lilsve*, no. 133. www.quebecoislibre.org. Retrieved 29/10/2020.

Zimmerman, J. (2017). Introduction. In J. Zimmerman *Re-envisioning Christian humanism*. Oxford: Oxford University Press.

CHAPTER THREE

Beyond Aesthetic Appeal to Healing Sounds: An Existentialist Reflection On George Ehusani's Liturgical Music

Anthony Okeregbe

1. Introduction

During an interlude in one of his sessions on art therapy during a course on psycho-trauma healing, Fr. George Ehusani picked up his guitar, plucked the strings in accompaniment to Prince Nico Mbarga's 'Sweet mother', a familiar song of global acclaim that pays tribute to motherhood. The hall was charged to frenzied nostalgia as everyone – Christians and Muslims, male and female, young and old – sang and shuffled to the music. Before he started the song, Fr. Ehusani had told everyone to mindfully reflect on the lyrics, and allow every word to sink in. Some learnt the lyrics for the first time from hearing others sing them. On and on the music went, and then it shifted to Bob Dylan's 'Blowing in the wind' and rested on R. Kelly's 'The storm is over'. At the end of the interlude, there was silence. The faces of many beamed, even as their eyes glittered from the reflection of light on threatening tear drops. Amongst the sated participants was a young woman who sought the attention of Fr. Ehusani, the facilitator. "I want to speak," she said. As she was handed the microphone, her sobbing but clear voice echoed in the silence: "Never in my life have I thought that this burden will be lifted off my chest." She continued: "After listening to these songs, especially 'Sweet mother', something in me broke..." And on she went unburdening and unearthing memories of bitterness, sadness, guilt and shame that seemed to have formed some incrustation in her mind. She was not alone. Before long, other participants expressed some form of release due to the effects of the songs. But let us ask: What broke when the young woman immersed herself in the music? What happened to these participants whilst they listened to the relay of songs to such an extent that they had to speak out?

Throughout history, wise men and philosophers have been known to draw connections between music and deep existential concerns. They have found that music has a part to play in the psychic balance of the human person. The ancient philosopher and mathematician, Pythagoras of Samos, is reputed to have been the first scholar to teach that music could be utilised as medicine for diseases of the body, the emotions and the soul (Dobrzynska, Cesarz, Rymaszewska, & Kiejna, 2006). Church Fathers like St Augustine and St Thomas Aquinas have taught on the intrinsic connection between music and divine encounter. Even metaphysical pessimists such as Arthur Schopenhauer and Friedrich Nietzsche had complementary submissions about music and human existence. For instance, Schopenhauer valued Baroque music as a means of taming the rapacious and whimsical nature of the will (Moges, 2006).

In religious experience, this invaluable dimension of music is further expressed as a vehicle for spiritual encounter and reconnection with the divine. Apart from the luminaries and maestros of great classical music, who have flourished in history, the contemporary period is also replete with outstanding composers of Christian liturgical music collections that are suitable for personal devotion and public worship. Amongst these are Joseph Gelineau, Carey Landry and the St Louis Jesuit group comprising Bob Dufford, Dan Schutte, John Foley, and others. Gelineau, who died in 2008, was a French Jesuit priest and composer of Christian liturgical music, who developed the globally acclaimed Gelineau psalmody – a method of chanting or singing the psalms in seminaries and churches worldwide. Like the Septuagarians that make up the St Louis Jesuits, Carey Landry, also a Septuagarian, is a former Catholic priest reputed as a foremost composer of Catholic liturgical music in the United States of America. In a less magisterial and nonprofessional manner, Ehusani follows the footsteps of these eminent composers of what has been dubbed Contemporary Catholic liturgical music. Although his songs, unlike those of the above composers, traverse certain genres, they have been characterised as vehicles of psycho-trauma healing.

With the foregoing as background, this paper seeks to re-establish the role liturgical music plays in fostering mindfulness, healing and spiritual wellness through a phenomenological analysis of selected songs in Ehusani's musical collection. Whilst this study does not deal with the musicology and discography of the songs, it employs media monitoring for selection and hermeneutically analyses the songs to unveil properties that make their melodies and lyrics instruments of healing, mindfulness and wellness. To this end, the study relies on the postulations of music therapists and psychologists of music in analysing the existential properties. Because this paper is a qualitative study, the scientific treatment of the impact of the songs on listeners is beyond its scope. The paper argues that Ehusani's liturgical music rises from mere aesthetic appeal and plain didacticism to prophetic ministration that leads to self-discovery and rediscovery of the wholeness of human existence.

2. Music, Liturgical Music and Music Therapy

As an art form and cultural activity that deploys sound as a medium, music may be regarded as a symbolic activity by which humans communicate. It is a creation of human intelligence which reflects the varied dimensions of the creativity and complexity of existence. In his bid to express the creative human agency in music, Levinson proposes a definition of music as "sounds temporally organized by a person for the purpose of enriching or intensifying experience through active engagement (e.g., listening, dancing, performing) with the sounds regarded primarily, or in significant measure, as sounds" (Levinson, 1990, p. 273). Kania, on his part, submits as follows: "Music is (1) any event intentionally produced or organized (2) to be heard, and (3) either (a) to have some basic musical features, such as pitch or rhythm, or (b) to be listened to for such features" (Kania, 2011, p. 12). In exploring the character and nature of music from the functional, operational, structural, socio-historical and essentialist definitions, renowned philosopher of music Steve Davies proposes that a successful definition is an intricate ensemble of variegated factors: it must balance all the stories, defining traditions of music, the universal elements, musical and non-musical factors that affect the diversity of music and the understanding of music makers and listeners (Davies, 2012).

Guided by the above submissions, music may be viewed as a veritable medium of entertainment that stimulates the good feeling of jollification and dissipation of pleasant energy. It affects moods by transporting an individual from one emotional state to another. Music is also affected by moods in the sense that its composition reflects the composer's emotional state. In all this, it modifies behaviour. Music is also a means of self-expression and identity creation. In addition, not only does it educate, but it also showcases culture as well as social history. While it does any of these, it sends various messages corresponding to the encoder's intentions and the decoder's desires. In short music is communication.

All over the world, singing has been recognised as a very powerful evocative dimension of the communicative function of music. This is especially true of liturgical worship, be it Christian, Islamic, Hindu, or any other. When songs are utilised in worship, they transport the singer to a realm outside of themselves and imbue them with some new reality and meaning. As an existential act of communication, liturgical singing entails a special transcendence that connects the human person with the source of their being. This transcendence symbolically takes the form of a vertical movement - from being a mere human act to that of the divine; it becomes the act of a lover attempting to connect with their source. Crichton explains this encounter lucidly when he highlights two points about singing. First, he speaks of singing as a profoundly human action that expresses not only our emotions but also the whole personality of the individual. He explains that in singing,

> ...the human person is saying all he can at a given moment, and when the verse and the music are the sort of words and music that are strongly evocative, they say more than we could say by rational discourse and carry us beyond ourselves (Crichton, 1980, p. 11).

Second, relying on the poignant statement of St. Augustine, "*Cantare amantis est*" (It is the lover who sings), Crichton presents this Augustinian conception of music as purely an act of worship and singing as the act of the singer seeking some connection with their beloved, and in the process is engulfed and overwhelmed by thoughts of their beloved. Hence, Crichton states that "song in worship is a sign, or even a sacrament of our love of God, a delighting in his goodness and beauty, a sign of the movement of the self to the supreme other to whom we would give ourselves" (p. 12). Singing is thus extendable as a relentless search for the vacuum or hollowness of our lives to be filled by the immeasurable love of God. In the parlance of theologians of music or connoisseurs of sacred music, what St Augustine appears to be describing so eloquently is the liturgy. Although the etymology of the word 'liturgy' relates to public service, as a Christian religious category, it is the formalised ritual or script for various forms of public worship in churches. In this sense, it accommodates the whole complex of official services, all the rites, ceremonies, prayers and sacraments of the Church, as opposed to private devotions. In this sense we speak of the arrangement of all these services in certain set forms (including the canonical hours, administration of sacraments, etc.), used officially by any local church (Fortescue, 1910: para. 5).

Thus, the liturgy is better understood as the official public worship of the church (para. 6). When music accompanies this form of worship, or music is composed around components of this form of worship, it is called liturgical music. It seems fitting, therefore, that the *New world encyclopedia*, (2018) defines liturgical music as "a form of music originating as a part of religious ceremony," which can be found in the "Catholic Mass, the Anglican Holy Communion service, the Lutheran mass, the Orthodox liturgy and other Christian services including the Divine Office" (para. 1).

In consonance with the *Vatican II document, Sacrosanctum Concilium*, liturgists have identified the goal of liturgical music as the glorification of God and the sanctification of the faithful (*Sacrosanctum Concilium*, 7, p. 112). However, the manner of interpreting the music that accomplishes this goal is a matter of contention, especially when in a loose sense, what may be termed Contemporary Christian Music (CCM) has been identified as liturgical.

Whilst some experts have identified this sanctification of the faithful as an instance of spiritual therapy, or healing, there is a positive sense in which music functions therapeutically outside worship. Music as an instrument of therapy is rooted in the assumption that it may be efficacious in the care and management of the human psyche. Despite the controversy around music as a veritable tool for clinical treatments and healing, some scholars strongly argue that music plays some vital therapeutic roles. Citing Ogunyemi (2002), Adeniyi (2018) avers that listening to certain music in a controlled fashion promotes health and wellbeing. In explaining the remedial potential of this controlled use of music, she defines music therapy as "the use of musical sound to help clinical patients to support and develop physical, mental, social, emotional and spiritual wellbeing" (Adeniyi, 2018, p. 138). In a specific sense, Maratos, Gold, Wang and Crawford (2008), building on the definition of Bruscia (1991), explain music therapy as "an interpersonal process in which the therapist uses music and all of its facets to help patients to improve, restore or maintain health" (p. 1). Bruscia's later definition, which has been further amplified by the work of Geretsegger, Elefant, Mössler and Gold (2014) describes music therapy as a "systematic process of intervention wherein the therapist helps the client to promote health using music experiences and the relationship that develop through them as dynamic forces of change" (Bruscia, 1998, p. 20).

The efficiency of this therapeutic medium lies in its touted ability to deploy the different levels of structure, namely, sound, harmony, melody, instrumentation, rhythms, form, etc., of different musical styles and idioms, to provide the variability and flexibility needed to counteract the more rigid characteristics of a pathology (Adeniyi, 2018). It is argued, therefore, that masterful control of these structures would bring about somatic registration that would reduce worry and control blood pressure, and so on.

Beyond the supposed somatic effect, music therapy is also posited as having an ethical goal, one that caters to the proper moral cultivation of the individual and corporate sanity of the society. This conception of music use elevates structured sound and musical arrangement from neutral amusement to moral education. Proponents of this position, among whom is Anthony Mereni, maintain that there is a correspondence between the moral health of an individual or society and the music that is generally accepted by them (Mesz, Rodriguez Zivic, Cecchi, Sigman & Trevisan, 2015; Mereni, 2014). Explaining the philosophical thrust of the Mereni music school, Olaleye states that the "Merenian music school is of the opinion that to build a civilized society good music disposes man to virtue whereas bad music disposes man to vice" (Olaleye, 2018, p. 15). It is on the basis of this submission that this school further posits that music "could express and encourage virtues, nobility, dignity, temperance, chastity" (p. 15), in the same manner it could also express and encourage vice – sensuality, belligerence, and indiscipline.

Whichever way the therapy goes, Koelsche (2009) tells us that music therapy works through the effect of the following: modulation of attention, modulation of emotion, modulation of cognition, modulation of behaviour and modulation of communication. In all, music-based therapy relies on receptive listening and the active method that involves playing of musical instruments and deploys highly sophisticated qualitative and quantitative scientific protocols to analyse clients or patients (Craig, 2020).

3. Ehusani's Liturgical Music

A multi-instrumentalist, Ehusani has had a flourishing hobby in music. Apart from personal satisfaction derivable from music, Ehusani has also extended this love to a level of quasi-musicianship; he now uses music as an instrument to complement his pastoral duties. So entrenched is the inevitable presence of musical activities in his personal life and pastoral cum administrative duties that one wonders what it would be like to dissociate music from his existence (G. Ehusani, Personal communication, April 8, 2011).

In line with the Jungian thesis, which posits that "every psychological problem is ultimately a matter of religion" (Moore, 1994, p. xii), Ehusani believes that music as art therapy could nurture the soul in such a manner that it generates positive energy for wholesome living and mindfulness. As suggested above, the music, fitting enough to bring this to fruition, should be rich in vital forces and positive vibes and be spiritually appealing so as to penetrate the core of our being. In other words, it should be able to connect psychological health and spirituality. Moore amplifies the necessity of this connection when he surmises: "A spiritual life of some kind is absolutely necessary for psychological 'health'; at the same time, excessive or ungrounded spirituality can also be dangerous, leading to all kinds of compulsive and even violent behavior" (Moore, 1994, pp. xii-xiii).

But the curious thing about this definitive presence of music in Ehusani's vocational life is that he was never trained in music. By his own admission, he was never in any choir neither did he express any passion for singing or music until he became a parish priest. In an interview granted Tony Okeregbe, Ehusani (2011) tells the story of the unexpected circumstances that ignited his interest in singing and music.

> I wasn't trained in the seminary to sing. I wasn't particularly passionate about it in the seminary, and I didn't really play any musical instrument in the seminary. But when I came out and became a parish priest, I saw the usefulness of music. It was in those days when people were translating English songs into Ebira, many of which did not make much sense to my people. So, I decided to champion the cause using our indigenous melody to do the Commons of the Mass liturgically (Ehusani, 2011, p. 96).

Also, by his own attestation, Ehusani states that music has added vitality to his ministry.

> It is a good source of distraction in the sense that you are able to entertain yourself and yet be productive. When I think of the tons of songs that I have put into over twenty CDs, I ask myself, 'What would I have been doing with that time that I used to do this if I hadn't engaged in it?' How do I compose my songs? It is this: if I am driving and a song occurs to me, I pull off the road and write the song down and then continue the driving. And you see, whenever I see a song that I composed twenty years ago, I know the melody since I didn't learn to read the solfa notation. It has worked very much for me and has brought a lot of young people to me, some of whom I have mentored. (Ehusani, 2011, p. 98)

A pleasant consequence of Ehusani's resolute self-help at music composition is the number and quality of songs he has successfully recorded. So far Ehusani has about 26 CDs of song collections, some of which have been uploaded on YouTube. Explored either professionally or simply for one's listening pleasure, the songs may be uplifting to the amateur listener as they may also be to a critic.

4. An amateur's analysis of Ehusani's songs

In an article celebrating the silver jubilee ordination anniversary of Fr. George Ehusani, Okeregbe reviewed 15 CDs comprising a jazz ensemble, psalms and canticles, devotional songs and poems (Okeregbe, 2006). A random selection from these collections is 'Jazz the gospel' (Ehusani, 2006), a 15-track danceable instrumental that combines keyboard, guitar and conga drums to create a jazzy fusion that is midway between Dave Koz and Majek Fashek.[1] This musical style has attained a dominant reggae rhythm in the devotional songs rendered in 'Fill me up' and 'Jesus loves me'.

True to its title in the CD 'Sing and Shout for Joy' (Ehusani, 2006), there is a drift from chanting to loud singing in one of the psalms and

---

[1] Dave Koz (David Stephen Kox) is an American smooth jazz saxophonist and Grammy Award nominee with a flourishing music career in his homeland and abroad. Majek Fashek (Majekodunmi Fasheke) was a Nigerian singer, multi-instrumentalist and songwriter of the reggae genre.

canticles. Contrary to the practice in traditional liturgical offices (periodic church prayers) where psalms and canticles are accompanied by the organ to provide the sacred ambience of worship, Ehusani's psalms and canticles follow a slow reggae rhythm dominated by the guitar. While this proves successful in some of the tracks, it becomes too hard for Track 4, 'You opened wide'- a solemn psalter rendered in minor key. One of the beauties of the musical collection is the crisp fluidity of former Miss Ifeoma Nnorom's soprano. Her sweet soft sonorous voice provides the much-needed harmony required by Ehusani's sharp grating voice. Nowhere is this vocal virtuosity demonstrated as in the selection of the poems- 'Love is beautiful' and 'Images of love', where the musical accompaniment attains its utmost melodic finesse and evocative ministration.

In the poem, 'The cross', the solemn mystery of the crucifixion is presented as 'School of love' in a mellow, meditative rendition that could finally penetrate any stubborn heart:

> Ah at Calvary
> Ah at Calvary
> I see love petrified
> And mercy exemplified
> In the twisted image
> And broken body
> Of God's direction

The same sonorous pungency is replicated in the poem 'Disarm our heart', where words and instrumentation employ contrasting imagery to transport an invitation to love. Consider the following:

> Disarm our hearts mighty God
> And teach us
> That we cannot shake hands
> With clenched fists
> Disarm our hearts wonderful counsellor
> And teach us
> That we cannot get a rose
> From a noxious weed

In the musical tribute to the Holy Spirit titled 'Come Holy Spirit', Ehusani's voice is at its best as a narrative and prophetic oracle. This seems to be the best song music in the entire collection. Here, there is a melodic balance and tonic harmony of pitch, sound quality and mood. In this collection, the subtle musical terror which jazzy-reggae melodies create is virtually absent. In tone, music and words, a prophetic voice, accompanied by the singing assembly, truly pays tribute to the Holy Spirit in worship.

Apart from the songs analysed above, Ehusani also used the ample time made available by the lock-down of the Coronavirus pandemic to compose and disseminate musical messages through some soulful songs. As may be observed in some samples of the 69 songs uploaded on YouTube, although the songs represent different genres of music, they express messages of comfort, hope, divine consolation and thanksgiving. It is for this reason that the following songs are selected for brief review: 'Slow me down, Lord', 'It's gonna be alright', 'Mysterious lover', 'As for me and my house', 'Darkness will pass away,' 'Love is beauty', and 'Fall afresh on me'.

4.1 *Slow me down, Lord*

> Slow Me Down Lord
> Ease the pounding of my heart
> Slow Me Down Lord
> By the quieting of my mind
> Slow Me Down Lord
> Amidst the turbulence of my day
> Give me the calmness of the hills
> Slow Me Down Lord

'Slow me down, Lord' is a mellow rendition interspersed with poem recital. It is a plea for divine solicitude amidst the drudgery of quotidian existence, and a call on God to arrest the seeming irrationality that characterises everyday living. In this appeal, the individual recognises the turbulence occasioned by their Sisyphian existence and invites some divine arrest. By this invitation, the individual also recognises the power of the Lord to bring about that arrest.

4.2 *It's gonna be alright/Darkness will pass away*

This is another consoling reminder of the faithfulness of God. Modelled after the act of solicitude of Julian of Norwich when the grave pestilence of Black Death afflicted England in the 14th century, this short two sentence song is a mantra of affirmation. Its lyric is simple: "It's gonna be well, for Jesus never fails." Another song in this mold is 'Darkness will pass away'.

> This darkness will pass away
> Better days are coming
> We shall see the sunshine
> The clouds shall clear

In this seemingly hopeless state of the COVID-19 pandemic and its uncertainties, these songs are harbingers of hope. They implore the believer to be joyfully expectant of God's power.

4.3 *Mysterious lover*

In 'Mysterious lover' Ehusani, in his characteristic reggae melody, presents a message of Christ the lover. In his simple narrative preluding the song, he attempts to convince his listeners that the same love that caused God to send His son to die for humankind while we were yet sinners, and that inspired Christ's work of mercy and compassion is still operative in all who abide in God.

> Mysterious Lover
> O Jesus Christ
> You died to save me
> I'll live to praise you

The mystery inherent in this love is aptly captured by the paradox in the song: Christ died to save. How can one die to save another?

4.4 *Love is beauty*

This song is suffused with powerful rhymes, and, like many of Ehusani's songs, it is rendered with Ifeoma Nwaoduah in simple reggae melody.

Notwithstanding its simple poetic form, it is loaded with strong philosophical themes. Whilst the song presents humanity as a fragile, weak, ephemeral existence that contrasts ultimately with the incomparable immensity of the divine, it posits that love can connect these two contradistinctive realms. The wordings of the lyrics are as metaphysically provoking as the mystery which love is. Follow the lyrics:

> Amid the fragile reality
> Of mortal humanity
> Love is the beauty
> That binds boundless divinity
> With finite humanity

4.5 *Fall afresh on me*

This is a poetic tribute to the Holy Spirit. It is a song chronicling the ubiquitous primordial powers of the Holy Spirit from Creation to Pentecost and to our time. It is a story-telling prayer also rendered in the characteristic jerky reggae tradition, with guitar progression interspersed by readings. The frequent interludes with some scripture recitals make this song a worthy dramatic solo performance:

> Spirit of the Living God
> Fall on me
> Spirit of the Living God
> Fall afresh on me.

Recital of scripture narrative

> Spirit of the Living God
> Fall on me
> Spirit of the Living God
> Fall afresh on me.

4.6 *Just like a river*

'Just like a river' is a refreshing pop rendition of a lover's admission of the overwhelming power of love. Like a true prayer of supplication and thanksgiving, the song seeks refuge in divine love. It expresses a plea to be transported to a plane where love, peace and forgiveness reign, one devoid of pain and violence and destruction. Infused with danceable and lively guitar rhythm, fantastically accentuated by Ifeoma's smooth vocal delivery, this song seems to express an eschatological feeling when taken literally. However, it is the serenity which comes from God's great love that this song presents to listeners.

4.7 *As for me and my house/The cross of Jesus has set me free*

'As for me and my house', an adaptation of the bible verse of Joshua 24: 15, is a declaration of self-affirmation rendered in 4/4 time signature. In a music composition or written song, a 4/4 time signature is one whose pulse or beat is counted 1, 2, 3, 4 and then repeated as necessary. This means that all the notes in each bar must add up to 4 quarter notes. This slow swingy beat, which synchronises with the bold narrative of the lyrics, invokes a powerful ambience of total submission to divine protection. The song '*The cross of Jesus has set me free*' is a reflective rendition set for the Passion. However, surprisingly it is rendered in an Afro-Juju melody and in danceable rhythm.

5. An Existentialist Evaluation

Given the above analysis, it is clear Ehusani's use of music and songs in his leadership trainings and psycho-trauma healing sessions may not be music therapy in the technical sense. This is because, as stated above, music therapy in the proper sense is a scientific and systematic study that deploys qualitative and quantitative research approaches in a controlled setting to attain wellness. It is this controlled setting and the possibility of repeatability that make the techniques of wellness scientific. Nonetheless, Ehusani's use of songs and music is therapeutic in a loose sense, owing to its goal of achieving wellness or good feeling. Thus, Ehusani's use of music is music therapy of a special kind, one in which the spoken word, the sung utterance, rather than the effect of sound, are construed to have healing powers, that is, powers for positive feeling of self and positive behaviour modification. In this sense, the pragmatic quality of Ehusani's songs may be appreciated within the Self-Affirmation theory of Steele. According to Steele (1988), individuals have the perceived ability to activate self-affirmation processes as a reaction to information that threatens the integrity of the self. In reaction to this threatening information about the integrity of the self, individuals are likely to maintain an experience of the self as positive, moral, adequate, good, competent, stable, through constant explanation and rationalisation (p. 262f.). Cohen and Sherman (2014) analyse this further by asserting that self-affirmation enables individuals to express and maintain flexible identities, by being competent in different areas of personal value to them. It also enables individuals to maintain self-integrity by acting in ways that genuinely merit acknowledgement and praise (p. 360). In the light of the Self-Affirmation theory, Ehusani's songs tend to promote healing through the effectuation of positive affirmation inherent in the songs. Positive affirmations are positive phrases or statements of self-motivation used to challenge negative and unhelpful perception about self and to boost self-esteem.

Whilst Ehusani's songs may not be deliberate mechanisms for music therapy in the strict technical sense, they provide therapeutic first aids that identify candidates for technical clinical music therapies. This, however, is not to say that they do not usher individuals into mindfulness. Because Ehusani's songs tend to boost a positive self-image and encourage an optimistic mind-set, they naturally lead to healing affirmation, that is, a positive statement about our physical and mental wellbeing. Thus, Ehusani's songs retain their ultimate value not necessarily in their sonic quality but rather in their word therapy. In the deployment of the therapy of the word, the patient or client is led or re-orientated towards an appreciable understanding of the meaning of their existence.

This is the psychotherapy philosophy which Frankl expatiated on when he explored the concept of logotherapy. Arising from his experiences as an Auswitz Concentration Camp survivor and as a practising psychiatrist, Frankl came to identify certain neuroses (noogenic neuroses) as those attributed to the failure of the sufferer to find meaning and a sense of responsibility in their existence (Frankl, 1989, p. 10). On the strength of his extreme experiences and professional observation, Frankl introduces logotherapy as a meaning-centred psychotherapy – that is to say a therapy "on the meanings to be fulfilled by the patient in his future" (p. 120). In his terse explanation of this therapy, Frankl tells us that "logotherapy...focuses on the meaning of human existence as well as on man's search for such meaning. According to logotherapy, this striving to find meaning in one's life is the primary motivational force in man" (1989, p. 121).

Re-echoing the inherent existentialist trait that resonate in all his works, Frankl goes further to explain that "this meaning is unique and specific in that it must and can be fulfilled by him (the individual) alone; only then does it achieve a significance which will satisfy his own will to meaning" (1989, p. 121). By this explanation, meanings become much more than defence mechanisms, mere rationalisations or reaction formations. They rather become ultimate values or ideals which the individual can live and die for. If this is the case, then meaning or finding ultimate meaning for one's existential situation tends to bring about hope.

Ehusani's use of music and songs appropriates instances of this logotherapy philosophy to ascribe meaning to human predicaments and conditions in order to attain mindfulness and wellness. Like Frankl's logotherapy, Ehusani uses rhythms as a vehicle to re-orientate the individual, be they clients or patients, to be mindful of the core of their existence, and how the healing powers of words connect them to mindfulness. In the parlance of one professional counsellor, Ehusani's songs and use of music may be described as "sermons with rhythm."[2]

Although the songs in Ehusani's liturgical music fundamentally express the communicative action between God the lover and the human person who is the loved, they highlight a truism emphasised by psychotherapists and care-giving professionals, namely, the freedom to take individual and personal action. Irrespective of their melodies, instrumentation, sonic quality and lyrics, Ehusani's songs affect people in different ways depending on the personal idiosyncrasies of the individuals; and in these different appeals, the individuals are the managers of the effects some songs have on them. The song is not the actor in the drama of the individual's existence, rather it is the individual who, through a conscious and deliberate exercise of freedom and will, creates, out of this morass of meaninglessness, a shareable field of interaction and spiritual connection between themselves and the divine for their own design. The capacity for openness and reaching out depends on their willingness to let go. Take for instance the lyrics of the song:

---

[2] I am indebted to Rose Okeregbe, who so described Fr. Ehusani's use of songs and music in his psycho-trauma healing sessions.

> This darkness will pass away
> Better days are coming
> We shall see the sunshine
> The clouds shall clear

The individual, be they a client or the ordinary listener, may choose to shroud themselves from the distressing importunities of life and allow the lyrics minister to them and the soporific melody of their desired song to transport them to another realm. They may choose to let loose from the chains of worries, depression and disillusionment and wallow in the reverie created by Ehusani's music. It may even lead the individual to console themselves and assuage their powerlessness by reaching to the source of their being or creating an imaginary all-powerful paternalistic being in order to give meaning to their life. In all this, it is the existential trait of freedom that is being expressed by the individual. The song shows the consciousness of the individual.

As existentialist thinkers would assert, consciousness is characterised by dignity and active intentions. Being conscious or aware or free entails that the individual must affirm or deny; hence, freedom involves the inevitability of choice. In this inevitability of choice, a responsibility is attached. Sartre expresses this inevitability of responsibility in freedom when he asserts that "freedom is the freedom to choose but not the freedom of not choosing. Not to choose is, in fact, to choose not to choose" (Sartre, 1969, p. 481). Moore, on his part, tersely captures this inevitable requirement of authentic existence when he stated: "No one can tell you how to live your life. No one knows the secrets of the heart sufficiently to tell others about them authoritatively" (Moore, 2002, p. xiii). Therefore, far from being talismanic, Ehusani's songs are solicitous in their auxiliary function of helping the individual to exercise their freedom.

In being open to the beauty and burden of freedom, the individual outlines what he or she wants to embrace: an attitude she wants to cultivate, a doctrine he seeks to understand, or a cause of action she desires to pursue. Thereafter, the typical probing that perplexes the individual comes to mind. What is at their disposal in the furtherance of this embrace with their existence? Are they being thrown into existence in a circumstance that is not of their making? Are they abandoned to the vagaries of both the factors of their constitution and experiences they must encounter? A proper response to these questions would be instrumental to an understanding of the individual's nature in existence. Heidegger uses the term facticity to refer to man's non-negotiated thrownness into the drama of existence. Man is thrown into something they have never bargained for, only to be left alone to sort out things for themselves. They are thrown into a world where they will not live forever, but have to struggle and eventually die. And, so, the moment an individual is born into this world, he/she is old enough to die (Heidegger, 1967, p. 160f.).

Thus, just as it is for Heidegger and Frankl, so it is for Ehusani. The facts of life are meaningful only to the individual who has thought them through personally, genuinely, but not through the prism of any publicly objectified position. They are meaningful also to the individual who has freely accepted the meaning they can genuinely make out of their reflection and are ready to accept the consequences as well as actively commit their existence to the cause necessitated by this facticity.

Although Ehusani's songs and use of music are meant to appeal to the general human community, the depth of meaningfulness they invoke have special appeal to the faith-based community, that is, a community of believers rather than of people with conflicting philosophical orientations. Philosophically speaking, faith is a trusting openness and response to the Unknown. But we can elevate this meaning of faith by asserting that this trusting openness to the Unknown is guided by the conviction that He who is greater than us all has a purpose for our being. Faith may then be a trusting openness to the divine will regardless of the human predicament. It is this virtue that John Paul II speaks of in his encyclical *Fides et ratio* (Faith and reason) (1998) as that gift of God which complements reason in the face of absurdities. When reason fails, as it often does, it is faith that justifies man's quest for the Unknown in the face of daunting absurdities (John Paul II, 1998, p. 48).

The Danish Protestant theologian and existentialist philosopher, Soren Kierkegaard, had argued from an existentialist perspective that living in faith is the authentic way to live in a world of absurdities and contradictions. Kierkegaard distinguished three stages in the exercise of freedom and the making of moral choices. These stages are the aesthetic, the ethical and the religious. Having criticised the aesthetic stage for seeking validation of freedom in man's capricious nature, and likewise the ethical stage for its dependence on fallible human reason,

Kierkegaard invites the individual to embrace the religious stage, which entails a response to a new awareness – of his finitude and estrangement from God to whom he belongs and from whom he must derive strength. However, the transition from this level to the religious stage is not achieved through an act of rationalisation, but by an act of commitment through a leap of faith. At this level, one is brought before the presence of God in a way that transcends any objective conceptualisation. It is a relationship that is both profound and fleeting, as if one is whirling in a vortex of immeasurable depth. Little wonder, then, that Johnson asserts:

The religious awakening is an Infinite and terrible experience; terrible because it has no recourse to the normal conventions that usually govern one's life: reason, rational inquiry, and objective analysis. None of these faculties that work so well in the first two stages has any meaning in the final stage (Johnson, 2002, para. 19).

Besides, one of the hallmarks of this relationship is its paradoxical nature because it cannot be discussed rationally or logically analysed. Here, as Stumpf (1991) interprets, "there is available no rational or conceptual or objective knowledge about this relationship. This relationship between God and each individual is a unique and subjective experience" (p. 482). Yet, it is owing to this profundity of meaning and logical cum communicative paradox, experienced in the religious stage, that the individual finds himself/herself in the realm of subjective truth – that highly personal mode of existence where one genuinely becomes an individual.

It is to the realisation of this stage, the spiritual realm or the supernatural world of faith, that Ehusani's 'music therapy' draws us. Ehusani's songs are better appreciated for drawing the individual to the consciousness of the religious state or, to use a more appropriate phrase, 'spiritual state'.

6. Conclusion

In the light of the conceptual clarification on music, liturgical music and music therapy, Ehusani's use of music may not be said to be music therapy in the strict scientific and technical sense. However, it may be construed as therapeutic in a special sense of being a Jungian-logotherapy influenced technique that uses positive affirmations through music or songs to nurture the soul, mind, and emotions. What one may discern from the analysis of Ehusani's songs is a theological anthropology which assumes that a person's action is the medium and the message of the gospel of love. According to Okeregbe (2006), in this theology of action, which finds credence in the 'humanist' crusades of Martin Luther King Jr., St Teresa of Calcutta and St John Paul II, man's ontological status as an image of God becomes the metaphysics on which their relationship with God and their fellow man is founded (p. B3). Ehusani follows the trail of this personalist spirituality by also using music as a vehicle for expressing the loving connection between the individual and God in whom they get their intrinsic worth and inviolable dignity.

References

Adeniyi, O. (2018). The application of folk music as therapy and social control for autistic children in Nigeria. In S. Olusoji, K. Oluseyi & F. Nweke (Eds.), *Music: A panacea for a country in distress: The contribution of Anthony Ekemezie Mereni* (pp. 137-147). Lagos: Department of Creative Arts, University of Lagos.

Bruscia, K. (1998). *Defining music therapy* (2nd ed.). Gilsum, NH: Barcelona Publishers.

Craig, H. (2020). What is music therapy and how does it work? Retrieved December 2, 2020 from http://www.positivepsychology.com.

Crichton, J. D. (1980). *Praying and singing.* London: Collins Liturgical Publications.

Cohen, G. L. & Sherman, D. K. (2014). The psychology of change: Self-affirmation and social psychological intervention. *Annual Review of Psychology,* 65. Retrieved November 11, 2020 from https://doi.org/10 .1146/annurev-psych-010213-115137.

Dagnini, J. K. (2010). The importance of Reggae music in the worldwide cultural universe. *Études Caribéennes.* 16 August, 2010. http://journals. openedition.org/etudescaribeennes/4740.

Davies, S. (2012). On defining music. *The Monist,* 95 (4), October, 535-555.

Dobrzynska, E., Cesarz, H., Rymaszewska, J. & Kiejna, A. (2006). Music therapy: History, definitions and application. *Archives of Psychiatry and Psychotherapy,* 8 (1), 47-52.

Ehusani, G. (2011). *Rev. Fr. George Ehusani in conversation, 2: The passion to serve humanity.* In T. Okeregbe (Ed.). Abuja: Lux Terra Leadership Foundation.

Ehusani, G. (2006a). Jazz the gospel. Audio CD. Lagos: Catholic Secretariat of Nigeria.

Ehusani, G. (2006b). Sing and shout for joy. Audio CD. Lagos: Catholic Secretariat of Nigeria.

Fortescue, A. (1910). Liturgy. *The Catholic Encyclopedia*, 9. New York: Robert Appleton Company.

Frankl, V. E. (1989). *Man's search for meaning.* New York: Washington Square Press.

Geretsegger, M., Elefant, C., Mössler, K. A. & Gold, C. (2014). Music therapy for people with Autism Spectrum Disorder. *Cochrane Database of Systematic Reviews 2014, Issue 6. Art. No.: CD004381.* Doi: 10.1002/14651858.CD004381.pub3.

Heidegger, M. (1967). *Being and time.* Maccquarrie, J. & Robinson, E. (transl.). New York: Harper and Row.

John Paul II, Pope (1998, September 14). Encyclical letter *fides et ratio.* Vatican City: The Vatican Press.

Johnson, D. (2002). Kierkegaard's stages toward authentic religious experience and the Bodhisattva Path to enlightenment. *Quodlibet Journal*, 4 (1), Retrieved on March 16, 2010 from http://www.quodlibet.net/articles/johnson-experience.shtm

Kania, A. (2011). Definition. In T. Gracyk & A. Kania (Eds). *The Routledge companion to philosophy and music*, 3. (p. 13). London: Routledge.

Levinson, J. (1990). *Music, art, and metaphysics.* Ithaca: Cornell University Press.

Maratos. A. S., Gold, C., Wang, X. & Crawford, M. J., (2008). Music therapy for depression. *Cochrane Database of Systematic Reviews 2008. Jan 23;(1):Art. No. CD004517.* Doi: 10.1002/14651858.CD004517.pub2.

Mesz, B. Rodriguez Zivic, P. H., Cecchi, G. A., Sigman M. & Trevisan M. A. (2015). The music of morality and logic. *Frontiers in Psychology*, 6:908. doi: 10.3389/fpsyg.2015.00908

Moges, A. (2006). Schopenhauer's philosophy. Retrieved on March 12, 2010 from http://www.galileanlibrary.org/schopenhauer.html

Moore, T. (1994). *Care of the soul: A guide for cultivating depth and sacredness in everyday life.* New York: Harper Collins Publishers Inc.

Okeregbe, T. (2006, November 5). Jazz of canticles and poems. *The Guardian on Sunday*. Lagos.

Olaleye, Olufemi. (2018). Thoughts and dynamisms of Merenian music school philosophy. In S. Olusoji, K. Oluseyi & F. Nweke (Eds.), *Music: A panacea for a country in distress: The contribution of Anthony Ekemezie Mereni* (pp. 9-19). Lagos: Department of Creative Arts, University of Lagos.

Reilly, S. A. & Dueck, J. M. (2016). *The Oxford handbook of music and world Christianities*. New York: Oxford University Press.

Sartre, J-P. (1969). *Being and nothingness*. London: Methuen Press.

Steele, C. M. (1998). The psychology of self-affirmation: Sustaining the integrity of the self. *Advances in Experimental Social Psychology* 21 (2), 261–302.

Stumpf, S. E. (1991). *A history of philosophy*. New York: McGraw-Hill Publishers.

The new world encyclopedia. Liturgical music. Retrieved on November 11, 2020 from http://www.newworldencyclopedia.org.

Vatican II Document. Vol. 1 Conciliar and Post Conciliar Documents (1965). Austin Flannery (Ed.) Dublin: Dominican Publications.

CHAPTER FOUR

An Expository Analysis of the Human Person and Human Dignity in George Ehusani's Christian Humanism

Philip Edema

1. Introduction

The focus of this chapter revolves around the human person, human dignity and African Christian humanism. These philosophical concepts on the face value look distinct, yet they are related. We are familiar with these concepts, especially within the context of the humanities and liberal arts. However, this chapter expositorily, analytically and conceptually examine how George Ehusani, a Catholic clergy and scholar, attempted to unravel the challenges bedevilling the human person in the twenty-first century especially with the advancements in science and technology. The work affirms that though humanity has benefited tremendously from the innovations of scientific and technological creations, it is essential that humanity tread with caution so as to avoid the half-truths these innovations offers us. This work concludes by arguing that the alternative to tackling the half-truths and abuses of technological innovations can be found in George Ehusani's African Christian humanism. These alternatives promote humanistic development, rather than materialistic development. The former emphasises the human person, human dignity, its ontology and the divine origin and the culture of dignifying life. This chapter is divided into four parts. The first part consists of the introduction, conceptual examination of the human person, human dignity, and humanism; second consist of Ehusani's narratives on the crisis of humanism in the twentieth century. The third part exposes elements of African Christian humanism proposed by Ehusani. The conclusion explains movement from a materialistic to humanistic paradigm as a way of entrenching humanistic development that is devoid of crass materialistic tendencies, to a humane and culture of life and dignity.

2. On the Nature of Human Person and Human Dignity

In this work, the concepts of the "human person," "human being" and "man" would be used interchangeably. The discourse on the human person in the history of philosophy is quite fascinating. The debate on 'who is the person?' has raised many contributions from philosophers of different orientations and schools of thought. In all of these analysis, interpretations and critical evaluations, the fact remains that the nature of the person is one complex reality. The more we attempt to understand it, the more elusive it appears. One thing is sure, that the human person is a valuable entity whose place cannot be taken for granted.

Historically, the word 'person' marks demarcation between pagan and Christian culture (Mondin.1985:243). The word is derived from the Latin word *persona*, meaning a mask, and the Greek *proposan*; meaning a face, role, character or part. Actors wear a mask in Greek and Roman dramas and the face, role, character or part is the action performed by the actors in a drama (Joseph Okemwa.1997:62). The term 'person' also has a theological origin, which is traceable to the patristic period; when the Church formulated the dogma of the mystery of the Holy Trinity and the Incarnation of the second person of the Holy Trinity (Okonkwo.2010: 62). The 'known' classical definition of Boethius (480-524 AD) states that a person is an individual substance of a rational nature. But not all substances are persons. This Boethius' definition attracted a barrage of criticisms; nevertheless, the definition remains classical.

Socrates concerned himself with the truth about man with his popular dictum, "Man know thyself". It was said that he was the first philosopher to consider man as a moral being. He equated knowledge with virtue. For him, virtue and good deeds follow from knowledge, while wrongdoing is due to man's ignorance (Copleston. 2003:108). He laid emphasis on the care of the soul because for him the soul is more important than the body (Arrington: 517). Aristotle describes 'the person' as a rational animal. In other words, rationality is what distinguishes man from other things in the universe. Aristotle used the doctrine of hylomorphism (the theory that all material things are a composite of matter and form) to explain the relationship between the body and soul. He opines that man is made up of body and soul with the soul being the animating nucleus. Body and soul forms an inseparable substance. He differed from Plato who argued that the soul is accidentally united to the body (Copleston. 2003: 328-329). For Plato, the human person is essentially the soul, spiritual, incorruptible, and therefore immortal.

Augustine a Neo-Platonists affirmed that man is the peak of God's creation. He shares similar views with Plato by reducing the essence of man to the soul. St Thomas Aquinas based his conception of man on the metaphysical explanation of Aristotle's hylomorphic doctrine. He advanced Aristotle's thought in arguing for the subsistence of the soul which in turn supports his argument of the immortality of the soul. He sees the soul as the first principle of life which animates all living beings (Adler. 1990). Simply, Aquinas' anthropology conceives man essentially as a composite of body and soul. The soul is not sub-ordinate to the body, but the body is subordinate to the soul (Copleston. 2003:339).

The idea of rationality and freedom of will was central in the Kantian understanding of man. For Kant man belongs to both the noumenal and the phenomenal world. With this, man could be conceived as having a dual nature. Thus, for Kant, since man belongs to the class organic or material beings, he forms part of the sensible order and is subject to the laws of nature. (Copleston. 203: 391). In addition, "man transcends the phenomenal or sensible sphere and forms part of the noumenal or suprasensible world because of his freedom; a property which is outside the causal principles of the world but which nevertheless belongs to man (Copleston. 203).

Furthermore, the centrality of the human person is fundamental in Kant's ethical theory. This was clearly delineated in the second formulation of the categorical imperative which states that, "act in such a way that you treat humanity, whether in your own person or in that of another, always as an end and never as a means only" (Immanuel Kant. 2006:38). Here, Kant affirms the dignity of person. The person is of important value that deserves respect at all times.

There are different components or parts that form the nature of the human person from the African perspective, especially in relation to the Igbo and Yoruba ethnic groups of Nigeria. For instance, the Igbo refer to these components when they attempt to describe and analyse what it is to be a person. They include: *mmadu* or *madu*, (human being) *muo* (spirit), *ahu* (body), *ihu* (face), *nkpuruobi* (seed of the heart), *chi* (destiny), *obi* (heart), *uche* (mind,), *Eke or Agu* (Ancestral Guardian). For the Yoruba ethnic group, the following components when put together and analysed, give us a better understanding of the person. They include: *eniyan* (person/human being), *ara* (body), *okan* (heart), *emi* (spirit), *ori* (destiny/spiritual head).

Although the intention of this work is not to go into details of these different components that express the real nature of the person from the Yoruba and Igbo ethnic groups. Studies have shown that:

> African perception of the person reveals that the person is a composite of different entities. Again...there is an agreement that the person consists basically of a material aspect and spiritual aspect. This presupposes dualism. However, what is unique about the African understanding of the human person is that there is not strict categorical difference between the spiritual and the material. The Africa conception of the human person therefore embraces and transcends the Western...it is a combination of the physical and metaphysical. It is diametrically opposed to the Western notion of person that revolves around functionalism and materialism. Again, in the African perception of the person, the individual is sometimes subsumed under the community. This is as a result of the belief of Africans that it is the community that shapes, determines the social, religious, political and as well as the moral status of every human person. (Edema Philip. 2015: 75).

Simply, in the African perspective, three aspects of the human person are realised; the transcendental, the communal and the individual. The person is not only one who lives in the world, but is one who also relates with the transcendental, that is, the divine.

3. Human Dignity

What does it mean to say that a human being has dignity? It is generally conceived that every human being has an intrinsic dignity that is not conferred on the individual by society but is simply recognised. The implication of this is that human beings by the virtue of their existence are persons of value, interest, respect, rights and essence. Saint Pope John Paul II rightly asserted "human dignity is rooted in person's creation in the image and likeness of God. It thus implies and requires uprightness of moral conscience and the pursuit of common good" (Okonkwo. 2010:171).

Kirchoffer and Dierickx (2012: 74) argued that the proper way to understand human dignity is through the multidimensional and historical approaches. They state that the multidimensional approach involves a philosophical observation that a human person exists as a being *per se*, and as a being situated in historical time; that is, as both an ontological and existential reality. By implication, "human dignity is simultaneously (i) already and always present for all human beings as human beings; and (ii) not yet fully realised as, human beings are subject to the moral ambiguity of historical circumstances, in which they nonetheless seek to realise the fullness of their dignity" (Kirchoffer and Dierickx.2012: 74-75). Put simply, human dignity is both 'already' and 'not yet' (2012).Indeed, all human persons already have dignity because they possess a broad range of capacities, such as reason and free choice, emotion, affiliation, imagination and play. Thus, to "respect human dignity, therefore, means to protect both our inherent potential and the realised sense of self-worth" (Kirchoffer and Dierickx, 2012: 74). Etienne de Villiers (2010: 268) summarily captures the essence and the content of human dignity thus:

> There is, first of all, an *ontological* dimension that entails that all human beings have human dignity, because it is bestowed on them as a gift in the act of God's creation and the justification of human beings. Secondly, there is an *experiential* dimension in that the human dignity that God has bestowed on every human being only becomes an experienced reality for an individual when it is internalised in a positive attitude of self-respect. Thirdly, there is a *normative* dimension in that human dignity holds normative implications for both the carrier of human dignity and for those who interact with him or her. Human dignity entails that the carrier has the responsibility to act in a dignified way, by fulfilling God's moral vocation with respect to him/herself, fellow human beings and nature. Other human beings, but also institutions such as the state, in turn have the responsibility to respect the human dignity of the carrier, both in withholding themselves from humiliating treatment and in enhancing the wellbeing of the carrier. In essence, human dignity is regarded to be inviolable, unique, inalienable and inherent in all human beings.

4. The Idea of Humanism

The idea of humanism is premised on the basis that human beings or persons are able to live together, collaborate with one another in order to transform the world to a better place. Essentially, humanism is mostly a human philosophy of 'good' life. The focus is on the human person, the here and now, and the humane. For humanists, it is about bringing values and meaning to life (Herrick. 2006:1). Herrick writes that "the word has developed since its use to describe a belief system that calls upon reason and values to enable us develop our lives and societies" (2006:1). It examines the nature of the universe, the nature of human beings and treatment of human problems. Humanism emphasises the use of reason to arrive at what is true, good and beautiful; and that human beings possess the capacity to solve their own problems by relying on reason and scientific method. Ultimately, humanists are of the view that human beings can attain good life by harmoniously combining personal efforts and self-development so as to contribute effectively to the welfare of their communities (Lamont. 1997:13).

Abam and Edema (2020) stated that humanism in true African sense, promotes communion among groups of people who together experience reciprocity of awareness. Furthermore, the virtue of being hospitable to strangers that flows from the African spirit of solidarity and togetherness is one that places Africans on the lead step to bringing about the spirit of humanism. Against this background, humanism encourages humankind to strive towards being accommodating to all irrespective of their colour, religion, ethnicity or background. Humanism transcends individualism. In the African sense, it is entrenched in the words 'I am because you are, because you are therefore I am.' Humanism is summed up not only in the worth of an individual since that individual is equally tied to a global community. To this end, by protecting the individual we are invariably protecting ourselves since our fates are bound in the collective (Abam and Edema. 2020). Oyeshile captures this better when he writes that:

> as Dasiens, both at the individual and ethnic group levels, survival is only possible if and only if we recognise the importance of others not as mere objects standing in the way of achieving our goal of survival, but as end in themselves who are not only important but inevitable and inescapable in the realisation of our goal of survival and freedom (Olatunji Oyeshile, 2005: 32).

5. Crisis of Humanism in the Twenty-First Century

George Ehusani's idea of Christian humanism emanated on his polarisation of the events of the twenty-first century, which he termed, 'Phenomenal Technological Advancement'. (Ehusan.1991:5). He described the twentieth century as the 'fastest' century there has been. Pellegrino (2008:1) quoting Gabriel Marcel on the beauty and danger of technology is apt here, "The problem in question is that of understanding what happens to human dignity in the process of technicalisation to which man today is delivered" (Pellegrino 2008: 1). Within this period, the world had recorded both the good and the bad.

Ehusani listed the good technological advancement and achievements such as, the discovery of the radio and telephone enhanced by the balloon and satellite communication systems. The advancement in communication has also made the exchange of goods and services easier. For instance, "an American could now wake up from a bed made in Korea, wash with soap made in France, drink coffee made in Colombia", etc., (1991: 5). Similarly, Ehusani affirmed that the technological revolution has reduced the world to one global village whereby, "white and black, Easterners and Westerners, Gentile and Jew, Catholic and Protestant, Muslim and Hindu, now belong to one great "world" house". (1991: 5).

Again, there has been spectacular development in the agricultural sector, breakthroughs in technological medicine, which has solved the problem of deadly diseases such as leprosy, small pox, malaria fever and tuberculosis (1991: 5-6). Medicine has expanded beyond what we use to know. For instance, Ehusani asserted that:

> ...today we have a whole range of technical equipment and procedures available for keeping people alive: from anti-clotting drugs to cardiac perfusion devices, from intravenous feeding to electroshock therapy for the heart, from respirators to nasal-gastric tubes, from ultra-sound to amniocentesis for pre-natal diagnosis, and from neurosurgery to effective antibiotics. With further conquests which medicine promises to make cardiology, gynaecology and genetic engineering, can it not be said that we are knocking at the door of physical immortality?

Pellegrino (2008:1) added that beyond the list of medical discoveries mentioned above, there are more like embryonic stem cell research, preimplantation genetic diagnosis, enhancements of human physical and mental capabilities, the practice of regenerative medicine, the uses of nanotechnology, and re-engineering the human species. It is worthy of mention that the exploration of these technologies has generated moral, religious, social and legal debates as it relates to the dignity of the human person. This further confirms Ehusani's fears in the above citation, 'that we are knocking at the door of physical immortality.'

Beyond the discoveries in medicine, Ehusani also mentioned the technological achievements of the computer. With this discovery, a lot of activities are easily carried out such as computations in various sectors of human life. Specifically, the computer is said to be capable of performing two billion calculations per second. It is also useful in digital library program such that it is possible for a student to access any material within a short time (1991: 6).

In contrast, Ehusani (1991:7) stated that the same twentieth century has been the 'bloodiest' in the history of humankind. By this, he meant, this century has suffered from two world wars which the world prays to never experience again. These events had further advanced and encouraged proliferation and accumulation of deadly weapons such as atomic weapons, bacteriological and chemical weapons of destruction. These weapons are not only deadly, they are also poisonous to the natural environment and has even robbed humanity of enormous human and financial resources which could have otherwise been used to fight poverty, ignorance and disease, which still hold most of humanity captive (1991: 7). Beyond the wars and proliferation of weapons in different parts of the world especially in Africa, there has been consistent act of terrorism perpetrated not only by the weak against the powerful, but often enough by the powerful against the weak. The consequences:

> Millions of human lives are destroyed in these wars and armed clashes; and many of those who survive are either reduced to the status of refugees, die of starvation or the epidemics that result from the wars, or remain physically or psychologically maimed for life.(1991: 8).

What is most worrisome is that the cases of terrorism, banditry and ethnic clashes are not decreasing especially in Africa, specifically, Nigeria. The numbers of IDP camps are increasing daily. For instance, the rising cases of insurgency in the Northern region of Nigeria have sent many people to IDP camps. Some are either kidnapped, like the Chibok girls case, while the rest are killed, recruited or maimed for life. This is properly described as the culture of death and human dignity further eroded. Human life is easily dispensable; the value attached to human worth is discarded.

Ehusani also identifies another culture of death that he considered a threat to human life and dignity and they include abortion, euthanasia, reproductive technology and genetic engineering. The controversy about these above listed medical practices and research is about the moral implications on the dignity of the human person. For instance, according to Ehusani, "millions of unborn children have died at the hands of their mothers! And as the medical procedures for abortions are becoming more sophisticated, so are the casualties increasing" (Ehusani 1991: 9). The question is who are the casualties? They are the unborn children who are considered persons especially among the pro-life scholars. The human embryos are not only potential persons; rather, they are already persons deserving the same rights as adult persons. In this case, abortion is immoral and unacceptable. Ehusani writes, euthanasia which was considered unacceptable world-wide when Nazi Germany practiced it during the World War II, is beginning to gain approval today among many people in the advanced nations (1991: 9). This kind of practice is considered as another threat to human life. Regarding the progress made in reproductive technology and genetic engineering; with practices in: In vitro fertilisation, artificial insemination, surrogate motherhood and embryo transfer and lately, cloning and embryonic stem cell research, Ehusani considers these technological procedures as dangerous, immoral and an attempt to remove the 'mystique' surrounding human generation. The consequence of these experimentations is that the dignity and uniqueness of the human person is undermined (Ehusani 1991: 9-10). For Karol Wojtyla, one thing that defines and dignifies the human person is the irreplaceable uniqueness of everyone and the interiority of spiritual life (See Edema 2015: 170).

Among other things that have degraded the human person in the twentieth century, which must be corrected is the war against the family system. The family plays a very fundamental role in society across the globe and its importance cannot be undermined as it were. Thus, Ehusani rightly observed that the war against the family which results in leaving the individual as a free and autonomous unit of society is erroneous. This kind of practice erodes the sense of community and ultimately causes the individual to lose his or her identity (Ehusani 1991: 10). Simply, communalistic living is far more productive than individualism. In addition, the increasing rate of divorce in our societies is a reflection of the general deterioration in human relationships (Ehusani 1991: 10). It is a matter of fact that division in the family does not produce any good result and the society often suffers for it. How else does one explain the increasing rate of street children who are mostly from broken homes? It is also true that these street children are easy targets for crime lords to recruit in order to perpetuate crimes and criminalities in different communities around the world. Recently, the Borno State governor had to cry out that the children situated at the IDP camps are easily recruited into the Boko Haram; it is so, because of poverty, displacement and irresponsibility of the Nigerian government to protect them *ab initio* from the attack of these bandits.

Another frightening aspect of this century is the level of abject poverty amidst affluence. In other words, "the phenomenon of starvation on the one hand, and what is cynically referred to as 'affluenza' on the other" (Ehusani 1991: 10). Pope John XXIII called the attention of the "world to the enormous wealth and unbridled luxury of the few which stand in violent and offensive contrast to the utter poverty of the vast majority" (1919: 10). This kind of attitude is inimical to progress; it is injustice to the poor and certainly inhumane to squander goods that other people need for their survival (1991: 10). Similarly, the human person has also been degraded in the technological and industrialised society, where idolatry of what Ehusani calls 'Economism' has its most appalling effect. He said:

> The attractions of efficiency and mass production have conspired to rob the factory workers of their creativity, affectivity, spontaneity and responsibility, making them mere cogs in the industrial mega-wheel, or turning them to what Yablonsky has called 'Robopaths'. Productive work has replaced meaningful labour, quantitative criteria have dislodged the deeply human yearning for quality and uniqueness, while a rift has occurred between work and leisure (1919: 11).

In essence, technology which is meant to free the human body and mind from toil and drudgery; to provide for the human person's material needs and to conquer diseases; to elevate culture through fostering reflection, through stimulating internal communication and through making possible a wide variety of rewarding jobs and tasks have been perverted (Ehusani 1991:12). By perversion, Ehusani meant that technology is now been used as the instrument of destruction of the environment, waste and pollution, upset of the eco-system, threat of annihilation because of the proliferation of nuclear weapons. Pope John Paul II also warns that there are three things we must avoid in relation to technology; first, technology should not be seen as an end in itself. Secondly, technology should not be used as a weapon of development and economic enslavement such that it creates advantages for some and leaving others in poverty, without preoccupying oneself with the true common good. And thirdly, technology should not be used as an attempt to enslave the acquisition or maintenance of power to manipulate and dominate the people (Battista Mondin. 1985:180). Rather than man controlling the pace of technology, the opposite is the case.

Another way whereby technology and the human person have been denigrated is through the advertisement and entertainment industries. There are subliminal messages in the kind of music, films and advertisement that are provided in the media space. These messages are meant to control and manipulate the moral weakness, ignorance and irrationality of the consumer (1991: 12). Ehusani made reference to the following:

> The young people enjoy 'heavy metal' music featuring such lyrics as "tear the baby out of your womb and stump it for fun". It is believed that this type of music plays a subliminal role in attracting young people into Devil worship, and sustains them through their sordid and sadistic rituals...No less offensive to human dignity is the amount of pornographic and sleazy materials traded on television, telephone, radio, newspapers and in fine arts. These materials glorify sensuality and promiscuity, demean fatherhood and motherhood, encourage all sorts of experimentation in sexual behaviour...Vulgar language is one of the subtle ways in which the dignity and sacredness of human life is being undermined in contemporary culture (1991: 12-13). These social ills are part of the unacceptable realities of the twentieth century which Ehusani considers toxic to the dignity of the human person.

6. An African Christian Humanism

The focus of this work is geared towards understanding some factors that has degraded the human person in the twenty-first century as pointed out by George Ehusani. It is true that man's creativity, wisdom and ingenuity has paved way for progress and development, yet some of the activities of this man, have not been favourable to man himself and to his/her immediate society. These problems, we have already analysed above. At this point, Ehusani provides a way forward in his African Christian humanism. According to Ehusani, "African Christian Humanism shall be seen as an alternative value system which deserves to be considered by a world in search of meaning...it rejects western secular humanism for its anti-supernaturalistic stance" (1991: 207-209).

What exactly is this African Christian humanism? Ehusani was concerned that when the missionaries arrived Africa, they failed to dialogue with the nature of the African culture and religion they met. As such what we had was not Christianisation of Africa; rather, what the missionaries succeeded in doing was the Westernization of Africa. Ehusani (1991: 209) quoted Fitzpatrick that:

> European missionaries, thinking sincerely that they were bringing the true faith to the African, were in actuality bringing them European culture in which the faith had been given expression for many centuries. The Europeans had lost the ability to communicate the Faith without its European cultural manifestation.

This for Ehusani is most worrisome and has been the base of the cultural and religious crisis affecting the human person in Africa. In other words, foreign religion without regard for our way of life has partly been responsible for the problems and challenges we enumerated. The point about culture influencing religion and vice versa is vital to a people's progress and development. This is perhaps the reason many Pan-African scholars would always blame the slow pace of development in Africa to colonisation and neo-colonisation. Thus, for Ehusani, "the missionaries proclaimed the Gospel and implanted the Church, but in many cases they did not touch the innermost depths of the local cultures" (1991: 206). The implication of this is that the 'foreign' faith and culture of the people was not properly blended to fit in into the people's way of life. If this is the case, then, proper evangelisation would not have taken place resulting in what Ehusani described as crisis of identity. In addition, "this insensitivity of missionary Christianity to the deeply spiritual values of the African heritage may result in the total loss of cultural and philosophical matrix which...constitute the foundation upon which a new faith can be built" (Ehusani 1991: 206).

From the foregoing, Ehusani asserted that when Mbiti describes the traditional African as 'notoriously religious', what he meant was that the Africans are deeply spiritual people who have so much respect for the divine and Supreme Being. It is difficult as it were to separate religion from the way of life of an average African person. Religion and religious activities pervades their thinking, their social lives, the names they bear, places, rituals, songs, greetings, the proverbs, festivals and ceremonies. One more interesting thing about the deep African consciousness of religion is that the traditional African cosmology, recognises that no item of the universe is a chance collation of atoms or molecules as we have in Western philosophy and evolutionary science, but that there inheres in the universe some natural, spiritual and mystical order, put in place by God. This aspect of African traditional religion was not a concept the early missionaries and ethnologists could relate to and as a result is called African traditional religion Animism (1991: 208). In addition, Ehusani stated that....

> early explorers could not comprehend the fact that the traditional African does not experience God in terms of concepts and theories. He or she experiences God as an awesome *Presence*, sustaining him or her long before birth... (1991: 208).

Pope Paul VI confirms the beauty of African traditional religion and the rich African legacy by describing that:

> The constant and general foundation of African tradition is the spiritual view of life...We have a deeper, broader and more universal concept which considers all living things and visible nature itself as linked with the world of the invisible and the spirit. In particular, it has never considered man as mere matter limited to earthly life, but recognises in him the presence and power of another spiritual element, in virtue of which human life is always related to the after-life (1991: 208).

This narrative of Pope Paul VI further confirms that the African perception of the divine from the perspective of religion is different, more engaging and more expressive of our reality and context. This is why Ehusani affirmed that African traditional religion rejects western secular humanism for its anti-supernaturalistic stance.

7. On the Meaning of Life

There is no denying the fact that Africans place so much respect and value to human life. Africans celebrate the birth of life in the person of a new-born baby and also celebrate the end of life, especially of an adult person old enough to die. This goes to show how the nature or idea of life is to an average African person. Africans are known to protect the sanctity of life and challenge whoever threatens human life. Life is seen as a precious gift that must be guarded jealously.

Having said this much on the value of life, Ehusani made reference to the fact that technological civilisation which is responsible for a lot of good things is also responsible for the abuses of secularism, whereby the sanctity of human life from conception to death is undermined. For instance, Ehusani argues that, Africa has now joined the rest of the world where deliberate termination of the life of the unborn child is considered in certain quarters as a civil right (1991: 212). This scenario is not only unacceptable, but offensive and incredible to the traditional African for whom the bearing of children is a blessing and not a curse. It is against the faith of the African Christian who considers human life as a gift of God. Similar to the abortion controversy is the challenge of population control. For the traditional African, "the more we are the bigger l am", shows the relevance and more importantly how Africans cherish population and the large family. However, the population control movement sees the arrival of an additional human being as undesirable. In other words, the coming of more children to the world is seen as a burden and Africans find themselves in a world in which people are not only counted and treated like statistics but are considered too many (1991: 212-213). These are the fallouts of abuse of technological innovations and secularism.

Beyond these, Ehusani made it abundantly clear that Africans do not just speak about the value of human life, but they do so in relation to the Divine Being-God. Put differently, "Africans also believe strongly that human life has a supernatural end and that physical death does not write 'finis' to human existence" (1991: 214). This explanation reveals the vital relationship which Africans continue to maintain with their departed relations in the form of the cult of Ancestors. This African belief is comparable to the Christian message of the Resurrection, which constitutes the centre of the 'Primitive Kerygma' (1991: 214). This foregoing justifies the assertion of Molefi Asante that for the African, "the human is divine". The human person transcends the merely physical and material world and that the person maintains a mystical communion not only with the Creator, but also with the elements of "the world in-between (1991: 214-215).

Respect for the elderly is so prized and important to the average African and is also related to the transcendence. For Ehusani, "old people are revered, not only because they are the forbearers of society, but also because they are now at the threshold of final fulfilment, and thus have reached the highest stage of transcendence possible in this world" (1991: 215). Benjamin Kiriswa as cited by Ehusani (1991: 215) said, that the traditional African respect for elders reflected reverence for God and the spirits of Ancestors". Consequently, longevity is more of a blessing within the African traditional society. The experience and words of the elders are cherished and disrespect for elders is not tolerated whatsoever.

Furthermore, euthanasia, which is known as mercy killing has no place in African Christian society. The aged are not considered a burden to be discarded. God gives life and takes it at his own time. It is not our duty to help one to die a mercy death. Life and death belong to God alone. On this, Ehusani (1991: 215) rightly observes that:

> In the African cosmology, the human reality stands in a class of its own, far above any other inhabitant of the universe. The African therefore sees as utterly degrading, the scientific approach to the human person which sees him or her as an animal little separable from the anthropoids. Such definitions of the human being as, for example, 'a rational animal' are very offensive to the traditional African who prefers to use divine or spiritual entities as the points of reference for the human person.

Consequently, Ehusani in furtherance to the above rejected the abusive nature of modern medicine whereby the divine origin and supernatural end of the human person is undermined. For instance, do we have the absolute right or authority to produce or dispose our kind or to introduce radical mutations into the nature of the human species? These techniques in question include: *in vitro fertilisation and artificial insemination, surrogate motherhood, extracorporeal gestation, fetal experimentation and sex pre-selection and lately, sex change, embryonic stem cell research, male pregnancy, cloning, etc.* Why Ehusani considers these techniques and procedures immoral and inhumane is the process involved. For example, they involve:

> the super-ovulation of the woman by artificial means for the procurement of a large number of her ova; the procurement of the male semen in the laboratory by way of masturbation; the freezing of live human embryos for indefinite periods of time; and the discarding or wilful destruction of embryos produced in excess, and the commercialisation of the womb, by which a woman gets pregnant only to surrender the fruit of the womb at any stage of its development for a fee. Experimentation with the foetuses has at times involved such a bizarre act as the slicing open of the rib cage of a still living human foetus (in order to observe the heart action); and the removal of vital organs of live foetuses for study (1991: 215-216).

These procedures are inimical to the traditional African who treats the foetus as human life, and also sees 'life' in the umbilical cord of a new born baby. This explains why the umbilical cord is buried in ritualistic manner, away from the public view. The traditional African attaches profound importance and dignity to the life of the new-born child. The average African believes strongly in the spiritual reality and connection of the child's umbilical cord and that is the sole reason it is disposed carefully for the protection of such child.

8. A Holistic Approach to Life

How should we approach the issue of human dignity such that the abuses against and ill-treatment of the human person can be reduced? What are the measures that must be put in place in the face of rapid technological creations and innovations for the protection of human life? To these, Ehusani asserted that the first thing we must take note of is the fact that, among the traditional African persons, the bifurcation of metaphysical and anthropological dualism that seems to divide reality as seen in western philosophy, science and theology does not exist. In other words, the African person does not have a problem in understanding the intersecting co-existence of both the physical and the visible, spiritual and invisible forces of the universe. In other words, there is no contradiction in them. There is a kind of symbiotic relationship between them; a harmonious interrelationship. The two worlds intersect in a dynamic communion such that the dichotomy between the sacred and the profane, matter and spirit, the supernatural and the natural, which defines the Western world view, is strikingly absent in Africa (1991: 291-220). Additionally, the idea of 'social dualism' does not exist in the mind of the traditional African. Simply, the individual and the community are not separated; they are one and the same. For Ehusani, "the community cannot constitute a threat for the individual, for it is precisely in community that individual existence is affirmed, as the saying goes: 'I am because we are, and since we are therefore l am'.

9. From the Materialistic to the Humanistic

At this point in our human and mortal existence, there is a need for us to pause and reflect on some critical issues about ourselves and our immediate environment. To what extent has technological advancement promoted the common good and human dignity? Has technological advancement solved all our problems or created more problems and challenges? There is no denying the obvious that science and technology have substantially assisted humanity to achieving the impossible. Nevertheless, the fears raised by George Ehusani are fundamental if we must promote the good of man. Science and technology ought to serve as a means to an end, not an end in itself. The fundamental challenges arising from reckless scepticism, secularism and abuse of technological innovations call for serious concerns. For instance, Ehusani (1991: 241) argued that we had been deceived by technological science which promised unending joy, peace and immortality; but it has failed to deliver any of these good, leaving us more confused and disoriented. What we see today is that people are "blinded by materialism, poisoned by consumerism, enslaved by greed and humiliated by aggressions, human beings appear to have lost their sense of meaning and purpose" (1991: 241). Thus, for Ehusani, there is a need for a paradigm shift; a movement from materialistic tendencies to a more humanistic world. A world where the interest and the collective good of all are given a humanistic consideration is germane; a more dignified society where human beings are regarded and accorded the respect that is due to them. This kind of society is possible when we promote the tenets of African humanistic value system (1991: 241).

In shifting to a humanistic paradigm, Ehusani, (1991: 242) warned that we should be wary of Western civilisation that parades half-truths as the 'TRUTH' where the world is stratified along the lines of First World, Second World and a Third World, where there are developed nations and developing nations. The yardstick for this stratification is purely economic or material advancement. This criterion is not enough as it only promotes materialism as a successful imperialist. Simply put ..."near-absolutisation and universalisation of purely economic category, is the triumph of materialistic reductionism, in which the world is judged, humanity stratified and development measured..." (Ehusani. 1991: 242). Ehusani rejects these "categories on the basis of reducing the human person by how much he or she eats, how fast he or she travels and how well he or she uses space and people, etc., but not by *who he or she is*". This narrow understanding of the human person today is responsible for the neglect of proper human development. The consequences are a new 'Dark Age' like sophistication in criminality, terrorism, nuclear weapon scare, 'High-Tech' baby-making, several abuses in biotechnology, and the age of widespread meaninglessness (1991: 242).

The way forward is to promote a humanistic value system and re-prioritising our developmental processes. Like Pope Paul VI said in his *Populorum Progression*, "human development ought to be the promotion of the good of people, every person, and the whole person". (See Ehusani, 242-243). In addition, Ehusani listed the following components of humanistic development: aside material development, development has to embrace the soul and the spirit of the human person and the physical environment; development must see the growth and fulfilment of the human person, as the goal of progress in science and technology, in economics, in politics and in religion; development must be a human fact; it must be more spiritual and cultural than economic and technical; development must not mean *'to have more'*, rather it must mean *'to be more'*; development must mean an ongoing commitment to advance from less human conditions of disease, hatred, crime, war, violence, nepotism, ethnic conflict, terrorism, racism, poverty, injustice, corruption, hopelessness, etc., to the more human conditions of health, of love, peaceful co-existence, equity, justice, community fellow-feeling, faith and hope; development must be understood in its material, moral, spiritual, social and environmental dimensions, if it is to be a truly human endeavour (1991: 243).Anything short of the listed components is absurd. The development makes meaning with the dignity of the person intact. Without this, the human person loses his or her sense of meaning and purpose and the entire reality becomes meaningless.

The Catholic Church which George Ehusani belongs to as a clergy man reminds us that personhood is rooted in a belief that dignity and rights are inherent in someone naturally. It does not matter whether these rights are recognised or not; what it means is that a person is defined by nature (See Dylan James). Thomas Aquinas added that as recorded in Gen 1:26, it was only man and woman God created in his image; this goes to show that this image is not something merely extrinsic to man, it is not something imprinted onto him, instead, it is something that holds from the very type of being that he is (See Dylan James). This analysis in itself places value on persons. In talking about the value, Immanuel Kant argued that human beings ought to be treated with respect, as ends in themselves. Karol Wojtyla provided a similar variant of Kant's second formulation that, "whenever a person is the object of your activity, remember that you may not treat that person as only the means to an end, as an instrument, but must allow for the fact that he or she too, has, or at least should have a distinct personal end" (Karol Wojtyla. 1981: 28).

The implications of Kant and Wojtyla's submission like Ehusani earlier noted is that, the weakest in our society must be protected and should not be exploited by the half-truths of science and technology. As Roger Scruton rightly noted, "personhood is not a property that 1 possess, but my way of being". (See Grzegor Holub. 2016: 177). Battista Mondin (1885: 257) affirmed that, "all humanisms which have thrived during the last few centuries agree in assigning to the man, to the human person, an absolute, inviolable, non-instrumental value, worthy of the greatest respect and consideration". In the light of these aforementioned, it becomes pertinent that we must care for one another and be responsible for the gift of life which has been entrusted to us. It is our duty to respect life and the conscious of the fact that freedom goes with responsibility. It is the eternal truth that must guide our actions and lived experience as acting persons.

10. Conclusion

This work set out to expose what George Ehusani calls the crisis of humanism in the twenty-first century. In achieving this, the paper discusses and analyses the nature of the human person, human dignity and humanism. These expositions gave the work the needed foundation towards understanding the context to situate the arguments of Ehusani. In the narratives, Ehusani hinged the cause of the crisis on half-truths coming from modern science and technological innovations and creations. This crisis is responsible for the dehumanisation of the value of the human person and when the person loses his/her sense of meaning, purpose, existence and essence, then the entire reality becomes meaningless and human purpose and achievements are subject to futility. The reason Battista Mondin (1985: 1) reminded us that man is the supreme question for man, such that every other interrogative, every other question- about the earth, the sky, the moon, the stars, the air, the water, atoms, cells, etc., even about God acquires relevance only with reference to our being. Ehusani therefore submitted that to retrace our steps, we must promote and entrench in our societies, African Christian humanistic value system. It is a moral system that is capable of showing that every human person, even the unborn deserves respect, dignity and equal treatment under the cosmos.

Consequently, this paper concludes that the discourse concerning the dignity and integrity of the human person must be given a profound attention in the twenty-first century owing to the fact that a lot of activities and programs from the medical fields, entertainment industry, political process and practices, labour industry, educational sector, the family, etc., are inimical to the well-being of the average person in our society. The language of 'modern man' is about excessive profit to the detriment of human dignity and integrity. Relevant agencies, the media, NGOs, and institutions are encouraged to use their spaces to canvas for existential humanism that is powered to promote the tenets and principles of human dignity in all ramifications. It is worthy of mention that the truth about the human dignity is constant, objective and natural to our existence. Importantly, human life is a special gift that ought to be valued irrespective of the ethnic group, tribe, or human activities as it were. In essence therefore, just as George Ehusani argued, the destruction and dehumanisation of the human person by whatever means cannot be justified; human dignity elevates the sacredness of human life and common good.

References

Abam Michael and Edema Philip. (2020). "Fela's Humanism and the Crisis of Governance in Nigeria". *Bodija Journal: A Philosophico-Theological Journal.* Vol. 10. 117-134.

Arrington L. Robert. (2001). *A Companion to the Philosophers.* Oxford: Blackwell Publishers.

Copleston Frederick. (2003). *A History of Philosophy. Greece and Rome.* I. London: Continuum.

Copleston Frederick. (2006). *A History of Philosophy. The Enlightenment.* VI. London: Continuum.

Copleston Frederick. (2003). *A History of Philosophy: Medieval Philosophy.* II. London: Continuum.

Dylan James. "Science and Modern Threats to the Human Person". *Faith Magazine.* Retrieved August 2011, from www.faith.org.uk.

Edema Philip. (2015). Ontological Personalism and the Ethics of Stem Cell Research. Thesis. Philosophy, Arts. University of Ibadan. i-xxix. +194.

Etienne de Villiers. (2010). "The Recognition of Human Dignity in Africa: A Christian Ethics of Responsibility Perspective". *Scriptura.* 104.

George O. Ehusani (1991). *An Afro-Christian Vision (OZOVEHE): Toward a more Humanized World.* Lanham: University Press of America, Inc.

Grzegor Holub. (2016). "Human Enhancement, the Person and PostHuman Personhood". *Ethics and Medicine.* 2 Vol. 32: No.3. 171-183.

Herrick Jim. (2006). *Humanism: An Introduction.* Ibadan: Gadfly Publishers.

Kant Immanuel. (2006). *Ground Work of the Metaphysics.* Mary Gregor (ed, and trans) Cambridge: Cambridge University Press.

Kirchoffer D.G. and Dierickx K. (2012). "Human Dignity and Consent in Research Biobanking". *SAJBL.* Vol.5. No.2.

Lamont Corliss. (1997). *The Philosophy of Humanism.* 8th Edition. New York: Half-Moon Foundation, Inc.

Mondin Battista. (1985). *Philosophical Anthropology.* Bangalore: Theological Publication.

Okemwa M. Joseph. (1997). *Self Determination and Freedom in the Acting Person by Karol Wojtyla.* Nairobi: Paulines Publications Africa.

Okonkwo C. Anthony. (2010). *Destined Beyond: The Truth of the Human Person, Concept and Transcendence in the Philosophy of Karol Wojtyla.* Ibadan: Don Bosco Publications.

Olatunji Oyeshile. (2005). *Reconciling the Self with the Other.* Ibadan: Hope Publication.

Pellegrino Edmund. (2008). "The Lived Experience of Human Dignity". Human Dignity and Bioethics: Essays commissioned by the President's Council of Bioethics. Retrieved February 2009 from, www.bioethics.gov/reports/human_dignity/chapter 20.

Thomas Aquinas. (1990). *The Summa Theologica*, Daniel J. Sullivan (rev.ed). Laurence Shapcote of the Fathers of the English Dominican Proince (literally trans.), 1941. 1.Q75, a 1, in Adler J. Mortiner (Gen.ed), Great Books of the Modern World. XVII. 2nd ed., Chicago: Encyclopaedia Britannica Inc.

Wojtyla Karol. (1981). *Love and Responsibility.* London: William Collins and Sons.

CHAPTER FIVE

From Pastoral Caregiving to Secondary Traumatic Stress: A Discussion of the Potential Risk Factors Among Catholic Priests

Richard Ehusani

1. Introduction

Pastoral work often involves providing care and support to vulnerable and suffering persons traumatized and distressed by life-altering events, including natural and human-made disasters, violent and sudden death of loved ones, sexual violence, kidnapping, major illnesses, and other emotionally stressful events and abuses (Hirono & Blake, 2017). In many such instances, the clergy are often the initial contact, and through their essential roles of listeners and voices of hope, they become the first resource for healing their parishioners. Empirical research has indicated that about 15% to 50% of individuals in the human service field who listen to or help traumatized or suffering persons will experience a secondary traumatic stress response because of their exposure to harmful material from their clients (Sansbury et al., 2015). *Secondary traumatic stress* is a term used in the mental health literature to describe the experience of psychological distress due to indirect traumatic exposure to the distressing experience of others (Butler et al., 2017).

Whereas research has focused on the risks of developing secondary traumatic stress and its impact on the secular populations of human service workers such as psychotherapists, counselors, doctors, nurses, and firefighters (Andahazy, 2019; O'Mahony et al., 2018), there is a paucity of research on secondary traumatic stress among the clergy who also function as frontline mental health workers (Hotchkiss & Lesher,

2018). The purpose of this paper, therefore, is to highlight the potential risk factors for developing secondary traumatic stress in persons engaged in pastoral work, with a specific focus on Catholic priests. The discussion shall include a brief description of the phenomenon of secondary traumatic stress and its prevalence among trauma workers, Catholic priests as trauma workers, the possible risk factors for developing secondary trauma among priests, and the need for more focused research on the impact of trauma work on priests' personal functioning and pastoral effectiveness.

2. Understanding Secondary Traumatic Stress

Secondary traumatic stress refers to the phenomenon whereby individuals become traumatized not by directly experiencing a traumatic event but by hearing about a traumatic event experienced by someone else. According to Figley (1995), the term describes the behaviors and emotions that naturally occur from knowing about a traumatizing event suffered by another. While the intent of engaging with traumatized persons is to relieve their posttraumatic stress and suffering, the helper or caregiver becomes indirectly or secondarily exposed to the sufferer's trauma-related material, including memories, thoughts, and emotions (Ecves, 2015). Such indirect exposure to trauma can lead the helper to emotionally engage with the same catastrophic event that disrupted the traumatized person's life (Coddington, 2017; Figley, 1995). In other words, the victim's behavior and emotionally distressing stories about the tragic experiences can so affect the helpers that they take on the same trauma. In contrast to primary or direct exposure, in which an individual experiences or observes a threat of or actual harm or loss (Quiros et al., 2020), secondary traumatic stress describes the state of being traumatized indirectly by witnessing or hearing about a traumatic event experienced by another.

Secondary traumatic stress symptoms are similar to those of posttraumatic stress disorder, a condition triggered in individuals directly traumatized by terrifying events (Passmore et al., 2020). The symptoms include intrusive thoughts, flashbacks, and recollections of the traumatic event; withdrawal from or avoidance of persons, places, things, and activities that are reminders of the traumatic event; and hyper-arousal involving persistent anxiety not experienced before the traumatic exposure and consisting of sleeping difficulties, irritability, difficulty concentrating, hypervigilance, or exaggerated startle response (American Psychiatric Association, 2013). With such symptoms, secondary traumatic stress could have a widespread impact on the sufferer's personal and professional life and diminish the quality of care that help-seeking victims of trauma require to heal.

3. Prevalence of Secondary Traumatic Stress

Research has been consistent in reporting a high rate of secondary traumatic stress in study samples of human service workers in various fields, including mental health, health care, child welfare, domestic violence, sexual assault, and social work. For instance, researchers found that 94% of 202 nurses in the emergency units (Ratrout & Hamdan-Mansour, 2020), 51.1% of 179 refugee services providers (Kim, 2017), and 63.8% of 193 Romanian social workers (Baciu & Virga, 2018) had symptoms of secondary traumatic stress due to their indirect exposure to traumatized clients. Although no study has specifically measured the prevalence of secondary traumatic stress among the clergy, the existing literature suggests an increasing rate of this emotional distress in caring professionals whose work-related contact with traumatized people and the associated psychological vulnerabilities appear similar to those of priests. This similarity between the much-studied populations of helping professionals and Catholic priests, in their engagement with suffering individuals, strengthens the justification for considering the potential impact of secondary traumatic exposure upon Catholic priests.

4. Priests as Trauma Workers

Priests, like mental health professionals, are in contact with suffering victims, often on an ongoing basis. Although many priests are not trained or equipped to provide trauma counseling (Hotchkiss & Lesher, 2018), they are often subject to the same stressors and psychosocial influences as other caregivers are. Trauma survivors often seek their priests' help, especially in places where mental health professionals are uncommon. For instance, in Nigeria, where people are still reluctant to seek mental health care because of the perceived associated stigma, the clergy is often the available and affordable option. Priests are typically on call to minister to those in need regardless of circumstance, adverse conditions, or time. As presiders over sacramental celebrations, Catholic priests provide emotionally demanding services such as reconciliation, anointing of the sick and dying, and funerals.

Additionally, priests often serve as chaplains to hospitals, prisons, and refugee camps, where they may encounter acute cases of trauma (Kane, 2017). In their pastoral caregiving, the prevailing attitude is sacrifice, without asking for anything in return, because a priest's caregiving enterprise is a critical part of his calling. The pressure of work is often high and continuous, expectations are superhuman, and self-care is scarce. By providing counseling, spiritual direction, and helping traumatized people search for meaning anchored in religious and spiritual principles, priests could develop secondary traumatic stress symptoms because of the traumatic exposure that often comes with these roles.

5. Potential Risk Factors of Secondary Traumatic Stress

Researchers have identified common risk factors of secondary traumatic stress among trauma workers. The factors mostly refer to either internal or external characteristics, or both, relating to the helper's personality traits, empathic engagement, prior experiences of trauma, level of exposure and caseload, years of working experience, the general influence of workplace factors, and the lack of social support (Bride & Kintzle, 2011; Ewer et al., 2015). These factors are quite applicable to Catholic priests. For instance, as empathic engagement is central to the development of secondary traumatic stress, so it is to effective pastoral care. Empathy is perceived by the clergy as other-centered, in which case pastoral contact begins and ends with the victim's good, and unlike trained therapists, the clergy are often lacking in critical self-awareness in trauma work. Also, as humans, priests could have personal trauma experiences, some of which may be unresolved. Such personal trauma history could be triggered now and again by a victim's story. However, beyond these general risk factors, Catholic priests may be more vulnerable to secondary traumatic stress for other reasons as follows.

6. Living the Vow of Celibacy

Whereas several studies have found that familial and social support strongly buffers against secondary traumatic stress (Diehm et al., 2019; Ludick & Figley, 2017), Catholic priests often live alone, with little to no immediate social support network of a family due to the vow of celibacy. More so, Chan and Wong (2018) and McMinn et al. (2008) have documented the benefits of spousal emotional support for married clergy, characterized by broad participation in the life of the church and preventing the experience of emotional isolation in the clergy. Thus, without downplaying the theological value of clerical celibacy which enables Catholic priests to be fully available for pastoral work (Kane, 2017), the lack of immediate social support network of a family with whom to share the load of ministry may be a unique factor that can increase the susceptibility of Catholic priests to secondary traumatic stress. More so, building a sustainable network of friends and colleagues is further hampered by the frequent reassignment of priests to different communities (Rossetti & Rhoades, 2013).

7. The Seal of Confession

Another potentially predisposing factor to consider is the seal of confession. Although all clergy members supposedly uphold the ethical value of confidentiality, the sacramental seal of confession forbids Catholic priests to share information from the confessional (Daly, 2013). The sacrament of reconciliation (confession) often involves listening to tales of human suffering and struggles and counseling victims of trauma. Those who approach this sacrament may also feel extreme trauma-related guilt for surviving a tragic event when others did not and engage in self-blame arising from the belief that they could or should have done something different when the traumatic event occurred or prevented the incident from occurring to another (Raz et al., 2018). Given the emotional demands of the sacrament of confession and the priests' potential exposure to traumatic material, they could be rendered susceptible to secondary traumatic stress. More so, because of their sacred vow to keep the confessional seal unbroken in whatever circumstance (Daly, 2013), Catholic priests may not share confessional information, even when the content of such information may be harmful to their mental wellbeing. Thus, the confluence of secondary trauma exposure and the inability to share emotional impacts, stress narratives, or any need for basic empathetic listening with family, friends, colleagues, or members of a support system, could lead to exhaustion, depression, disruptions in sleeping and eating patterns, and burnout.

8. Dealing with Difficult Questions

Following any tragedy, trauma, or a major loss, the survivors usually struggle with existential questions that frequently cause them to undergo a crisis of philosophy and faith (Ogden et al., 2000). It is not uncommon for priests to deal with existential doubts and resentment toward God. Often, the bereaved or traumatized shun any spiritual activity or gathering because they cannot reconcile the evil they currently face with the God of goodness and love portrayed in religion. God becomes the object of their psychological frustration as they struggle to understand *why* and make sense of the tragic events. Questions arise about divine providence and free will, sin and salvation, the afterlife, and the meaning of our very existence. As parishioners seek answers to such extremely deep, thought-provoking, and difficult questions, the priests' meticulously cultivated and reinforced belief systems can profoundly suffer after prolonged periods of empathetic listening. Such questions often go unanswered, doubt arises, and confidence erodes. Secondary traumatic stress can result from continual exposure to such narratives of ontological disruption during trauma. Constantly ministering to those in spiritual crises, especially when unanswerable questions arise, can cause secondary spiritual crises among priests. Even the strong and steadfast priests could be vulnerable.

9. The Church Culture

Church or clerical culture seemingly reinforces perfectionism. Parishioners see their priests as God's representatives who should always be available to all and be exceptionally compassionate toward the suffering and traumatized members of the community they serve (Proeschold-Bell et al., 2016). Likewise, the priests see their ministry as a divine calling to serve. This call may motivate priests to keep working and showing the expected positive emotions, even when they inwardly feel negative emotions, such that the desire to care for others may inhibit their taking time for self-care activities (Case et al., 2019). By their calling, priests are expected to teach others how to experience a positive quality of life and find meaning in times of suffering and distressing circumstances (Kim, 2017). The 'wounded healer' image, which suggests that healing capabilities can emerge from the experience of being wounded (Roots & Roses, 2020), gets used for priests often, sometimes dangerously suggesting that the wounds of caregiving should be accepted or endured without question. Such internalized expectations of perfection could prevent priests from sharing their psychological struggles and seeking help. Thus, cases of depression, emotional isolation, and addictive behaviors could arise among priests, especially in rural areas where they have no access to supportive resources. Consequently, priests may become irritable and unable to display compassion and empathy, counseling interactions with suffering parishioners may become nontherapeutic and potentially harmful, and the pastoral ministry of the Catholic church as a whole may become less fruitful. These aspects of the church's culture might increase the risk of secondary traumatic stress among priests secondarily exposed to trauma.

10. Battling Stigma and Shame

Priests often have to battle the stigma brought on by the misconduct of other clergy members. In today's media-driven society, if a priest commits a crime in the United States or Japan, the priests in Mozambique or Nigeria hear about it and are sometimes painted with the same brush. Unlike psychotherapists or other mental health professionals who may get sued for malpractice generally outside media scrutiny, the clergy suffer greatly from guilt by association, as abuses of varying severity perpetrated by one priest get played out in the news media and seen as the norm and not exceptions. Additionally, priests may find themselves in the difficult situation of ministering and providing counter-narratives to individuals who directly experienced trauma perpetrated by fellow priests. Such secondary battles and added stressors caused by situations outside the priests' immediate control can result in a unique type of secondary guilt and shame that could, in turn, exacerbate secondary traumatic stress symptoms and adversely impact their pastoral effectiveness.

11. Conclusion and Recommendation

This paper set out to highlight the potential risk factors for developing secondary traumatic stress among priests. The factors discussed indicate a personal, social, and spiritual cost associated with priestly ministry. Priests tend to seek spiritual and salvific gratification by helping others navigate their stress, fear, anger, sadness, and trauma. As in other trauma-related caregiving professions, the desired outcome of any pastoral counseling session is the formation of a new hope, which can lead to a return to a previous normal or the forging of a new normal. In the process, priests could be exposed to various stressors, social ills, suffering, and extreme traumatic material. The veil of confidentiality under which they work can also be a burden because they take on trauma and cannot talk about it. Seeing their work as a divine call, priests hear stories of human tragedy for a living, which can lead to secondary traumatic stress, existential crises, and burnout.

The scarcity of research focused on secondary traumatization related to priests suggests that priests are barely aware of and prepared to manage this potentially harmful aspect of their work. Thus, there is an almost ethical and moral obligation upon researchers to explore whether and how these caregivers experience secondary traumatization, what the experience is, and how they cope with it. Such research efforts will benefit priests who might become more aware of the risk of secondary traumatization and how to develop preventive or coping strategies and improve the quality of service for individuals who rely on priests for pastoral care. More focused research may draw the attention of the church hierarchy to the need to provide adequate mental health support for priests and highlight the need for specialized training of priests and seminarians in working with trauma. Additionally, the church could fund and benefit from such research directly as the mental wellbeing of the individual priests and parishioners would mean well for the entire church.

References

American Psychiatric Association (APA). (2013). *Diagnostic and statistical manual of mental disorders* (5th ed.).

Andahazy, A. (2019). Tuning of the self: In-session somatic support for vicarious trauma-related countertransference. *Body, Movement & Dance in Psychotherapy, 14*(1), 41–57. https://doi.org/10.1080/17432979.2019.1577758

Baciu, L., & Vîrgă, D. (2018). The Prevalence of secondary traumatic stress among Romanian social workers: A replication study. *Social Work Review / Revista de Asistenta Sociala, 17*(3), 151–164.

Bride, B. E., & Kintzle, S. (2011). Secondary traumatic stress, job satisfaction, and occupational commitment in substance abuse counselors. *Traumatology, 17*(1), 22–28. https://doi.org/10.1177/1534765610395617

Butler, L. D., Carello, J., & Maguin, E. (2017). Trauma, stress, and self-care in clinical training: Predictors of burnout, decline in health status, secondary traumatic stress symptoms, compassion satisfaction. *Psychological Trauma: Theory, Research, Practice & Policy, 9*(4), 416-424. https://doi.org/10.1037/tra0000187

Case, A. D., Keyes, C. L. M., Huffman, K. F., Sittser, K., Wallace, A., Khatiwoda, P., Parnell, H. E., & Proeschold-Bell, R. J. (2019). Attitudes and behaviors that differentiate clergy with positive mental health from those with burnout. *Journal of Prevention & Intervention in the Community, 42*(1), 94-112. https://doi.org/10.1080/10852352.2019.1617525

Chan, K., & Wong, M. (2018). Experience of Stress and coping strategies among pastors' wives in China. *The Journal of Pastoral Care & Counseling: JPCC, 72*(3), 163–171. https://doi.org/10.1177/1542305018782518

Coddington, K. (2017). Contagious trauma: Reframing the spatial mobility of trauma within advocacy work. *Emotion, Space and Society, 24,* 66–73. https://doi.org/10.1016/j.emospa.2016.02.002

Daly, B. (2013). Seal of confession: A strict obligation for priests. *Australasian Catholic Record, 90*(1), 3–21. https://search.informit.com.au/documentSummary;dn=246200005249472;res=IELNZC

Diehm, R. M., Mankowitz, N. N., & King, R. M. (2019). Secondary traumatic stress in Australian psychologists: Individual risk and protective factors. *Traumatology, 25*(3), 196–202. https://doi.org/10.1037/trm0000181

Evces, M. R. (2015). What is vicarious trauma? In G. Quitangon & M.R. Evces (Eds.), *Vicarious trauma and disaster mental health* (pp. 9-23). Routledge.

Ewer, P. L., Teesson, M., Sannibale, C., Roche, A., & Mills, K. L. (2015). The prevalence and correlates of secondary traumatic stress among alcohol and other drug workers in Australia. *Drug & Alcohol Review, 34*(3), 252–258. https://doi.org/10.1111/dar.12204

Figley, C. R. (1995). Compassion fatigue as secondary traumatic stress disorder: An overview. In C. R. Figley (Ed.), *Compassion fatigue: Coping with secondary traumatic stress disorder* (pp. 1–20). Brunner/Mazel.

Hirono, T., & Blake, M. E. (2017). The role of religious leaders in the restoration of hope following natural disasters. *Sage Open, 7*(2). https://doi.org/10.1177/2158244017707003

Hotchkiss, J. T., & Lesher, R. (2018). Factors predicting burnout among chaplains: Compassion satisfaction, organizational factors, and the mediators of mindful self-care and secondary traumatic stress. *The Journal of Pastoral Care & Counseling: JPCC, 72*(2), 86–98. https://doi.org/10.1177/1542305018780655

Kane, M. N. (2017). Stress and relaxation among aging Catholic priests. *Journal of Spirituality in Mental Health, 19*(1), 1–19. https://doi.org/10.1080/19349637.2016.1157566

Kim, K. (2017). The power of being vulnerable in Christian soul care: Common humanity and humility. *Journal of Religious Health, 56,* 355-369. https://doi.org/10.1007/s10943-016-0294-8

Kim, Y. J. (2017). Secondary traumatic stress and burnout of North Korean refugees service providers. *Psychiatry Investigation, 14,* 118–125. https://doi.org/10.4306/pi.2017.14.2.118

McMinn, M., Kerrick, S., Duma, S., Campbell, E., & Jung, J. (2008). Positive coping among wives of male Christian clergy. *Pastoral Psychology, 56*(4), 445–457. https://doi.org/10.1007/s11089-008-0122-5

Ludick, M., & Figley, C. R. (2017). Toward a mechanism for secondary trauma induction and reduction: Reimagining a theory of secondary traumatic stress. *Traumatology, 23*(1), 112 123. https://doi.org/10.103 7/trm0000096

Ogden, C. J., Kaminer, D., Van Kradenburg, J., Seedat, S., & Stein, D. J. (2000). Narrative themes in responses to trauma in a religious community. *Central African Journal of Medicine, 46*(7), 178–184.

O'Mahony, S., Ziadni, M., Hoerger, M., Levine, S., Baron, A., & Gerhart, J. (2018). Compassion fatigue among palliative care clinicians: Findings on personality factors and years of service. *The American Journal of Hospice & Palliative Care, 35*(2), 343–347. https://doi.org/10.1177/1049909117701695

Passmore, S., Hemming, E., McIntosh, H. C., & Hellman, C. M. (2020). The relationship between hope, meaning in work, secondary traumatic stress, and burnout among child abuse pediatric clinicians. *Permanente Journal, 24*(1), 29–34. https://doi.org/10.7812/TPP/19.087

Proeschold-Bell, R. J., Eisenberg, A., Adams, C., Smith, B., Legrand, S., & Wilk, A. (2016). The glory of God is a human being fully alive: Predictors of positive versus negative mental health among clergy. *The Journal for the Scientific Study of Religion, 4*, 702. https://doi.org/10.1111/jssr.12234

Quiros, L., Varghese, R., & Vanidestine, T. (2020). Disrupting the single story: Challenging dominant trauma narratives through a critical race lens. *Traumatology, 26*(2), 160–168. https://doi.org /10.1037/trm0000223

Ratrout, H. F., & Hamdan-Mansour, A. M. (2020). Secondary traumatic stress among emergency nurses: Prevalence, predictors, and consequences. *International Journal of Nursing Practice, 26*(1), e12767. https://doi.org/10.1111/ijn.12767

Raz, A., Shadach, E., & Levy, S. (2018). Gaining control over traumatic experiences: The role of guilt in posttraumatic stress disorder. *Journal of Aggression, Maltreatment & Trauma, 27*(5), 461–474. https://doi.org/10.1080/10926771.2017.1389792

Roots, & Roses. (2020). Wounded healer experiences in art therapy. *Journal of the American Art Therapy Association, 37*(2), 76–82. https://doi.org/10.1080/07421656.2020.1764794

Rossetti, S. J., & Rhoades, C. J. (2013). Burnout in Catholic clergy: A predictive model using psychological and spiritual variables. *Psychology of Religion and Spirituality*, 5(4), 335 341 https://doi.org/10.1037/a003 3639

Sansbury, B. S., Graves, K., & Scott, W. (2015). Managing traumatic stress responses among clinicians: Individual and organizational tools for self care. *Trauma*, *17*(2), 114 122. https://doi.org/10.1177/14604 08614551978.

CHAPTER SIX

A Critical Look at George Ehusani's Prophetic Imagination

William Ikhianosimhe Orbih

1. Introduction

George Ehusani is not the first person to use the phrase "prophetic imagination." At the very least, Walter Brueggemann used it before him. It is the title of Brueggemann's 1978 book. The question of how and where Ehusani might have first come across the phrase is, however, not as important as highlighting how significant it is to Ehusani's life and career as a priest, theologian, poet, musician, social activist and commentator. This article expounds on Ehusani's understanding of prophetic imagination and how this theological concept provides us with an essential introduction to the life, theology and expansive ministry of Ehusani. In other words, this article argues that "Prophetic Imagination" is not just the title of one of his poems in the *Flames of Truth* collection but a theme that runs through the entirety of Ehusani's scholarly, pastoral and social work. It is responsible for his vast works and interests, versatility and fruitfulness, unquenchable zeal, and relentless courage in his work for God and humanity. It is the window through which he sees the world and judges the times. Most importantly, his prophetic imagination is shaped by the richness of the long humanistic tradition of his Christian faith.

Thus, along with a critical analysis of the poem in question, an appraisal of some of Ehusani's significant works is equally important. Two of Ehusani's best known books are: *An Afro Christian Vision ("Ozovehe"): Towards a more Humanized World* (1991) and *A Prophetic Church* (1996). Like virtually every other intellectual production of Ehusani, they give us a crucial glimpse into the length and breadth, the nature and shape of Ehusani's prophetic imagination. Seen from a holistic perspective, the poem "Prophetic Imagination" published in 2006 becomes more of an invaluable attempt by Ehusani himself to put into words a reality that is only too evident in his life and entirety of his works. It becomes, so to say, Ehusani's autobiography or memoir, written in the esoteric, albeit accessible and precise language of poetry—a genre he has mastered over the years.

The aim of this article is, therefore, twofold. The first is to demonstrate how the theological concept of prophetic imagination is one of the dominant themes in Ehusani's vast and versatile body of works. To do this, it will critically appraise some selected works of Ehusani to highlight prophetic imagination alive and at work and how his understanding of prophetic imagination evolved over the years. Next, it will also show how Ehusani himself understands it by a literary analysis of his poem, "Prophetic Imagination." By moving from his first published book in 1991 to his 2006 poem, this article hopes to demonstrate how Ehusani's prophetic imagination has always been active through his life and ministry. It will also show how he grew increasingly aware of his vocation as a social prophet and the usefulness of prophetic imagination in the context of the social injustices and unrest that characterise modern Nigeria, and how this evolving understanding finds climax in the poem. To conclude, this article will briefly discuss how prophetic imagination can be a panacea for the urgent task of rescuing Nigeria from chaos, anarchy and doom.

2. 'Prophetic Imagination' in the Works of Ehusani: An Overview

An Afro-Christian Vision: "Ozovehe!" (1991) is a fitting place to begin a critical analysis of Ehusani's prophetic imagination as it appears in his vast bibliography across different genres. Not just because it is his first published book, but because in this work, which is an adaptation of his doctoral dissertation, we already see his prophetic imagination at work. Ehusani's prophetic vision or imagination of the human person is shaped by both African traditional humanism and Christian theological anthropology. The African worldview, he explains, is anthropocentric. The human being is at the centre, is of supreme importance, and indeed, inviolable. Human life is noble, and human blood is sacred. Family life and the human community are highly valued. According to him, "the African tradition is characterised by an emphasis on community and progeny, and wholesome human relations and hospitality are distinctive marks of the traditional African" (1991, p. 24). It is for this reason that when asked, "what is the human person? The African answers by saying—"The human person is life": Ozovehe!" (p. 3).

Ehusani notes that although the immensely rich Africa's past is now almost completely eroded by the forces of Western materialism and consumerism, it has been miraculously kept alive in the beautiful tradition of African names. According to him, In Africa, unlike in Shakespeare's *Romeo and Juliet*, a name is not just a symbol of identification. It expresses a depth of meaning and is an essential vehicle of cultural identity (pp. 123-5). The presence of so many names across the different cultures and languages of Africa expressing the dignity of the human person proves the traditional African belief in the "immense dignity of the human person amidst God's creation" (p. 143). Ehusani would insist that, whereas human life is a good desired by all people everywhere, the way the African society is systematically organised around the propagation, promotion and protection of life is worthy of special notice....Life and its protection is the central preoccupation of the African family, clan and chiefdom, whose legal and authority structures have in turn been designed to foster life. Human actions are good or bad to the extent that they promote or threaten life. It could be said that for the African, authority is there to make the flame of life burn more brightly; that the Ancestors are there to make the stream of life surge more fully; and God is there to make the human person more *living* (p. 210). In other words, African names which emphasise the dignity of human persons are an expression of the ethos of the larger society.

However, while the African world view is anthropocentric, at the heart of the Christian worldview is the creation of the human being in the image of God. This doctrine of the *Imago Dei* is the theological framework that Ehusani uses. According to this framework, the human person is never conceived except relationally. Primarily, the human being is considered in his or her relationship with Yahweh. Human origin, history, and destiny are seen in the context of this relationship to the divine. This relationship is one of utter dependence, albeit balanced dynamically with true human autonomy. This dynamic relationship with God and the ability for humans to freely enter into a real relationship with God distinguishes humans from the rest of creation. "The human being is like the rest of creation in materiality, mortality and dependence, but he or she towers above the rest of creation and is more like the creator in freedom, dominion, transcendence, intelligence, spirituality, creativity, and above all personality" (p. 43). This is consistent with what *The Catechism of the Catholic Church* teaches when it describes the human being as "not just something, but someone" (no. 357). Explaining what this means, Paulinus Odozor, in *Morality, Truly Christian, Truly African*, comments that the high point of human creation was the conferment of personhood on the human individual. This is what "enables the human person, a finite being, a being who is not God, to receive and be in dialogue with God." Odozor subsequently notes that it is in being a person and naturally relational that the human being is most like unto God (2014, p. 216).

Because of this special likeness to God, the human being is the summit of creation and exercises dominion of divine conferred responsibility for all other creatures. The human being is not just in a vertical relationship with God but in a horizontal relationship with other human beings, and thus, the human being is social by nature. In the New Testament, Christ reveals to us how infinitely valuable human life is to God. While the human being was created in the image of God, sin perverted this nature. The incarnation is a testament to this truth. Ehusani (1991, p. 56) explains that the incarnation "reveals that the human being is so vast that he or she can contain the divine presence." The redemptive death of Christ restored human nature to its original dignity, raising human dignity and conferring on human beings the privilege of being children of God (p. 51).

The centrality of the human being in the African world view gives us what Ehusani describes as an Afro-Christian vision. The Afro-Christian vision is, therefore, a dynamic dialogue of Christian anthropology with African humanism. It is a dialogue that recognises Africa's rich heritage as a gift of God, the locus of God's salvific activity and the matrix upon which a Christian theology fully accessible to the culture can be constructed. One point of notable intersection in dialogue is the dignity of human life. As he succinctly puts it, "The Christian tradition confirms the African emphasis of life" (1991, p. 210). This intersection makes the dialogue a pathway to a truly humanised world (p. 204). By the way, Ehusani's ultimate aim in proposing an Afro-Christian Vision is his vision of a truly humanised world. This is because the context in which he writes is a world, although witnessing spectacular and technological achievements, marked by a shameful degradation of the human person (p. 17). According to him, this is the paradox of the age. Phenomenal technological advancement in communication, agriculture, medicine and industrialisation has occasioned an alarming decline in the level of sensitivity to the inviolability and sacredness of life, the beauty and importance of family and community and a growing disillusionment to the meaning and purpose of human existence (pp. 5-21).

However, while Ehusani's sight is awakened to this awful reality of the contemporary world, his imagination is prophetic and enlivened by the richness of African humanistic heritage, especially when this rich African heritage is further enriched and elevated by the Gospel of Christ and is thus adequately equipped to stand as an alternative value system to the system obtainable in the world (p. 28). He is convinced that while African heritage has something to offer the world today, this becomes even more obvious, when this African heritage is seen through the Christian message. While African tradition is rich in itself in its holistic view to life, it is further enriched by the Christian tradition in its proclamation of the divine purpose of the human being and the ultimate destiny of the human person in Christ. For instance, while John Mbiti (1969, p. 6), in *African Religions and Philosophy*, rightly notes that "to live here and now is the most important concern for African religious activities and beliefs," it is the place of Christianity to enrich this worldview with the good news of eternal life. Ehusani thus calls for the Christianization of Africa's richness. This must be clearly distinguished from what might be described as a mere modernisation of African culture. Like Elochukwu Uzukwu (1996, pp. 4-6), Ehusani is obviously wary of a modernisation that amounts to nothing other than radical secularisation of an otherwise religious continent.

Ehusani's prophetic imagination is thus an embodiment of the Afro-Christian vision of human dignity. It envisions a future where the dignity of every human person is recognised, respected and protected. He looks back with nostalgia to the African humanistic worldview, and he looks forward to the depth of the mystery of the human person already and yet to be fully revealed in Christ in the eschaton ((1991, p. 2). This imagination is far from being passive and romantic. Instead, it propels one to proclamation and action. For the alternative future that exists safely in the mind of the prophet to become a reality, concerted work is needed. The prophet must be ready to put in the work needed and motivate others to do the same. Propelled by this imagination, which he excellently describes in his first book, Ehusani became a relentless crusader for social justice in Nigeria.

Ehusani's social activism was at its fearless peak during the military regimes of the 1980s and 1990s. He was actively involved with the National Democratic Coalition (NADECO), formed in 1994 to prevail on General Sani Abacha to step down for M. K. O Abiola, the winner of the 12th of June 1993 presidential election. NADECO was a collaboration of activists in a relentless quest for the respect of human life, justice, peace, and a return to civilian rule and democracy in Nigeria, and Ehusani was an integral and visible part of the Catholic Church's contribution to the effort (Kukah, 2017). He wrote ferocious satires decrying the injustices of the military regimes of Generals Muhammadu Buhari, Ibrahim Babangida and Sani Abacha. He would compile 48 of these articles in a volume titled: *Nigeria: Years Eaten by the Locust* (2002). As the name suggests, Ehusani describes Nigeria's gory military years as the years eaten by the locusts. According to Taiwo Abioye, in *Language and the Moral Imperative in George Ehusani's Writings*, "the title of the book is a metaphorical configuration of a nation completely covered by locusts that eventually consume it" (2019, p. 20). While this sounds gloomy at face value, an understanding of the source of this choice of metaphor, perhaps, suggests more hope and less gloom. This title is culled from the book of the Hebrew prophet Joel: *"I will repay you for the years the locusts have eaten—the great locust and the young locust, the other locusts and the locust swarm—my great army that I sent among you"* Joel 2:25 (NIV). This was far from being a prophecy of gloom or doom. It was one of hope. Joel was speaking hope to a people who had just barely recovered from the battering of their exilic experience. The years of the exile were the years eaten by the locusts, which God was now going to restore.

By adopting this line from Joel, Ehusani invariably draws our attention to the prophets of Israel and their role in society. In his 1978 book *The Prophetic Imagination*, which is based on an analysis of prophecy in Israel's history and tradition, Walter Brueggemann outlines the threefold task of prophets in a society that thrives in self-deception. Firstly, it is the role of the prophet "to offer symbols that are adequate to the horror and massiveness of the experience which evokes numbness and require denial." Secondly, it is the role of the prophet "to bring to public expression those very fears and terrors that have been denied so long and suppressed so deeply that we do not know they are there." Thirdly, the prophet is required "to speak metaphorically but concretely about the real deathliness that hovers over us and gnaws within us and to speak neither in rage nor in cheap grace" (1978, pp. 49-51). Ehusani's interest and literary style in *Nigeria: Years Eaten by the Locust* perfectly fits this framework suggested by Brueggemann. While the very title of many of the articles accentuates this framework, Ehusani's writing style, in general, embodies it even more. He invokes the metaphors one finds in the writings of biblical prophets, such as dreaming and vision.

Abioye rightly identified the importance of metaphors and other literary devices in many of Ehusani's articles in the book. Her study and analysis of several of Ehusani's writings left her in awe of the enigma that Ehusani is. Most interestingly, she sees Ehusani's fearlessness, his commitment to truth, and his social and literary brilliance through the lens of Brueggemann's *Prophetic Imagination*. For her, Ehusani is an example of true prophets, who, as Brueggemann notes, "understood the possibility of change as linked to emotional extremities of life. They understood the strange congruence between public conviction and personal yearning. Most of all, they understood the distinctive power of language, the capacity to speak in ways that evoke newness "fresh from the word" (p. 97). Moreover, Abioye notes that it is not just the case that most of Ehusani's works can easily be located in the biblical tradition of prophecy, but that "Ehusani sees himself as a prophet with a sacred mission whose conscience cannot be stifled" (p. 97).

No doubt, Ehusani has always seen himself as a prophet with a sacred mission. In *A Prophetic Church,* initially published in 1996 (reprinted with major additions in 2003), Ehusani extensively reflects on what it means to be a prophet in Nigeria. According to him,

> Prophets are the visionaries of their time. When all others are blind, prophets are the ones that are granted to see the handwriting on the wall, to interpret the signs of the times, and to see the light beyond the tunnel. Equipped as they are with superior knowledge and perception, prophets analyse the situation on the ground in light of God's wisdom and commandments. Prophets refuse to be defiled by the corruption of the moment; they refuse to be engulfed by the darkness of the surrounding environment. They possess the vision of life as it ought to

be, and it is this vision that propels them in their difficult assignment. Prophets speak for God under different circumstances. They are endowed with rare courage not only to denounce evil in general but also to name the specific human agents of evil in society. They remind society that our God is a God of truth and that peace is the fruit of justice. They warn evildoers of the inevitability of nemesis while giving the much-needed hope to a suffering people. They tell the poor and the oppressed or the victims of injustice not to despair, because God is capable of intervening and turning things around. Prophets give the reason for the poor to hope. They assure "the remnant of Yahweh" that all is not lost (2003, p. 68).

The context of this sterling reflection is the Nigerian society, and its target audience is the Nigerian church. It is a paradox of the Nigerian society that stimulates this work. This is the irony of a country endowed by the Creator with enormous natural resources and abundantly blessed with human resources that yet has a majority of its citizens living in abject poverty (pp. 17-19). "Though their land is rich and their people intelligent, they are living in misery" (p. 19). It is not perchance that majority of Nigerians live in abject poverty. It is due to the actions and inactions of "a corrupt, selfish, greedy and callous elite," a succession of despotic rulers, decadent administrators, visionless leaders and reckless managers" (p. 19). However, it is not to the elite of the Nigerian society that the book is directed. Instead, it is to the church and to the Christians who make up the church. It is an indictment on the Nigerian church and Nigeria's religious establishment in general. Paul Knitter (2013), in his "Inter-Religious Dialogue and Social Action," notes religion's complicity in the suffering of the world and thus its social responsibility in work to alleviate suffering in the world. "Religion has either contributed to this suffering by taking sides with the exploiting perpetrators of such suffering, or it has served as a distraction from this suffering" (p. 139). If this is true, then it is only logical, argues Knitter, that religion is involved in social action. Ehusani, like Knitter, does not deny religion's complicity in Nigeria's woes. His call on the Christian church to take on social action, however, goes beyond the logic of restitution.

Ehusani's call on the Christian church to take up its responsibility as a witness for justice and truth to a society of injustice, poverty and oppression is based on the nature of the church as prophetic. As he puts it, "Nigeria is in urgent need of a prophetic church. Our land perishes for lack of knowledge, so we need a Church of prophets, visionaries and seers" (2003, p. 71). He thus urged the Christian church to be more committed "to the interest of the poor, oppressed and marginalised people, and of those who struggle for justice" (p. 37). He, however, clarifies that while Nigeria is in need of a prophetic church, Christians must realise that Christianity is a prophetic religion. "Christianity does not promote social indifference. Christianity does not, at any time, endorse the status quo where the status quo is unjust or oppressive. Instead, Christianity raises the consciousness of adherents to their responsibility for the creation of a better world in the service of the kingdom of God" (p. 40). In addition, the God of Christianity is a God who is interested in the spiritual and material welfare as well. He loves his people (p. 44). He takes side with his people in their strife and does not just stand aloof as a neutral observer (p. 45). He groans with anguish for them in their suffering and oppression (p. 45). He is a God of holiness and justice. He is a defender of the poor and the weak, the protector of the widow and the orphan (p. 46). He delivers his people from oppression. He is an incarnational God who visits his people and overhauls the power structures in their society that gives some people so much power and wealth while others suffer abject poverty and powerlessness (p. 48). He meets his people, encountering them in the form they can relate with (p. 56). Above all, in Jesus Christ, we encounter a God who "always takes a stand." As Ehusani emphasises, Jesus "did not vacillate. He was always on the side of the poor, the lowly, and the oppressed" (p. 59).

This above is the theological basis of Ehusani's urgent call for a prophetic church. He called for much more than prophetic utterances and powerful statements, but rather for more concrete prophetic actions (p. 71). Ehusani argued that a prophetic church must go beyond pious exhortations and passionate appeals to the oppressors of the Nigerian people and learn to engage in practical prophetic action that would put more pressure on the oppressors (pp. 109-10). He also called on the Nigerian Christian elite to take more active responsibility in shaping the direction of society (p. 76). He even laments that while Nigeria can boast of many theological experts, most of these experts often seem to be out of touch with the reality on the ground (p. 62). Ehusani equally challenges the hierarchy of the church to an alternative self-perception and the perception of the church's social engagement. Ehusani insists that "Bishops, priests, nuns, and theologians, need to abandon the perception of the Church in terms of power and privilege and begin to assume the posture of weakness and vulnerability through sharing the life of the powerless Christians in the slums and shantytowns, the detention cells and prisons, the factories and plantations, the dirty neighbourhoods and crime-ridden alleys, where people live, suffer and die" (p. 79). In general, Ehusani calls for a re-imagining of the church in Nigeria, a re-imagining of ecclesia structures, its agenda, its focus and its evangelisation.

In *A Prophetic Church*, therefore, the emphasis is on activism. It calls for more action to resist, upturn and eradicate injustice. "The time has come for some form of action" (p. 111). For Ehusani, while the church cannot be faulted in her social teaching, it is in practical action that the church often leaves so much to be desired (p. 112). In order to be truly prophetic, therefore, the church must become more proactive. In the penultimate chapter, Ehusani suggests practical actions the church can take in response to injustice and oppression. This ranges from staging peaceful demonstrations, anti-establishment rallies, organising mass rallies, encouraging non-violent acts of civil disobedience, staging protests and boycotts, among other things. The dominant metaphor for the prophetic church for Ehusani comes out clearly in the story of young Moses in Egypt, which he references. As he notes, Moses, on seeing "a powerful man mercilessly beating a weaker man and almost suffocating him to death," responds with concrete action by brutally defending the weaker man (pp. 63-4).

However, it is important to point out that while Ehusani's emphasis in *A Prophetic Church* seems to be activism, there is an essential place for prophetic vision. Prophets, for him, are first visionaries before they are actors. The edge they have over everyone else in society is their keen vision and foresightedness, that is, the ability to see and interpret the signs of the times and see the light at the end of the tunnel. Their prophetic vision is their shield against corruption and the defilement of society. It is the source of their relentless courage in their fight against injustice and the oppressive powers of society. "Their only source of strength," says Ehusani, is the "oracle of God they bear" (p. 69). The divine oracle is their message of judgment against the oppressor, while being at the same time, their message of hope for the oppressed. Consequently, while the oppressors "are often threatened by the presence and message of the prophets, the poor find consolation and encouragement in their ministry" (p. 69). However, this rich and succinct reflection on the primacy of the prophetic vision is not Ehusani's last word on it. The subject would appear again in one of his poems. There, the prophetic vision would have become prophetic imagination, and prophetic action will seemingly be further deemphasised. In other words, while in *A Prophetic Church*, Ehusani writes succinctly about the nature of the prophetic vision, he seems to be only interested in the vision of the prophet, in so far as it is to be seen as the ground for the prophetic action. In "Prophetic Imagination," written ten years after *A Prophetic Church*, Ehusani would revisit the concept of prophetic vision/imagination, and this time, discourse it for its own sake.

3. 'Prophetic Imagination' according to Ehusani

The poem 'Prophetic Imagination' is one out of the 45 poems in Ehusani's 2006 poetry collection *Flames of Truth*. This is his third poetry collection, and it is preceded by *Fragments of Truth* (1997) and *Petals of Truth* (1998). Both earlier poetry collections followed closely the publication of *A Prophetic Church* in 1996 and several of the articles that will eventually be collected in *Nigeria: Years Eaten by the Locust* (2002). Therefore, it is not surprising to notice how many of the themes in these books resonate in the poems and vice versa. For example, the literary style and content of the article "Count Me Out," in which he broods over the Nigeria's deplorable condition, finds much resonance with six poems titled Protestation (I-VI) in *Petals of Truth*. In both the article and poems, Ehusani stages a personal defense. He dissociated himself from the atrocities in the land. He emphatically declared that he did his part in trying to salvage Nigeria from "political profligacy" (1998, p. 36). He saw the handwriting on the wall early enough and shouted with all his strength, even though no one was willing to listen or heard his strenuous voice of protestation (*Petals of Truth*, p. 35; *Nigeria: Years Eaten by the Locust* p. 62). Thus, he claims no part in the Nigerian mess, nor did he cast his vote for the entrenchment of jungle justice in the land (1998, p. 39). Similarly, in his poem "Freedom" in *Fragments of Truth*, we find "Those were years/ Eaten by the Locust", and we almost immediately recall the volume *Nigeria: Years Eaten by the Locust*.

In general, many of his poems are reflections on the Nigerian predicament and his passionate commitment to social justice. As Abioye explains, "they are not just metaphorical representations of our social realities but a critical interrogation of the forces and ideological configurations behind the socio-economic and political harshness being witnessed by the vast majority of Nigerians" (p. 51). They, therefore, include themes such as detainees without trial in "Detainees," homelessness in "Under the Bridge" in *Petals of Truth* (pp. 59-61), military dictatorship in "Stillborn," and hunger and abject poverty in "Hunger" in *Fragments of Truth* (pp. 27-8, 132-3). Of course, these are themes he also writes extensively on in his non-poetry works. What one notices is how these themes oscillate across the genres of Ehusani's writings. Sometimes, one can see his poems echoing an earlier issue Ehusani had written about in an article or book or capturing the thought more profoundly and succinctly. At other times, one sees his article advancing an idea already hinted at in a poem. In some case, one can even notice a gradual evolution of thought or approach. The poem 'Prophetic Imagination' published in 2006, when read in light of his earlier musings on the topic of prophetic vision in *A Prophetic Church*, presents an excellent example of this.

In this poem, Ehusani captures his understanding of prophetic imagination in a free verse made up of 32 lines that are divided into four stanzas. Whereas in *A Prophetic Church*, Ehusani had been interested in prophetic vision to the extent that it is the foundation of and energy for the urgent prophetic action the church and Christians need to embark on, "Prophetic Imagination" seems to be a reflection on prophetic imagination/vision for its own sake. Since it is a relatively short poem, it can easily be reproduced in full below.

> Prophetic Imagination
> Is the spiritual defiance of what is
> In the name of what ought to be
> It visualises an alternative future
> To the one fated by the momentum
> Of current contradictory forces
>
> Prophetic Imagination
> Breathes the fresh air
> Of a time yet to be

Into the suffocating atmosphere
Of present reality
It is the unrelenting commitment
To a new inevitability
Anchored on God's promised intervention

Prophetic Imagination
Is the rejection of the old world
Dominated by the powers of evil
Reflected in the regime of hatred, injustice, violence and war
In favour of a new world
Overwhelmed by the forces of good
Characterised by the civilisation of love, justice and peace

Amidst widespread debauchery
Multiple tragedies
Despondency
Discouragement
And despair

Prophetic imagination is pregnant with hope
For long-standing victims of injustice
It energises the remnant few
Who hunger for righteousness
With the luminous visitation of dawn
Announcing the birth of a new day (2006, p. 103).

The first impression one gets on approaching the poem is just how it reads as an attempt to define or at least describe the nature and content of prophetic imagination. It is as if it is a response to the question: 'What is prophetic imagination?' to which Ehusani responds by providing not one but four different definitions. Whether 'defining' is what Ehusani saw himself doing might be difficult to ascertain, what is essential is that by the end of this relatively short poem, Ehusani had indeed exhaustively described prophetic imagination. Each stanza is devoted to a specific aspect of prophetic imagination: the essence and purpose, content and context, not necessarily in this order. The first stanza speaks of prophetic imagination as spiritual defiance, while the second stanza describes it as an unrelenting commitment. In the third, the focus is on the context in which prophetic imagination operates. In the last stanza, Ehusani shifts focus from the imagination to the identity of the prophets who embody it.

By describing prophetic imagination as spiritual defiance from the very inception of the poem, Ehusani leaves us in no doubt of the theological basis of this poem. The theological basis of the poem is the Judeo-Christian tradition of prophets. If this poem is a definition, then it is a theological definition. Although Ehusani does not intend to limit readership to those who share his Judeo-Christian convictions, neither does he intend to hide these convictions. In this, as in all his writings, Ehusani displays vastness in both the Jewish tradition of the Old Testament and the Christian tradition of the New Testament. In the Old Testament, prophets are often depicted as rebelling against the unjust, idolatrous and oppressive status quo. Prophet Elijah, for instance, rebelled against the worship of Baal that had become prevalent among the people of Israel during his time. Even when he thought he was alone in doing this, he carried on (Cf. 1Kings 18 & 19). He also rebelled against the oppressive regime of Ahab and Jezebel. While many New Testament authors encouraged Christians to resist the corruption of their time, we find many stories of the early Christians in the Roman empire defying edicts of emperor worship and refusing to be conscripted into the army of the empire. Ehusani shows how this act of defiance, resistance or rebellion is first and foremost a spiritual act. According to him, it involves visualising an alternative future. For Elijah, that will be the future when true worship of the one true God is established. For the early Christians, this is the future where true religion would have wiped out what Augustine, in books 2, 6 and 8 of the *City of God*, will decry as the folly and illogicality of pagan worship. For the early Christians refusing to fight in wars, this would also be a visualisation of a civilisation of peace in the manner one finds in prophecies of Isaiah (see Isaiah 2).

Prophetic imagination is not just spiritual defiance; it is also an unrelenting commitment. In this verse, Ehusani points us to the basis of the relentlessness of prophets. According to him, "it is anchored on "God's promised intervention." This is consistent with the image of God Ehusani advances in his *A Prophetic Church*, where he describes God as a God of well-being (2003, p. 42). God does not just take the side of the oppressed and fight on their behalf; God has promised a new future of glad tiding to the poor, liberty to the captives, recovery of sight to the blind, freedom to the oppressed and a year of favour for everyone (Cf. Luke 4: 18). God himself will intervene, even as he intervened and brought the people of Israel out of captivity in Egypt. God intervened with a mighty hand, bringing his people out of captivity and dividing the Red Sea for them (p. 45). God will intervene, even as he intervened during the era of the judges when he responded to the desperate cry of his people and raised judges to destroy their oppressors (p. 47). God will intervene even as he did during the time of the kings, defending the weak and lowly against the excesses of the rich and powerful (p. 47). God will intervene, just as he did during the era of the prophets when he gave righteous judgement against the unjust structure in Israel's society (p. 47). God's intervention is inevitable. The emphasis, therefore, is not what the prophet does or should do; it is what God has promised and what God will do. Thus, prophetic imagination visualises this future promised by God, is assured of its inevitability and can, thus, breathe the fresh air of a time yet to be even when the prophet lives in the time that is. In other words, the prophet can breathe the fresh air of freedom, even amid present oppression and captivity.

However, while God's promised intervention lies in the future, there is a sense in which it is already truly present in the prophetic imagination. Unrelenting commitment does not, therefore, imply patient anticipation or even an inactive disposition or posture. It is the ability to live in the future even now. It is a rejection of the old/present world characterised by evil, hate, injustice, violence and war, in favour of a new world characterised by love, justice and peace, because the prophet, in a sense, already lives in this new world. The future of justice, freedom, peace and love is alive in the imagination of the prophet. The prophet defies injustice by living in a future of justice. He or she defies hate by living in the civilisation of love. He or she defies oppression by living in the freedom of the spirit. The future promised is already here. The present doom is already in the past. He or she defies unrest and war by living in peace. The prophet is already living in a future made possible by God, and it is by merely living in it, the prophet invites everyone else to live in this future. As Brueggemann puts it, it is the task of the prophetic imagination and ministry to bring people to engage in the promise of newness that is (already) at work in our history with God (59-60; parethesis mine). It is in this sense that Brueggemann calls prophets "future-tellers." In other words, the emphasis is not on prophetic action but on prophetic living. This is prophetic imagination at its best. This is what we see when God, through prophet Isaiah, declared: "See I am doing something new! Now it springs forth, do you not perceive it? In the wilderness, I make a way, in the wasteland, rivers" (Isaiah 43:19).

Yet, it is essential to note that the prophet's manner of living in the future does not amount to a denial of the present realities. It is not a denial of widespread debauchery, multiple tragedies, despondency, discouragement and even despair. Rather, even amidst these awful realities, the prophetic imagination is replete with hope. This is hope even in the midst of ongoing tribulation. This is hope amidst the ruin. This is hope even when there seems to be no hope. Reflecting on the theology of Christian hope in *Born from Lament,* Emmanuel Katongole (2017) observes that "there is something about Christian hope that is revealed only through tribulation" (p. 33). Several pages down, Katongole cites O'Connor on the nature of biblical hope. According to Kathleen O'Connor,

> Biblical hope does not emerge from proper reasoning or new information. It is not optimism or wishful thinking. It is not a simple act of the will, a decision under human control, or a willful determination. It emerges without clear cause like grace, without explanation, in the midst of despair and at the point of least hope. It comes from elsewhere, unbitten, illusive, uncontrollable, and surprising, given the pit, the place of no hope (O'Connor, 2002, p. 57, cited in Katongole, 2017, p. 55).

Ehusani will most likely agree with both Katongole and O'Connor on the nature of Christian hope. He would even add that there is something in Christian hope that energises. As he puts it,

> It energises the remnant few
> Who hunger for righteousness
> With the luminous visitation of a new day (p. 103).

Prophetic imagination as replete with energising hope echoes what he had said about the oracle of God as the source of the prophet's strength in *A Prophetic Church*. The oracle of God, the promise of God, the inevitability of God's intervention is the energy that keeps prophetic imagination going. It is also the prophetic message that energises the "long-standing victims of oppression." Thus, one of the roles of the prophetic church, in Ehusani's opinion, is "to make an intervention in God's name on behalf of the distressed people of our land" (2003, p. 72). The church does this not just by prophetic action but primarily by a display of prophetic hope.

4. Conclusion

One of the effects of Nigeria's socio-political woes since independence is that many Nigerians have given up on the Nigerian experiment. Many Nigerians today are cynical about the possibility of Nigeria becoming a more just and less corrupt country. These Nigerians no longer believe that a civil, clean and prosperous country is possible. Many Nigerians no longer believe that Christians and Muslims can live peacefully or that people of different tribes can live together amicably. For them, Nigeria is a jungle, a no man's land. Survival is the name of the game, and an individual should do whatever it takes to survive, irrespective of the repercussion on the society at large. The unfortunate consequence of this negative mindset is that Nigeria continues to sink deeper and deeper into chaos, anarchy and doom. The less Nigerians believe in their country, the less they will be committed to the hard work necessary to make Nigeria prosper. For instance, an individual who does not believe that Nigeria can ever be a clean country will likely not imbibe the discipline of properly disposing of waste. Yet, Nigeria can only become a clean nation when every Nigerian commits to cleanliness. If this is true of every facet of society, then it is evident that one cannot overemphasise the importance of a positive mindset in the prosperity of society. In other words, our society will automatically change when we all learn to be the change we want to see.

This is the meaning of prophetic imagination, in a very general (secular) sense. The point is that while we all must continue to call for change relentlessly, it is more crucial that we endeavour to be the change we want to see. We must not only envision a better Nigeria; we must even now begin to live as though Nigeria is already better. Prophetic imagination is not ultimately about prophetic speech and activism; it is prophetic living. It is an invitation to begin to live even now in a new Nigeria devoid of tribalism, corruption, filth, oppression, injustice and unrest. It is an invitation to defy the culture of greed and corruption, refuse to perpetuate injustice in one's sphere of influence, and stretch out a hand in fellowship and harmonious living with the other person irrespective of creed, language and tribe. It is to refuse to give up on the Nigerian project. Above all, it is the opposite of cynicism, despondency and hopelessness. In the case of Ehusani, the darker the terrain turned, the more he became aware of his call to light a candle and prophesy. Through the years, he has grown increasingly aware that his call is not just to activism but to live prophetically even now, this future of brightness. He currently lives that prophetic life through his LUX TERRA Leadership Foundation.

References

Abioye, T. (2019). *Language and the Moral Imperative in George Ehusani's Writings*. Abuja: Lux Terra Leadership Foundation.

Brueggemann, W. (1978). *The Prophetic Imagination*. Philadelphia: Fortress Press.

Ehusani, G. (1991). *An Afro-Christian Vision "Ozovehe!" Towards a More Humanized World*. Lanham, NY: University Press of America.

_____ . (2003). *A Prophetic Church*. Ibadan: St Pauls.

_____ . (2006). *Flames of Truth*. Ibadan: Kraft Books Limited.

_____ . (1997). *Fragments of Truth*. Ibadan: Kraft Books Limited.

_____ . (1998). *Petals of Truth*. Ibadan: Kraft Books Limited.

_____ . (2006). *Nigeria: Years Eaten by the Locusts*. Ibadan: Kraft Books Limited.

Katongole, E. (2017). *Born from Lament: The Theology and Politics of Hope in Africa*. Grand Rapids, MI: William B. Eerdmans Publishing Co.

Knitter, P. F. (2013). "Inter-Religious Dialogue and Social Action." In Catherine Cornille, *The Willey-Blackwell Companion to Inter-religious Dialogue*. Indianapolis, IN: John Willey & Sons. Ltd.

Kukah, M. H. (2017). "George Omaku Ehusani: 60 Years of Grace." The Guardian Newspaper, 5th of December 2017. Retrieved 15th of August, 2020 from https://guardian.ng/opinion/george-omaku-ehusani-60-years-of-grace/.

Mbiti, J. S. (1969). *African Religions and Philosophy*. New York: Anchor Books.

O' Connor, K. M. (2002). *Lamentations and the Tears of the World.* Maryknoll, NY: Orbis.

Odozor, P. I. (2014). Morality: Truly Christian, Truly African. Notre Dame, IN: Notre Dame Press.

Saint Augustine (1972). *City of God.* Translated by Henry Bettenson. London: Penguin Books.

Uzukwu, E. E. (1996). A Listening Church: Autonomy and Communion in African Churches. Maryknoll, NY: Orbis Books.

CHAPTER SEVEN

Re-Imagining Leadership to Reclaim the Failing Promise of Nigeria

Pat Utomi

1. Introduction

Nigeria has known challenged times. The celebration of political independence in 1960 and the freedom of Republic status in 1963 were still very visible in the rear-view mirror when election-related violence disrupted the peace of Western Nigeria. It brought in its wake a bloody coup d'état, a counter-coup that was even more bloody, a pogrom that consumed the lives of tens of thousands of innocent southerners in Northern Nigeria, beginning on the 30th of May 1966, and then a civil war of epic genocidal proportions for 30 months between July 1967 and January 1970 (Utomi, 2015: p. 3f.; Dudley, 1993; Decalo, 1976; Dent, 1978).

But there were bright moments. Reconciliation did not only mark the tone on which the war ended, it signalled the coming of a new beginning that heralded the programme of 3Rs (reconciliation, reconstruction and rehabilitation) with which the Federal Government of Nigeria flagged off the post-war era. It also gave impetus to infrastructure development occasioned by the quadrupling of oil prices, following the Yom Kippur Arab-Israeli war of October 1973. It would be recalled that the Arabs tried to use oil as a weapon by cutting off supplies to Western Europe and the US with the supply/demand effect of jerking up crude oil prices. Nigeria had found oil in commercial quantities in Oloibiri in its Eastern region in 1956 (Ihediwa, 2015). Oil price swings would then come to define the character of the Nigerian economy. Structural crisis would build up and Structural Adjustment Programmes would bring some relief, but the challenges of oil price volatility did not abate.

By 2020 Nigeria was back in economic misery history-making, as a recession, for the second time in five years. This was the result of the three-shock economic tsunami: the global perception of economic mismanagement, which resulted in the Forbes article of May 28, 2019 that said Nigeria was a money-losing machine (Rapoza, 2019); the supply chain dislocations which cut off raw materials shipment to manufacturers as a result of COVID-19 lockdowns; and a COVID-19 stimulated crash in crude oil prices, which sustained budgeting in Nigeria, all came together in a highly troubling admixture. The alchemy with combustible potency would trigger questions about the nature of the state and the quality of its leadership.

2. On the role of the Church in advocating good leadership in Nigeria

Why does Nigeria stumble from crisis to crisis, even with enormous factor endowments in agriculture, solid minerals, crude oil and human capital? Many years ago, the celebrated Nigerian novelist Chinua Achebe tried to capture it in a famous statement: The trouble with Nigeria is leadership (Achebe, 1984). What is the phenomenon known as leadership? How are stakeholders such as the church, foundations committed to advocating for good leadership? And how do citizens engage with it, so that true leaders can be formed based on a philosophy for saving Nigeria, and helping it claim its promise?

Among these stakeholders is the Church. And one of those championing the desired civic engagement is Rev. Fr. George Ehusani, a priest of the Catholic Diocese of Lokoja. In a 1996 book, *A Prophetic Church*, Fr. Ehusani articulates the mission of the church and the imperative of social impact. He points to the prophetic role in the mission of the church and passionately points to its deployment in the challenged Nigeria with much hunger for leadership:

> Prophets are visionaries of their time, when all others are blind, prophets are the ones granted to see the handwriting on the wall, to interpret the signs of the time and to see the light beyond the tunnel. Equipped as they are with superior knowledge and perception, prophets analyze the situation on the ground in the light of the common good and in the light of God's wisdom and commandments. Prophets refuse to be defined by the corruption of the moment; they

refuse to be engulfed by the darkness of the surrounding environment. (Ehusani, 1996, p. 14)

This visionary status of the prophet charts a role for the church to play in the elevation of the dignity of the human person. As a critical mission of the Catholic Church, this role of promoting the dignity of the human person has received greater amplification in the social teachings of the church, especially in Papal encyclicals since Leo XIII wrote *Rerun Novarum* in 1891 during the oppressive conditions of the Industrial Revolution (Pontifical Council for Justice and Peace (2004). But 130 years after, as we enter the fourth Industrial Revolution the prophetic voice of the church seems even more needed in countries like Nigeria. And priests, like Fr. George Ehusani, using the technology of the times must continue to speak from the pulpit, write in newspapers and use the internet to help people, who are, increasingly, just statistics, find their voice.

Ironically, Stephen R Covey, the personal effectiveness guru and author of the seven habits of highly effective people, noted, in his last book: The 8th Habit, that helping people find their voice would be the most important habit of the 21st century (Covey, 2004). This suggestion by Covey becomes even more pertinent as we see the government of Nigeria drift more towards fascism in its effort to muzzle civil society, as was evident in the cowardly shooting on October 20th, 2020 of peaceful protesters by armed soldiers, when young people protested police brutality under the banner of #EndSARS. As the government of Nigeria issued a statement that they would meet peaceful protest with force, threatened anyone who dared to protest after the 'Lekki Tollgate Massacre' was exposed by a CNN television investigative report, resulting in weakening the first round of protests, it was quite obvious, that the public authority better understood power than leadership.

They had failed to show compassion, a major attribute of leadership, but were anxious to use power base elements at their disposal to make the people do what they would ordinarily not want to do for fear of a more negative outcome. Faced with those conditions, many well-educated young people began to emigrate from Nigeria or planned to do so, as many of their parents did, when President Muhammadu Buhari was previously in power, as military head of state. These issues have raised a great question for people in positions of authority in Africa, in general, and Nigeria in particular. Why have they persisted in the preference to use power, which Dahl views as the ability of A to make B do what B would not like to do (Dahl, 1955), than to exercise influence which Maxwell (1997) defines as "inspiring people to own a cause of action and passionately pursue or support the attainment of the set goals" (Maxwell, 1997, p. 13)? The latter has been called Leadership. It is proven to be less costly than use of power and by far more effective.

3. Leadership Deficit and Nigeria's Myriad Problems

In the light of the above, we need to raise questions on why leadership is scarce and how leadership could help solve a myriad of problems assaulting the dignity of the human person in Nigeria (Utomi, 2014; Taiwo, 2011).

At a time of rapid change requiring the steady hands of consummate leaders, there seems to be a dearth of leadership talent. The mission of this navigation to the end of a world of global, political, corporate and family leaders, is, without doubt, of missionary dimensions. The means by which people of compassion, sense of service and knowledge can emerge to set clear goals and inspire their attainment is pursued as conversation for living. Leading is not a formula. It is capacity deployed in situational contexts, with actors of varying goals, and motivations (Hershey and Blanchard, 1977).

We live in a world full of challenges, and one which is peopled by many of varied aspirations. Thanks to Abraham Maslow and those who followed in his work path, we also know that man has needs and is never satisfied as such, because achieving at one level disposes us to a higher level of desire (Maslow, 1962).

The need to find the most cost-effective ways of overcoming the many challenges of today's world, from war and peace, to environmental challenges of a planet imperilled, calls for capable leaders. These troubles, which include overcoming the dislocations of a rapidly changing world that is driven by technology, shifting demographic trends, change in culture as well as to help achieve the goals of commercial enterprises and citizens in search of a better life, have created a great need for people of influence.

As people who help find and navigate a path to destinations not hitherto imagined within reach, the need for leaders is enormous. All through history, the pursuit of the better life and moving creation towards its perfection (as laid out in Christian tradition in Genesis: 2:15) has made yesterday's impossible today's routine and, very likely, tomorrow's obsolete, in the creative destruction tradition that the economist, Joseph Schumpeter identified as being largely made possible by leaders (Schumpeter, 1934).

Yet, remarkably, the word out there is that leaders seem to be harder to find, relative to the need. At the level of global leadership, the point has often been made of the twentieth century that its first half was marked by the influence of outstanding personages. They came from science, like Albert Einstein, who would be picked by *Time* magazine as the man of the century, and Sigmund Freud. There were those from the social movements – people like Mahatma Gandhi and Susan B. Anthony; and from politics, - the likes of Winston Churchill and Franklin Delano Roosevelt. There are many who will argue that with a few sprinklings like Martin Luther King Jnr in the 1960's, the former Tanzanian president Julius Nyerere and, Mother Teresa later, the close of the century had just one man standing at global leadership level: Pope John Paul II. Nelson Mandela would later begin to set his roots as the twenty-first century's first global leader.

For a century dominated by the rise of the private sector through quantum leaps in wealth creation, the crises of global leadership from private enterprise in a globalising world would prove even more terrifying that leaders could not be found in desired numbers.

In quick order, the world would witness iconic news magazines question the influence of elected political leaders at the first meeting of the expanded G7 in France, when the Russian president, Vladimir Putin joined the leaders of the United States, Germany, Britain, France, Japan, Canada and Italy, for the first time to become the G8, or as was joked about at the time, G7½ (seven-and-a-half). It was said that CEOs of several global corporations, like Jack Welch and Bill Gates had more real influence on the global stage than those gathering in France. Yet within a few years, the cry was for Main Street to rescue Wall Street.

Questionable values had led to the demise of many leading corporations and a major US business leader who had led Medtronic to much success, Bill George, wrote his book, *Authentic Leadership*, as a critique of the failings of the corporate world, with ideas on how to stay authentic (George, 2003).

Even more powerful in communicating the leadership chasm in corporate America was a book with a title that jumped at me from a Boston bookstore shelf in 2003. I had arrived on one of my fairly frequent visits to the United States, since I returned to Nigeria after my graduate studies twenty-one years earlier, and gone into a bookstore for a skim of new offerings as had become a habit. The new book that advertised itself was titled: *Value Leadership – The 7 Principles that Drive Corporate Value in any Economy*. Its author, Peter S Cohan, caught my attention on the first page with a magnificent statement on corporate values. He writes: "It's hard to imagine a better one." This is because this statement was from Enron's 2000 Annual Report; it is also hard to imagine a better example of the chasm that separates word and deed in too many companies (Cohan, 2003). As Jeff Skilling, Enron's CEO at the time would say, the statement of values was "good optics". Authentic leadership is surely beyond good optics. Indeed, part of the trouble with leadership is that many leader-wannabes are reading cookbook prescriptions that offer twenty-one or twelve steps to good leadership.

4. What Happened to Leadership in the 20th Century?

To reflect on what happened in the twentieth century and to understand why leaders have become scarce, it is useful to get a sense of what leadership is, and who leaders are. This is not so easy a task because the pervasive sense of the concept makes it bestride all human endeavour and so, explanation has been sought from the perspectives of several academic disciplines, and the realms of praxis. My academic background in several disciplines, including political science, business management, policy economics and media communications, with perspectives on leadership, and my active role on the Christian speaking circuit through much inspiration from preachers and faith-based writers on leadership as reference, provides enough variety of approaches to know that communicating a clear sense of leadership and what leaders do, is not so easy. Yet, it is imperative that it be made crystal clear, such that a 9-year-old can understand.

The nexus from which I draw meaning is further compounded, but also enriched by my active involvement as a business, political and church leader, and founder of a leadership think-tank and advocacy organisation. These are in addition to my academic role in which leadership is a core part of the framework I use to teach a course titled, "Political Economy of Growth and Economic Development". In essence, these disciplines and praxis see leadership as the exercise of goal-directed influence in as cost-effective a manner as possible, through the deployment of assets of confidence in the one who leads, such that the synergy which results in attaining that which was thought improbable, crystallises.

The personal effectiveness guru Stephen R Covey suggests that for leadership to take place two dimensions need to align. These are knowledge and a sense of service. So, a team or a person that is knowledgeable and has a sense of service towards those that follow them is more likely to see tomorrow more clearly, chart a course towards the tomorrow they see, and stretch the talent of the followers, obtaining synergy from the pool such that goal attainment brings fulfilment. In the main, leadership is joy from focus on the good of others.

If this be leadership, why did it wane in the course of the twentieth century? A good track of explanation can be drawn from shifts and trends in the core of how a sense of service is conditioned in culture.

The renowned Catholic Bishop of New York, Archbishop Fulton Sheen, lamented the loss of a sense of sin during the twentieth century. This lamentation, in many ways, summarises the shift in culture and paradigm for judging social action. Partly to blame was the effect of the work of one of the leaders of the early twentieth century scientific community, Sigmund Freud. He brought with psychoanalysis, the projection of some of our actions on our earlier experiences, but this psychoanalysis also focused man on himself. The rise of the ego and the social movement of the 1960s, as the mantra of the generation of the anti-Vietnam War movement and Woodstock, became more 'me, myself and I'. It had to rub off on a phenomenon that is essentially other-centred behaviour, leadership.

It seems reasonable to conclude that the more self was caused to matter, the less effective leadership became. This is an interesting paradox because the more successful leaders ultimately were not masochists, but their self-interest was better advanced in long term perspectives. It seems clear that deferred gratification, as a value, would show how better off people were if they prepared and acted towards others in a manner that resulted in 'common good' goals being achieved. True leaders saw the 'common good' as a better way for advancing their self-interest.

Culture matters and the habits of culture tint the prism through which reality is seen as well as the values that shape choice. The hedonism and artefacts of instant gratification that would signpost the new challenge of leading in the second half of the twentieth century began a detour from authentic leadership. The result of the trends in popular culture that focus on the individual, it seems, sets the generation of the early twentieth century apart from the latter, in terms of care for others. Care and commitment to the common good may be the reason corporations, nation-states and social movements began to worry about missing leaders at a time when the need for leaders to show the way to overcoming a myriad of social problems was rife.

Business schools, in response, began to pay more attention to the leadership question and personal effectiveness gurus, like Stephen R. Covey, established a strong presence as global thought leaders. Coming from faith-based domains, televangelists and teachers like John Maxwell and Myles Munroe became leadership development icons, just as the Sultan of Sokoto sponsored a volume on the leadership thoughts of his forebears – the founders of the Sokoto Caliphate, the bastion of Islamic leadership in west and central Africa.

To help shape a generation, help young people become persons of influence for good and to move the world to a place of greater peace, personal fulfilment and happiness, I founded the Centre for Values in Leadership (CVL). Its aim is towards becoming a global centre of excellence to develop young people that will lead Africa away from the years of Afro-pessimism, pervasive corruption and income inequalities – these have triggered injustice, consequent civil strife and insurgencies in an era of economic growth, social harmony and dignity amongst the peoples of the world.

Before this era, most of the huge literature on leadership had come from political science and the study of power. It was clear that CVL's mission was to provide platforms for coaching and directing the development of a habit of service in the next generation. This was coupled with a desire to promote continuous personal growth such that a generation of service and knowledge could become clearly discernible, lest the impression also arises that leaders are the few and the strong, like the advertisement for the US Marines.

The CVL message also showed that all could and should lead, as a person may, in one context be a leader, and in another, be a follower. More important, however, it was to indicate that the people who may be more responsible for inspiring goal-directed behaviour may not be the ones with the big title, but those with the right configuration, even if they be located in the middle of the pack. The thrust from the lessons in Robin Sharma's *The Leader who Had no Title*, would therefore be part of how organisations and societies see socialisation into leadership effectiveness (Sharma, 2010).

This is even more so when emotional intelligence domiciles primal leadership in one who has no title in the group. Examples abound of how those gifted with emotional intelligence, as Daniel Goleman often points out, may be the bus driver in the company. However, they could set the tone of the workplace (Goleman, 1998).

So, leadership development would not be a niche enterprise but a mass programme if the world were not only to be freed from the leadership challenge of the late twentieth century but also find the creativity to liberate a world held hostage by violence. This is especially for the voiceless and the angry in a global space where the resources of the planet are more than ample to ensure the banishment of poverty that degrades the dignity of the human person. Yet, poverty and disease continue to hold many back even though, as Angus Deaton rightly points out, far more have escaped misery in the second half of the twentieth century than in the millennia prior (Deaton, 2013). Much credit for that also goes to leadership in Asia and resurgent Brazil.

5. Leadership and the Scourge of Poverty

Peter Drucker once asserted that the quality of life of the average African at the beginning of the 20th century and that of the average European were only marginally different, but by the end of the century the difference in the quality of life of both groups was like night and day. What is more remarkable for me is that by the middle of the century self-government had begun to arrive in Africa.

Ownership of Africa's slide in the quality of life of its people needs therefore to be domiciled at the steps of African leaders who set the course of Africa's journey through most of the 20th century. Yet, ironically, the ultimate leadership icon to come out of the second half of the twentieth century would be an African leader, Nelson Mandela. Mandela's now famed meeting with Hakeem Baba Ahmed in which he was visibly unhappy with leadership in Nigeria seems now the appropriate peg for the synthesis of what went wrong in Africa, particularly in its most populous country that was expected to be light of the nations, Nigeria.

In the framing of the question, from the perspective of Franz Fanon and the burden of each generation to discover its mission and fulfill or betray it, can we say the leaders of Africa's first half century either failed to discover its mission regarding its well-being or betrayed it, as evident from Nigeria's position on the UNDP's Human Development Index, Millennium Development Goals and other measures of life and the Good Society? Not even the exploration of the vast natural resources discovered across Nigeria and many other parts of Africa like Democratic Republic of Congo (DRC) have helped in the journey away from poverty which crushes the dignity of the human person. Why is Africa poor and not growing as has happened in South East Asia? Explanations are legion. From the economic policy choice and geography arguments to the culture, and institutions-based explanations, there is no escaping the place of leadership in the widening gap of the 20th century.

We may lament the resource curse phenomenon until we see the relatively superior performance of natural resource endowed countries like Indonesia that make it clear that leadership matters. The imagination with which Norway, Alaska in the United States and others manage the impact of natural resources on national income provides lessons. Years ago, I tried to domesticate those lessons in the distribution of those incomes by inviting to Lagos the Norwegian economist at Columbia's Earth Institute, Martin Sandbu, and featuring him on Patito's Gang. As Africa has gone from the immediate post-independence decade to the decade of coups and then civil wars, and a time of Afro-pessimism, the new context of renewal hope should be a time for leadership that can recognize that the dignity of the human person is central to all progress. It should shape a time where getting rid of poverty is more important for the challenge of now than the kind of priorities that tend to dominate decision making in African states.

6. Economic Growth in Africa

For many years, the discussion of economic growth in Africa focused on the structural challenges of the late 1970s and the structural Adjustment programmes consequences upon them. The prolonged period of slow economic growth marked by television images of famine and war beamed around the world by television cameras, establishing a season of Afro-pessimism, led to schools of thought about why growth was slow on the continent.

Among two of those dominant schools was the Destiny or Geography orientation, which more or less blamed slow growth on Africa's geographic location that made malaria a source of enough health challenges to take away from productivity, among others. Sometimes associated with this approach, sometimes referred to as destiny determination position, is Jeffrey Sachs whose counsel inspired Nigeria's Roll Back Malaria programme of 1999 which was quite poorly implemented.

The counter view, which significantly featured Paul Collier of Oxford University's Centre for African Economies, stated that growth was slow in Africa because the leaders made wrong policy choices. This point is powerful in illustrating how leaders must have both knowledge and a sense of service in the example of one African leader from the first decade. Julius Nyerere, one of my favourite people, had a great sense of service. Had he a better understanding of economics, Tanzania would be paradise today. But he made the wrong economic policy choices. His sense of service would prove inadequate compared to Lee Kuan Yew who had both.

Comparatively, in Nigeria's contemporary experience in which people lacking in both knowledge and a sense of service captured the state and acted capriciously in a manner that sometimes left the state smelling like a criminal enterprise, politicians used and still use state apparatus to pursue rent opportunities often to the detriment of the common good. Nigeria's dominant political leaders, owing to lack of knowledge, are unable to muster enough vision even though they keep announcing visioning initiatives from Vision 2010 to Vision 2020. As Fr.

Ehusani and others keep pointing out from the Bible reference in Prov. 29:18, "without vision a people perish".

This poor vision is further compounded by the lack of a sense of service which leads to pervasive corruption and disruptive policy inconsistency noted in the indicting Forbes article cited earlier. Other explanations of why growth has been slow in Africa emphasize the value of institutions for progress. This point was stoutly made by US President Barrack Obama on his first visit to Africa. In Accra, President Obama lectured that what Africa needs are strong institutions, not strong men. As we know, Africa tends to have more of the latter. This is essentially the same as the point made by the Peruvian economist Hernando de Soto in *The Mystery of Capital* which tells the story of how institutions, representational systems, facilitate assets becoming capital (De Soto, 2000).

The absence of these institutions in most poor countries made their wealth of assets dead capital. In most of my research pursuits, my central concern continues to be the question of how institutions affect economic performance, a subject to which I am in much debt to the Nobel Laureate Douglass North and Raghuram Rajan and Luigi Zingales in their journeys of discovery in the books *Institutions, Institutional Change, and Economic Performance* (North, 1990) and *Saving Capitalism from the Capitalists* (Rajan & Zingales, 2003).

I have no doubt that institutions are critical for economic growth, but unlike de Soto, I do not discount culture. I am convinced that culture matters and that it shapes human progress. Values determine a work ethic, context of trust, attitudes to instant or deferred gratification, and many others. But, more importantly, leaders set the tone of culture. Among the enduring examples of how leaders shape culture is the Singapore story where Lee Kuan Yew used politics to shape culture and change the country, moving it, in the words of the title of his memoirs, in one generation, *From Third World to the First* (Yew, 2000).

7. Conclusion

In an October 2019 lecture organised by the Acton Institute at the Gregorian Pontifical Urban University in Rome, I looked at models of economic development in Africa and how values such as are advanced in papal encyclicals that constitute the social teachings of the Catholic

Church can shape economic choice, and how leadership could use that tone to shape human progress.

I was also acutely aware that other faiths orient to more effective leadership in their teachings. In the Nigerian experience, the leadership philosophies of the founders of the Sokoto Caliphate, which were rooted in Islamic teachings, served equally well. For example Shaykh Uthman Ibn Fadoye (Usman dan Fodio) admonishes the leader:

> I warn you to avoid oppression, wanton damage, spilling of blood without the sanction of law and nepotism, because if you indulge in partiality and class distinction, your authority would be broken, and this would destroy satisfaction, understanding and good relation. (Bobboyi, 2015, p. 25)

But leadership in Nigeria has been slow to learn from these principles from the various Faiths. This has elevated the expectations of activists and social philosophers like Rev. Fr. George Ehusani and the institutions they have founded such as the Lux Terra Leadership Centre. Their work should play an enduring role in the emergence of institutions that will provide boundaries within which leaders can work to advance humanity's material and social growth and development.

References

Achebe, C. (1984). *The Trouble with Nigeria.* Ibadan: Heinemann.
Bobboyi, H. (September 25, 2015). "Practices wherewith a state cannot survive." *National Mirror.* Lagos, Nigeria.
Cohan, P. (2003). *Value Leadership: The 7 Principles that drive Corporate Value in any Economy.* New York: Wiley.
Covey, S. R. (2004). *The 8th Habit: From Effectiveness to Greatness.* New York: Simon and Schuster.
Covey, S. R. (1992). *Principle Centred Leadership.* New York. Free Press.
Dahl, R. (1955). The Concept of Power. *Behavioral Science.* Vol. 2 No 5.
Deaton, A. (2013). The Great Escape. Princeton: Princeton University Press.
Decalo, S. (1976). *Coups and Army Rule in Africa.* New Haven: Yale University Press.

Dent, M. (1978) "Corrective Government: Military Rule in Perspective". *Soldier and Oil.* Keith Panter-Brick (ed.). London: Frank Cass.

De Soto, H. (2000). *The mystery of capital: Why capitalism triumphs in the West and fails everywhere else.* London. Bantam Press.

Dudley, B. (1993). Instability and Political Order in Nigeria. Ibadan: Ibadan University Press. 1993,

Ehusani, G. (1996). *A prophetic church.* Ede: Provincial Pastoral Institution Publications.

George, B. (2003). Authentic leadership: rediscovering the secrets to creating value. San Francisco: Jossey-Bass.

Goleman, D. (1998). Working with Emotional Intelligence. New York: Bantam Books House.

Greenleaf, R. K. (1977). *Servant Leadership,* New York: Paulist Press.

Hershey P, and Blanchard. K. H. (1977). *Management of organizational behaviour-utility human resources.* New Jersey. Prentice –Hall.

Ihediwa, N. (2015). "Interpretation of the July 1966 Counter Coup, Igbo Massacre and the Subsequent Civil War as 'Final Solution' on the Igbo question in Nigeria." *Igbo Nation: History and Challenges of Rebirth and Development Vol.1.* T. Uzodinma Nwala, N. Aniekwu and C. Ohiri-Aniche (eds). Ibadan. Kraft Books.

Maslow, A. (1962). *Towards a psychology of being.* New Jersey: Van Nostrand.

Maxwell, J. C. (1997) *Becoming A Person of Influence.* Nashville: Thomas Nelson.

North, D. (1990). *Institutions, institutional change and economic performance.* Cambridge:Cambridge University Press.

Pontifical Council for Justice and Peace. (2004). *Compendium of the Social Doctrine and Church.* Ibadan: Paulines Publication Africa.

Rajan, R. & Zingales, R. (2003). *Saving capitalism from the capitalists.* Princeton: Princeton University Press.

Rapoza, K. (May 28, 2019). "Nigeria has become Africa's Money-losing Machine' *Forbes.*

Schumpeter, J. (1934). *The theory of economic development: an inquiry into profits, capital, credit, interest and the business cycle.* Cambridge MA: Harvard University Press.

Sharma, R. (2010). *The Leader who had no title.* London: Simon and Schuster.

Taiwo, O. (2011). *Africa Must be Modern.* Ibadan: Kraft Books.

Utomi, P. (2015). "The Pursuit of Poverty". *Nigeria's Political Economy and the Courtship with Poverty.* Pp.3-43. Okom, M. P., Godfrey Ozumba, Rose Ugbe, Victor Lukpata and S. Ijor (eds). Calabar: Pumoh Ltd.

Utomi, P. (December 17, 2020). "The Troubles with Nigeria." *ThisDay.* Lagos. Nigeria.

Utomi, P. (2020). *Why Not- Citizenship, State Capture, Fascism and the Criminal Hijack of Politics in Nigeria.* Ibadan: Kraft Books.

Utomi, P. (2015). *Why Nations are Poor.* Lagos: CVL Leadership Series.

Utomi, P. (2014). *The Art of Leading.* Lagos. CVL Press.

Utomi, P. O. (1982). "Bureaucratic Power and the Public Policy Process. A Nigerian Case Study." Unpublished Ph.D Thesis. Indiana University Bloomington.

Lee, K. Y. (2000). *From Third World to First: The Singapore story, 1965-2000: Singapore and the Asian economic boom.* New York: HarperCollins Publishers.

CHAPTER EIGHT

Peacebuilding and the Imperative of Ongoing Interfaith Dialogue and Conflict Management

Anthony Azuwike

1. Introduction

Peace is tranquility and freedom from disturbance. It is the fruit of an active engagement with the various facets of and elements within society to attain relevant social welfare, equity, justice, and social cohesion, hence the word "peacebuilding." The central underlying principle of peacebuilding is justice, and the absence of justice results in injustice which often gives rise to conflict and unrest. Peace is not the absence of war, rather a state of harmony and justice accomplished through fairness and equity. Like every other thing of value, peace is not a product of wishful thinking, rather a product of hard work. As the Second Vatican Council put it, "peace is rightly and properly called 'the effect of justice.' It is the fruit of the harmony built into human society by its divine founder, and it is brought about by men as they strive to attain an even more perfect justice" (Gaudium et Spes, 1965: p. 2).

The word "peacebuilding" is attributed to the Norwegian sociologist, Johan Galtung from his 1975 pioneering work "Three Approaches to Peace: Peacekeeping, Peacemaking, and Peacebuilding." In this seminal work, Galtung suggested that peace has a structure different from, perhaps over and above, peacekeeping and ad hoc peacemaking. In his view, the mechanisms that peace is based on should be built into the structure and be present as a reservoir for the system itself to draw up. More specifically, structures must be found that remove causes of wars and offer alternatives to war in situations where wars might occur (www.peacebuildinginitiative.org). Therefore, peacebuilding aims to resolve injustice in non-violent ways and transform the cultural and structural conditions that generate deadly or destructive conflict. It bothers on developing constructive personal, group, and political relationships across ethnic, religious, class, national, and racial boundaries. This process includes violence prevention, conflict management, resolution or transformation, and post-conflict reconciliation or trauma healing, before, during, and after any given case of violence, Rapoport A. in *Peace: An Idea Whose Time Has Come* (1992: p. 25).

Nigeria is a classic example of a multiethnic, multireligious, multicultural nation and, therefore, has known its fair share of conflict. These conflicts are often occasioned by an admixture of social, cultural, and (extremist) religious factors, bias, and intolerance. More than anything else, however, religion appears to be Nigeria's most troubling factor. This is because Nigeria's ethnic delineations follow a pattern of religious affiliation which sees Nigeria divided into what could broadly be termed Muslim north, Christian south, and a mixture of both in the south-west. Unfortunately, these ethnoreligious affiliations often interfere with the social and political life of the nation, thus consistently raising the question of the place of religion in the country's constitutional order. It becomes imperative, therefore, that every possible avenue of peacebuilding must be explored, including and most importantly promoting and sustaining interfaith dialogue at all levels. A robust interfaith programme of dialogue will mitigate conflict and eliminate conflict breeding situations. It will also ensure that in the event of a conflict, society is not caught off-guard as it will leverage the understanding already built in time of peace in managing the conflicts that may arise.

The purpose of this paper is to make suggestions on how the Nigerian society can engage in a robust interfaith dialogue that will build peace, mitigate and manage conflict. The analysis and recommendations would mostly border on the two predominant religions in modern Nigeria. The reality of intra-religious acrimonies, which is a given within the Nigerian society, does not often rise to the level of intra-religious violence. Thus, because most of the crises witnessed in the country are mostly inter-religious - between Christians and Muslims, the focus will be on building bridges towards the peaceful coexistence of the adherents of both religions.

2. Brief Theoretical Foundation

According to Song, cultures do not correspond in any neat way to national or societal boundaries, and many cultures have long interacted and influenced one another through relations of trade, warfare and conquest. Today, due in part to interactions through the global economy, transactional communications networks, and the increasing migrations of peoples across borders, people in many parts of the world live in multicultural contexts and possess multiple identities, *Justice, Gender and the Politics of Multiculturalism 33* (2007). Nigeria is not an exception.

Song is an expert in multicultural theory as it affects internal minorities. Though her studies focused specifically on the inner minorities of the United States, they could very well be applied to other cultural and social groups even if they are not to be precisely referred to as "minorities." Of note, in *Justice, Gender and the Politics of Multiculturalism 33* (2007), is Song's observation that the term "minority" refers not to a group's numerical strength in the population but to groups that are marginalized or disadvantaged in some way (p. 3). This is essential to understanding the Nigerian social experience. For example, one or two large ethnic groups, which are by no means lacking in numerical strength, have been visibly and actively marginalized since the civil war for various (unjustifiable) reasons. There is, however, an aspect of number in classifying a group as a minority or majority because, in a multicultural, multireligious nation like Nigeria, a group that makes up a quarter of the population can hardly be categorized as a minority group.

The interaction between the majority and minority religious, ethnic, social, and political groups within Nigeria highlights the interconnection between majority and minority groups which, as Song suggests, has shaped cultural conflicts (p. 5). While cross-cultural experience has enhanced equality in certain societies, they have reinforced unequal and oppressive norms and practices across other cultures; Nigeria is a good example. For instance, the mixing of the Christian and Islamic cultures, except perhaps in western Nigeria has produced a clash of culture and civilization in recent years, which only looks to a modern democratic state for solutions. Unfortunately, the democratic state has so far not lived up to its role in the peacebuilding process.

In many respects, it is arguable that a particular section of Nigeria has mostly treated Nigeria as their exclusive heritage and patrimony since independence and has leveraged most of the privileges the country provides. Extending some of such privileges to the "non-privileged" segments of the country is often conceived as an accommodation comparable to the advocacy of Song *et al* in favor of American minority groups. However, if the core value of liberal democracies is the equality of all citizens (p. 3), then the principle of equal treatment is violated when a purported "majority" group usurps what should be shared national privileges and offers mere "accommodations" to the "minority" groups. Even so, whereas accommodations are well advocated for American social, religious, linguistic and gender minority groups, the experience of the religious and cultural minority groups in Nigeria is different as Christians and southerners are often left out in the scheme of things.

It becomes clear from the foregoing that while Song argues that treating members of minority groups with equal respect requires social accommodations under certain circumstances, my view is that accommodations are not necessary for equal respect with particular reference to Nigeria. This is because the nation's Constitution has in-built provisions meant to accord equal recognition and respect to the two dominant and often conflicting religions that to correspond to the two broad but not strict geographic circumscriptions – Muslim north and the Christian south. Though the actual expression of this constitutional equality is often lopsided, the Constitution's intent is reflected, for example, in the inclusion and national observance of the major Christian holidays, like Good Friday and Christmas, and Muslim holidays, such as *Ramadan* and *Eid-Al-Fitr* in the national calendar.

Grounded in the idea that citizens should treat one another with equal respect – a core value of the liberal democracy, Song argues that justice requires special accommodations under certain circumstances (p. 9). While this holds true for inner minorities of the U.S and other nations, it has proven problematic in Nigeria, more so since the supposed majority group has consistently exploited "accommodations" to the detriment of other groups. In my view, the better idea is that citizens express mutual respect for one another simply by accepting a set of basic constitutional rights and opportunities that apply equally to all while the state maintains uniform treatment of all, especially in sensitive religious matters [emphasis, mine]. Other intra-social, cultural and religious accommodations can be worked out among the concerned groups without the direct involvement of the state, which often gives rise to allegations of lopsidedness whenever differential treatments are proffered.

My view, however, does not imply a repudiation of Song's egalitarian approach, which she admits is open to differential treatment under certain circumstances. However, in the specific Nigerian context, my position is related more to that of many liberal theorists who maintain that justice should be "culture-blind" and that justice requires a common set of rights and opportunities for all individuals, regardless of religious, or ethnic affiliation (p. 10). I am open to leaving the choice of specific policies and resolutions to be decided through democratic deliberation (p. 10). This idea finds expression in the Constitutional Conferences that have taken place in the country's political history. But again, these conferences (with the possible exception of the 2014 Constitutional Conference), have mainly provided avenues for bigotry and the inflammatory rhetoric that demonstrates the deep divide between the presumed majority and the supposed minority.

Song supports a deliberative approach to particular cultural (social and political) dilemmas, which has several advantages over approaches that give little or no role to the participation of those affected by the dilemmas in question (p. 10). The Nigerian dilemma, however, is that those who argue for state accommodations argue on the strength of their number and their supposed right over the rest of the nation. Moreover, accommodations that consistently favor a dominant group can easily cross the line into injustice and oppression by hegemony, especially when corresponding accommodations are not accorded other groups for the simple reason that their voices on the political table are thin.

Empirical deliberation research suggests that when a diverse set of people come together to talk over a consequential decision, they tend to attenuate many of the problems associated with mass democracy. As Michael Neblo *et al.* note, deliberation, although hardly a cure-all, works by posing a different question to the democratic citizen than politics dominated by interest-group and partisan blood sport. Instead of asking people, "What do you want?" a deliberative frame asks them, "What should we do?" (http://science.sciencemag.org/). Scholars have found that the effects of this small shift can be profound, and there is strong evidence that deliberative institutions positively influence citizens, especially in consolidated democracies [emphasis mine]. Deliberative moments present opportunities for elected officials to persuade - on the merits, something often missing from the current political system. When leaders participate in deliberation, they very often succeed in changing citizens' minds (p. 10).

Treating all members of the composite groups- majority or minority as equals by giving them a real voice (as opposed to a nominal or symbolic voice) in governance provides a more effective mode of conflict resolution. As Song aptly suggests, 'by drawing on the voices of affected parties, a deliberative approach can help clarify the nature of the interests at stake, as well as help identify the complex sources of cultural conflicts which are [...] in some cases, practices that threaten the basic rights of vulnerable members (p. 11). Deliberation can often expose these practices and can even make it clear that there is no reason why a particular community should take precedence over others in a liberal democratic state.

Two of Song's submissions ring particularly true when brought to bear on the Nigerian situation. First, she notes that many cultural conflicts arise out of intercultural interactions; what appear to be *intra*-cultural conflicts may have been fueled by intercultural connections (p. 36). This is true from the intercultural perspective in the sense that the Boko Haram uprising, for example, has been linked to a reaction to the growth of Christian evangelical movements and their perceived aggressive proselytization (Sanusi, 2007). These conflicts which allegedly began as a push back against Christianity have now seen Muslim leaders and ordinary Muslims unsympathetic to Boko Haram's extremist ideologies constituting a good number of its victims, underscoring the *intra*-cultural conflict dimension.

3. John Inazu and the Concept of Pluralism

A plural society is a society divided by segmental cleavages (Harry Eckstein, 1966). Such segmental cleavages may be of a religious, linguistic, regional, cultural, racial, or ethnic nature. Nigeria is one such pluralistic society replete with segmental cleavages and in which it has been found that democratization is often more difficult than, for instance, in states where people see themselves as members of the same community (John Stuart Mill). Confident pluralism recognizes that we have better and worse ways to live out our confidence and negotiate the pluralism around us (John Inazu, *Confident Pluralism* 2016, p. 4-5). Inazu's theory admits that we retain some modest unity in our diversity – a modest unity that also includes two premises, inclusion and dissent.

Inclusion allows those on the fringes of the civil and political society to be admitted into the mainstream, while *dissent* allows people the space to dissent from the norms established by that same society (p. 9).

Jean Jacques Rousseau had stressed the impossibility of living in peace with those we presume as damned. Taken literally, Rousseau's words may imply a justification of the often-overheated rhetoric coming out of the conservative and the liberal elements of western societies over issues like gay rights, abortion, and social welfare. On a grimmer level, Rousseau's prediction finds concrete expression in the gruesome murder of innocent people in the hands of religious zealots in the Middle East, Africa, and around the world. John Inazu criticizes Rousseau's assertion by declaring that the impossibility of living in peace with those we think are damned ultimately leads to what Shadi Hamid calls "the end of pluralism," (p. 6), which is a nightmare. Inazu thus declares that confident pluralism insists that our shared existence is not only possible but also necessary.

I would, however, like to recast Rousseau's words in terms of a call for tolerance rather than a statement of the undesirability of peaceful living with people of differing worldviews, faith, or practice. Rousseau could not have been calling for a world that accommodates no difference seeing that the mindset that views people as damned is the reason for such atrocities as are committed by radical groups like ISIS, al-Qaeda, Boko Haram, and the rest. This is what makes such worldviews dangerous. Under the illusion of "saving others from damnation," violence finds justification – a pointer to the biblical prophecy that "the hour is coming when everyone who kills you will think he is offering service to God" (John 16:2). Jesus, however, puts it in the right perspective when he says in the very next verse, "They will do this because they have not known either the Father or me" (John 16:3), which means that those who kill in the name of God lack authentic faith and knowledge of God and of his holy prophets. The knowledge of God and of his word put into proper use, is the path to peace among religious adherents. And we must recognize, as Abner Green notes, that "we do better by recognizing that difference is something we cannot get past." (Green 2012, p. 23). Therefore, we must live our difference with grace.

Furthermore, Inazu's "common ground imperative" is worth considering. This imperative presupposes that though it is not always possible to have relationships with people who differ from us in important and often insurmountable ways, sometimes the best we can do is coexist. This coexistence is what is being called for in the Nigerian social and political circumstance. Though we may retain our primordial views, we can always work together towards a common ground in spite of our differences (Inazu, p. 12). Inazu's common ground makes an interesting parallel to Aristotle's "excess and deficiency" in his appeal for a middle way or a common ground. In this perspective, the appetite's excess is licentiousness, its deficiency is frigidity, and its middle way is moderation. Anger's excess is rage, its deficiency is cowardice, and its middle way is courage. Reason's excess is demagogy, its deficiency is ignorance, and its middle way is wisdom (Aristotle, 1996, ps. 268 -71).

Beautifully too, the middle way is an important concept in Islam (Hakan Yavuv & John Esposito 2003, p. 118). For instance, the Qur'an defines the Muslim community as the *ummeten vasatan*, or the community of the middle way (Qur'an 2: 143). The Bosnian politician and author, Alija Izzetbegovic, wrote a book to demonstrate that Islam is the middle way between materialism and spiritualism (Yavuv & Esposito, p. 118). Similarly, the Turkish preacher, former Imam and founder of the Gülen movement, Fethullah Gulen, interprets the important Islamic concept of *sirat-i mustakim* (the straight path), which is recited in a Muslim's prayer forty times a day, as the middle way between *ifrat* (excesses) and *tefrit* (deficiency) (Gullen, 1980). The understanding of the middle way was also crucial in Bediuzzaman Nursi (1873 -1960) who had a great influence on Gullen. Nursi would repeatedly state that Islam is a middle way, a path of moderation, rather than extremism (Yavuv & Esposito, p. 118). This should be an exemplary model to those who choose the way of extremism in the name of God, rather than the path of moderation and tolerance.

4. Negotiation: Lessons from the Northern Ireland Peace Process

There is need for negotiation as an important aspect of peacebuilding. Nigerians can coexist only if all ethnic and religious groups agree to live together in peace. Indeed, it is only through compromise and tolerance that the dominant ethnic and religions groups will be able to collectively achieve the better future that Nigerians deserve and yearn for. Since what is sauce for the goose is sauce for the gander, the leadership of Nigeria should speak to those across the ethnic, religious, and political divide to reassure them that their core interests are recognized and that what is in the interest of one group needs not be inconsistent with the interests of the other.

5. What We Can Do

In proposing solutions to the Nigerian problem, we can look at countries that have been successful in not only negotiating peace but also improving their economy at the same time. A prime example is Northern Ireland, a country that was bedeviled by intractable religious crises but eventually succeeded in achieving peace. Though the conflict between the two main religious groups, the Protestants and the Catholics, began over 400 years prior, violent clashes between the two groups claimed over 3,000 lives in the second half of the 20th century, (http://www.english-online.at/history/northern-ireland/northern-ireland-troubles-and-conflict.htm.).

Up until 1972, Northern Ireland was allowed to rule itself. During this time, the Catholics, who lived in the Protestant province, had no easy life. They lacked equal rights and opportunities compared to the Protestants and were discriminated against in all aspects of life. They barely found work, got less money from the government, and were often harassed by the police. In the late 1960s, riots broke out between Protestants and Catholics in Belfast and Londonderry. The violent decades that followed became known as "the Troubles" (p. 34). Towards the end of the century, a new peace agreement was signed that helped to bring peace to Northern Ireland.

Precisely in the 1990s, the British government started working on a peaceful solution to end the troubles. The British and Irish governments tried to get political and paramilitary sides to the conference table, and as time went on, both sides realized that violence could not lead to a solution. The Irish Republican Army (IRA) promised to end all violent activities, and finally, the talks resulted in a historic agreement signed on Good Friday 1998.

Despite this treaty, not everything went according to plan in the succeeding years due to mutual distrust amongst the paramilitary groups. Finally, after years of squabbles and disagreement, the leaders of the Catholic Party, Sinn Fein, and the protestant Democratic Unions Party came to a historic agreement in 2007 to share power in the Northern Irish government. The cooperation between the two groups is a sign that a lasting peace could finally come to Northern Ireland.

6. Lessons for Nigeria

There are lots of parallels to be found between Nigeria and Northern Ireland before the peace accord. Thus, Northern Ireland's path could be a model for Nigeria because, like Northern Ireland, identity and economic problems tied with religion are the major issues. The difference is that in Northern Ireland, the two groups, Catholics and protestants, were essentially of the same Christian faith though of different denominations. In Nigeria, the issues are majorly between two fundamentally different religions, though with commonalities. There is also an ethnic tug of war laced with the struggle for political control, which translates into the control of the vast oil resources.

Fundamentally, the union of the Protestants and Catholics in Northern Ireland was never a happy marriage (Arthur, 2000). However, efforts were made to keep up appearances. For a time, it seemed that reconciliation had been effected until violence reappeared to the disappointment of those who had thought that a new era had dawned and that the loveless marriage might finally produce offspring (p. 31). They were left with only one choice: to self-immolate or seek the help of a "counselor." The same can be said of the constituent parts of Nigeria. Though marred with antipathy from the onset, efforts to keep up the appearances of unity by the major ethic delineations of Nigeria continued, until the violence of the thirty-month war of 1967 - 70 marred the marriage altogether. After the Nigerian civil war, which the Gowon led administration described as "no victor, no vanquished," reconciliation appeared to have been achieved and a new day seemed to have dawned. But that is not completely the case, as events have led to further acrimony and ill-feelings. Like Northern Ireland, Nigeria is left with a hard choice: to self-destruct or seek the help of "marriage counsellors." But it must be noted that the best marriage counselors in this case must be ourselves.

John Darby argues that Northern Ireland's conflict is remarkable for the limitations it places on violence rather than for the violence itself. He argues that "the long familiarity with inter-community conflict has led to the evolution of effective mechanisms to control it [...] They have amounted so far to a major and effective control against the conflict expanding into a genocidal war" (Darby 1986, ps 10;30). It is highly doubtful if such could be said of Nigeria and her efforts to manage crisis situations. The government and her security apparati mostly adopt reactive measures instead of proactive measures against violence and incidents of terror attacks such that the cumulative loss of lives and property could now be very well measured in genocidal proportions.

The "hypothetical tranquility of communal deterrence" on which Nigeria is currently riding has been a disincentive against negotiation. We like to believe that as long as our cities and creeks are not up in flames, there is peace. But this kind of peace is both deceptive and unsustainable due to its innate short lifespan. Hostilities in the country could potentially escalate to epic proportions if not properly managed by bringing aggrieved parties to the table. The occasional lulls in intercommunal conflicts and terrorist outbursts should not be an impetus for government to sit on its palms. It should rather be an occasion to usher in negotiators because such lulls are deceptive. Experience shows that in Nigeria, such relative peace can be so easily upset at the slightest provocation. Such social volatility succeeded in driving manufacturing to an all-time low in Northern Ireland because companies had to flee for their safety. The same scenario has played out in Nigeria where industrialization has greatly been affected. Companies have fled the restive parts of northern and southern Nigeria because of violence and recurrent cases of kidnapping of both locals and expertrates.

An identifiable factor in the Northern Ireland crises, which is deeply shared by Nigerians, is the lack of a collective sense of nationhood. Thus, managing our plural identities remains a great challenge. Nigerians continue to view themselves primarily in terms of our ethnic, religious, and regional identities rather than our common identity as Nigerians. Some in their religious fanaticism, cannot as yet distinguish between our democratic dispensation and a theocracy. Bishop Matthew Kukah was thus right in suggesting that we should consider banning the usage of Christians and Muslims as categories for defining ourselves as the two words have become inherently divisive and conflictual only triggering a sense of identity consciousness of "us and them (Kukah, 2015). As was the case in Northern Ireland, the institutional religions not only walk a fine line between the pastoral and the political but often dabble wholly into politics in many cases. This means that, as John Dunlop posited, "by providing an uncritical chaplaincy services to political ideologies, we confer a quasi-religious character upon them" (Dunlop 1986 p.18-20). Dunlop's suggestion, therefore, is apropos for Nigeria: "politics needs to be desacralized so that they can become manageable and, in the process, the churches will be set free to be church" (p.18-20) and mosques set free to be mosques [emphasis, mine].

An important question for Nigeria is the same question raised by the 1985 Anglo-Irish Agreement leading up to the 1988 Belfast Agreement: When is the most important time to engage conflicting parties in mediation and negotiation? Arthur suggests that it is wise to view the 'ripe moment' as a process rather than a specific point in time" (p.18-20). It calls for a proactive role on the part of government. In other words, government must be engaged at all times in order to keep conflict under control and decide at what point it becomes necessary to engage third party mediators. Nigeria must work towards such an arrangement that recognizes the right of citizens to determine their constitutional future and respects the equality and the rights of all citizens to hold political positions regardless of their ethnicity or religion, along with fixing a broken economic system that perpetually keeps the masses poor.

It must be said that ethnic, political, and religious grievances do not just go away until affirmative steps are taken by all concerned, including the government and the civil society to heal rifts and establish justice and peace through equity. Thus, the Nigerian government needs to take active steps to promote the peace that is critical for national development. Additionally, because the common aspirations of people change, we must all realize that "peace is not something that can be attained once and for all, but something that must continually be built up." (p.18-20). This is the meaning of peacebuilding.

Furthermore, Northern Ireland's experience is a testament to the fact that apart from dialogue, whenever a nation's economic lot improves, religious tensions and other tensions subside. For much of the post-war period, the Irish economy significantly underperformed compared to its European neighbors. In the mid-1990s, when the economy picked up and outpaced other European countries, things began to change. From about 1995 to 2002, the nation's productivity increased, the fiscal position of the Irish state became very strong, and the unemployment rates fell to around four percent (http://ec.europa.eu/ireland/key-eu-policy-areas/economy/irelands-economic-crisis/indexen.htm). Around these times, the news of frequent religious crises in Northern Ireland abated. A good strategy, therefore, would be to pursue peace negotiations alongside plans for a robust economic development. Nigeria must address its security problems by negotiating peace which allows investments to return.

7. Wisdom from Paul Ricoeur

Paul Ricoeur is a philosopher of conversation and mediation who embodies the Socratic dictum that truth is a dialogic event (Paul Ricoeur 1995, p. 1). He acknowledges that in every dialogue, there is a middle ground between the factions; a middle ground, which is often hidden, and which dialogue helps uncover. Ricoeur's attempt at rapprochement, however, never purchases mediation at the price of ignoring important differences (p. 1). Thus, recognizing, but not capitalizing on important differences amongst the constituent groups making up the Nigerian state is an important first step in any peacebuilding effort. This difference is obvious in the culture, religion, economy and economic philosophy (emphasis, mine). In this respect, rather than the cliché of "One Nigeria," recognizing the differences amongst the respective people and building on those differences as strength rather than weakness, would be a basis for a harmonious relationship. Just as America is great because of its strength in diversity, our differences can be harnessed as building blocks for a great nation. Identifying and recognizing our differences therefore, without trying to elevate one over another, would constitute a great asset in our peacebuilding efforts.

According to Paul Wallace, editor of Ricoeur's *Figuring out the Sacred*; "Truth happens in the space opened up in the conversation between newly found dialogue partners – whether these dialogue partners be human interrogators, literary texts, works of art, or cultural artifacts." (Wallace, *Figuring out the Sacred* P. 1). The constituent parts of Nigeria are partners made so through the 1914 amalgamation, though sometimes, uncomfortable bed partners. This means that there is the need to continue to find space to engage in dialogue so that truth may happen. So far, this has remained a deferred dream and an ideal yet to be realized.

In building the much-desired peace in Nigeria, religion, which is our most troubling factor, has a role to play, incidentally. Thus, Ricoeur's thoughts regarding the recovery of the sacred becomes relevant. He argues that an authentic response to the question "who are we" is founded, in part, on a recovery of the sacred by taking up residence in the world of mythopoetic literature. This underscores the place of religion and of sacred texts such as the Bible and the Qur'an in the quest for peace (p.1). Ricoeur knows fully well that beyond cumulative reason, there could be a world of transcendent possibilities (mediated through the sacred texts) that can refigure and remake the world of the reader

(p. 2). This, he says, "is only possible through a self-critical, always revisable, and never certain hermeneutical solemn pledge that leads to a discovery of the task of becoming an integrated self." (p. 2).

Reading scriptural texts cognizant of their subtle differences allows people to learn the various forms of identify-formation within the texts that can inspire people to move from being nomads without hope to being authors of their own life's story (p. 2). Nigerian religious adherents (Muslims and Christians alike) must be readers and writers of their own life's story; and the power to do this may be found in the experiences and the master stories of the Bible and Qur'an's greatest heroes, taking into consideration the fact that life is full of discords and accords. This is true because Islamic history, for instance, is filled with positive chapters of cultural and religious coexistence and cooperation between Muslims and non-Muslims, as seen in the oft-cited examples of medieval Spain, India, and south-east Asia. In this vein, Mike Ghouse argues:

> When Prophet Muhammad (pbuh) initiated the inclusive Madinah Treaty, he showed us the way — a spiritual leader can also be a civic leader and work with people of other faiths with respect and dignity. He would not have invited Jews, Christians, and others to sign the treaty, had he believed that Islam was the only way (http://www.huffingtonpost.com/mike-ghouse/two-islams-the-mangledup-_b_5748280.html.)

Such positive examples can shine a bright light on Nigeria's path to peaceful coexistence. Thus, as against a citizenry that envisions itself in terms of ethnicity, language, religion, or region, we must strive for an integrated vision of self. This vision, I imagine, could also be realized through the nation's Constitution which is our first and common "holy text" and has the potential to unite the nation.

While our distinctive and distinguishing identities and attributes may never be ignored, a vision of Nigeria beyond our dividing factors would help transform the expression, "One Nigeria" from a mere cliché to the reality of one nation united. Ethnic politics, religious rivalry, and the struggle for the control of oil wealth have been Nigeria's most dividing factors and her greatest obstacles to growth and development. As Lamido Sanusi notes, "the failure of the Nigerian political elite to forge a true national consciousness, corruption and absence of a social safety net for the poor, historical identities and the search for authenticity, the struggles between and within the religions have all contributed to generating religious and social tensions in Nigeria." (Sanusi, 2007). How to unite and transform these variables of ethnicity, religion, and oil wealth into a catalyst for growth and development has been the country's greatest challenge. Unity, however, is no substitute for justice. As Odimegwu Ojukwu observed, "Nigeria's unity is enhanced only when oppression of any ethnic group ceases and the political system is adjusted to accommodate the legitimate aspirations of every group… and the members of every constituent group feel equal and secure in the country" (Ojukwu, 1994). This is an important dimension that must never be ignored.

8. Listening to the Parties

Political scientists suggest that the ability to develop the most appropriate and enduring solution to a conflict lies in the accurate identification of the cause(s), (Hauss, 2003). The identification of the causes of conflict can best be achieved through listening. Listening to the disagreeing factions in Nigeria tell their stories openly and candidly, regardless of who they are, would be a great way forward. Listening to the parties makes clear the causes and the sources of conflict and reveals, to a great extent, why people act and react the way they do.

In general, the two most identifiable strands of conflict within the African continent are: identity-based conflicts and interests-based conflicts. Nigeria is divided along ethnic, linguistic, cultural, religious, class, and political lines. By listening, therefore, we can differentiate between identity-based conflicts and interests-based conflicts, know how conflicts arise, and determine which instruments or avenues of peace negotiation to adopt.

A great parallel to the Nigerian situation is the Sudanese situation before the independence of South Sudan. The northern Sudanese are Arab while the southerners are black African. The oil reserves are in the south while there is none in the north. Islam is an integral part of the northern Sudanese culture, while the southern Sudanese are Christians and animists. So, a threat to Islam is a threat to the northern Sudanese culture. The establishment of Sharia law by the northern-Sudanese-dominated government in 1982 was, therefore, a way of asserting their Muslim identity (Zwier, 2015). The government sought to defend their Islamic culture by pushing the religion to all parts of the country such that the more secure the Northerners felt about their religion, the more the southerners felt their own culture and religion were being threatened. The increased acrimony resulted in a war; however, war did not have to be the answer. Given the situations in Sudan, a well-planned programme of dialogue and peaceful negotiations could have led to ways the two parts of Sudan could both maintain their identity and culture and carefully reach a political compromise to save the country from the eventual break up. Such dialogue and negotiations could help in the Nigeria case, given the similar polarity between the North and the South.

In his book, *The Power of Ethical Persuasion* (Patrick Miller & Tom Dusk, 1994), Tom Rusk, an expert in teaching community mediation, noted the importance of talking as well as getting the parties to listen to each other; a strategy that is applicable in any mediation setting. According to Rusk, "there is no necessary connection between listening and agreeing with the opponent's position" (p. 7). Nonetheless, listening to the opponent is necessary.

Talking or negotiation as a problem solving-strategy is inevitable, as demonstrated by the "orange" illustration in Paul Zwier's book, *Advanced Negotiation and Mediation Theory and Practice* (2016):

> Imagine that two parties were sent to a late-night grocer shortly before closing. Both want an orange. They each reach for the orange at the same time and each establishes a firm grip on the orange. In deciding who gets the orange, the parties' immediate option may be to resort to violence with the stronger party winning the fight and getting the orange. However, talking to each other would reveal the reasons why each wants the orange. Supposing one wants the orange for its juice to make a cake and the other wants the orange for the rind to make garnish for a drink. A win-win solution could be reached if they both agree to split the cost of the orange, one peels it and takes the rind while the other takes the rest home (p. 3).

The orange story demonstrates the advantage of "problem solving" as a means of achieving peace. By recognizing and addressing the underlying needs of the parties, creative solutions can possibly emerge. Thus, if the disagreeing parties in Nigeria would sit and talk frankly and understand the needs of the others, they could all be smiling home with a fair share of their desired interests; ownership issues can be transformed from the concept of exclusive control to that of sharing different economic benefits (p. 5), and some of the accruing economic resources can be used to sponsor social, intellectual, and cultural exchanges between the different ethnic and religious groups. Such exchanges might lead to social cohesion, rather than the violence that is commonplace. Not talking often leads to demonization and too often to violence (p. 21).

9. Education as a Path to Peace

Any program for peace and economic advancement in Nigeria must include greater educational development. Quality education has a direct bearing on national prestige, greatness, and cohesion. In addition, the knowledge and skill that young people acquire help determine their degree of patriotism and contribution to national integration and progress (Stella Anasi, *Curbing Youth Restiveness in Nigeria: The Role of Information and Libraries*). Between the years 2000 and 2004, about 30% of Nigerian youth, ranging from ages ten and twenty-four, was not enrolled in secondary school (Population Reference Bureau, 2006). The lack of educational opportunity denies the youth the opportunity to reach their potential and makes them disorientated and readily available for antisocial behaviors.

The first Western style educational institutions in Nigeria were established by the Christian missions at the dawn of the 19th century. This happened mostly in the south. While across southern Nigeria, there was a growth in western-type schools, with some children of the southern elite going to the Great Britain to pursue higher education (Bourne, 2015), the British Crown's policy of indirect rule and validation of Islam, did not encourage the operation of Christian missions in the north (Garba, 2012). Lugard's respect for the emirs and his deference to Islam made him slow to launch a drive for western-style education in the north while Christian missionaries in the south were spreading education and spearheading enlightenment. This meant that by independence in 1960, regional differences in modern educational access were marked. The legacy, though less pronounced, continues to the present-day and accounts for the imbalance between the northern and southern educational achievement. Accordingly, peacebuilding and conflict management must involve finding ways to bridge the gaps in educational access for the youth in all regions of the country. This is necessary because exposure to educational opportunity will reduce youth unemployment, stimulate economic growth, and, to a great extent, reduce the propensity of the youth to fall prey to jihadism, terrorism, and militancy – the ills that currently threaten Nigeria's unity and peace.

In this vein, universities have a unique role in building the social cohesion of the nation's youth. Like everywhere else in the world, universities are a confluence point for young people drawn from many different places and backgrounds and united for a common pursue: the pursuit of learning, which includes their mental, social, and scientific development. Young people often develop tolerance for differences as they engage in social interaction and live and study side by side with one another. In response to Mark Jurgensmeyer's question regarding where the future generation of Palestinians and Israelis might come together, a member of Hamas was quoted to have said, "it would be in a university." He imagined a situation where his child and an Israeli child could, someday, relate to one another as friends and fellow students in a neutral arena – "Perhaps on your campus of the University of California," he suggested (Jurgensmeyer, 1995). This shows that schools symbolize a unity beyond ethnic and ideological boundaries.

10. The Role of Libraries

The primary role of the library is to acquire, process, preserve, and disseminate recorded information (Stella Anasi, *Curbing Youth Restiveness in Nigeria: The Role of Information and Libraries*). Studies demonstrate that libraries are important, not only in educational endeavors but also in the promotion of peace and social unity. It has been suggested that libraries have a place in curbing violence and youth restiveness (Omotayo, 2005; Echezona, 2007). Libraries can help enlighten the youth and other members of the community by presenting them with intellectual resources and reliable information that could help their mental development, guide them in promoting peace and reducing occasions of violence, acrimony, and confrontation.

The Nigerian government must invest in the provision of libraries and equip them with up-to-date materials, books, and information technology aids. As is the case in most advanced societies, the governments should ensure that Library services are available not only in the Universities and other institutions of learning but also in cities and villages around the country. The government can seek partnership of the many multinational oil companies operating in Nigeria to make library facilities available in all educational institutions, urban centers, towns and villages. Libraries can be places where people access information that promotes peace, unity, progress and peaceful coexistence amongst all communities. They could be centers of formal and informal education with learning and recreational facilities where idle youths and other members of the community can find fulfilling engagement. Such meaningful engagement would help redirect people's minds and energies to wholesome activities instead of violence.

11. Conclusion

To think that peace and equity will be easily achievable in Nigeria is to be naïve. Peace and justice are ideals that often emerge from a people's deliberate choices. Although there are no set of rules or academic postulations that would automatically resolve the myriads of problems that Nigeria faces, dialogue, negotiations, and compromises could be the way forward. To preserve the unity of the nation, Nigerians must make choices that would uphold the peace of the nation. The nation's leaders must make political decisions whose goal is the attainment of equity, justice, and peace. Urgent steps must be taken to assuage the current nagging issues; otherwise, the social division will continue to intensify, the violence will increase, investment will be scared off, alienation will continue to grow, and the best minds in the country will continue to flee elsewhere in search of greener pastures. Depending on what choices we make as a country, the future of Nigeria will either be that of a vicious circle or a virtuous one.

References

Abner S. Green. (2012). *Against Obligation: The Multiple Sources of Authority in a Liberal Democracy.*
Aristotle. (1996). *Poetics.* ...268-71
Arthur, Paul. (2000). *Special Relationships: Britain, Ireland and Northern Ireland Problem.*
Anasi, Stella. *Curbing Youth Restiveness in Nigeria: The Role of Information and Libraries.* http://digitalcommons.unl.edu/cgi/viewcontent.cgi?article=1404&context=libphilprac. Last visited, March 11, 2017.
Bourne, Richard Bourne. (2015). *Nigeria: A New History of a Turbulent Century.*
Darby, John Darby. (1986). *Intimidation and the Control of Conflict in Northern Ireland* vii-ix.

Dunlop, John. (1986). *Irish Challenges to Theology* 18-20.

Echezona R. I. (2007). *The role of libraries in information dissemination for conflict resolution, peace promotion, and reconciliation. African Journal of Libraries, Archives, and Information Science 17* (2) 143-152

Eckstein, Harry. (1966). *Division and Cohesion in Democracy: A Study f Norway.*

European Commission Directorate-General for Economic and Financial affairs (2006), http://ec.europa.eu/ireland/key-eu-policy-areas/economy/irelands-economic-crisis/index_en.htm. Retrieved March 17, 2016.

Garba, Safiya. (2012). *The Impact of Colonialism on Nigerian Education and the Need for E-Learning Technique for Sustainable Development*, Journal of Education and Social Research 2 (7) 56.

Gaudium et Spes. (1965). *The Constitution of the Second Vatican Council on the Church in the Modern World.* General Conference and Council, Oslo, Norway.

Gaza, (1995). *Terror in the Heart of God* 241.

Ghouse, Mike. http://www.huffingtonpost.com/mike-ghouse/two-islams-the-mangledup-_b_5748280.html. Last visited, August 25, 2016.

Gullen. (1980). Ahlaki Mulahazar, Vols. 1-14

Hamid, Shadi. (2014). "The End of Pluralism," *The Atlantic*, July 23, 2014.

Hauss, Charles. (2003). Beyond Intractability, http://www.beyondintractibility.org/bi-essay/addressing-underlying-causes. Last visited, July 10, 2017.Inazu, John. (2016). *Confident Pluralism* 4 -5

Jurgensmeyer, Mark. (1995). Interview with Imad Faluji, journalist and member of the policy wing of Hamas.

Kukah, Matthew. (2015). *The Muslim Agenda for Nigeria: Challenges of Development and Good Governance*,' Keynote address.

Lamido, Sanusi. (2007). *Islam and Muslim Politics in Nigeria.*

Lamido Sanusi. (2007). *Islam and Religious Politics in Africa*, 184

Neblo, M. A., Minozzi, W et al. (2017). "The Need for a Translational Science of Democracy" available at http://science.sciencemag.org/. Last visited, May 2, 2017.

Ojukwu, Chukwuemeka Odimegwu. (1994). *Nigeria, the Truths that are Self-evident*, The Sunday Magazine 15, 18.

Omotayo. (2005). *Women and conflict in the new information age: Virtual libraries to the rescue.* 71st IFLA

Patrick Miller and Tom Dusk. (1994). *The Power of Ethical Persuasion: Winning Through Understanding at Work and at Home.*

Peace Building Initiative – History www.peacebuildinginitiative.org. Retrieved, September 25, 2020. Population Reference Bureau, 2006.

Qur'an 2:143.

Rapoport, A. (1992). *Peace: An Idea Whose Time has Come.*

Ricoeur, Paul. (1995). *Figuring out the Sacred; Religion, Narrative and Imagination* 1.

Song, Song. (2007). *Justice, Gender And The Politics Of Multiculturalism.*

Wallace, Mark. (1995). Introduction to *Figuring out the Sacred,*"

Yavuv & Esposito. (2003). *Turkish Islam and The Secular State* 118,

Zwier, Paul. 2015. *Advanced Negotiation and Mediation Theory And Practice* 296.

CHAPTER NINE

A Critical Analysis of Social Activism in George Ehusani's Writings

Abiodun Jombadi

1. Introduction

Discourse is one of the most important means of expressing opinions and ideologies. Religious sermons, for instance, are aimed at persuasion with the speaker's intention often to influence the audience to adopt, reinforce or modify certain beliefs (Akhimien & Farotimi, 2018). Groups, in today's world, are able to keep power not by force or economic control but through implicit use of persuasion in discourse that leads to consent. van Dijk (1996) observes that an understanding of opinion and what function it serves is essential because it is by way of opinion that the relation between ideology and discourse can be understood. He believes that an analysis of opinion must incorporate relating society, discourse and cognition. He further explains that opinions are located in our minds and are a type of belief. According to him, opinions are usually regarded as subjective evaluations by which someone thinks something to be true yet might be considered as false by someone else.

This suggests that speakers/writers can reveal their feelings towards specific issues, convey certain points of view, values and thoughts, make evaluative judgements or take positions when they interact with others through implicitly or explicitly expressed opinions. The expressions, referred to as stance, are either "in relation to propositions in an ongoing communication activity or in relation to other social actors directly or indirectly involved in the communication" (Ajiboye & Abioye, 2019, p. 118).

Religious discourse embodies useful insights into language. It portrays the ways religious personas utilise language resources to express their stance on social issues from a religious perspective with the intention to affect the lives of individuals and communities in general. For instance, the work of Chruszczewski (2006 cited in Alsohaibani, 2017) shows how the texts of prayers, such as benedictions recited at certain times, form a Jewish religious discourse. This discourse can distinctively unify diversified Jewish communities, thereby creating an integrated Jewish religious community. Significantly, religious discourse is effectual in influencing decisions and mobilising change judging from the crucial role the power of words plays in shaping realities in the minds of its hearers.

This study conceptualises George Ehusani's writings as (socio-)religious discourse since they appraise social issues from a religious perspective. As Alsohaibani (2017) posits, when studying the effect of religion on language, we cannot disregard the influence of religion on people's beliefs, values and attitudes towards their language, otherwise expressed as their language' ideology'. Therefore, within the appraisal mechanism and critical discourse analysis, the paper analyses selected writings of Ehusani as a representation of social activism laced with identifiable stance and ideology.

2. Existing Studies and Statement of the Problem

Religious discourse has been studied from diverse approaches. Non-linguistic studies have considered religious discourse in relation to education (Arman, 2020), sociology (Munson, 2012) and religious studies (Jemiriye, 2020). Linguistic studies have considered religious discourse from the perspectives of Conversational Analysis (Akhimien & Farotimi, 2018), Stylistics (Patricia, 1994; Ogunbode, 2008; Emike & Abdulraheem, 2015; Adjei, Ewusi-Mensah & Logogye, 2016), Discourse Analysis (Adegoju, 2002; Mooney, 2006; Szudrowicz-Garstka, 2012), Systemic Functional Theory (Adeniran, 2004), Politeness (Olanrewaju, 2004; Oloruntimilehin, 2012), Lexical Studies (Zuckerman, 2006; Esimaje, 2014), Sociolinguistics (Chruszczewski, 2006; Crystal, 2014) and Textlinguistics (Adam, 2008). None of these works ventures into assessing religious discourse as a resource for analysing social activism embedded in stance and ideology. The current work, which intends to bridge this gap in the analysis of religious discourse, therefore, analyses the evaluative language of selected George Ehusani writings and its potential for (re)shaping realities in the minds of Ehusani's readers and effecting social change in the polity. The study attempts to answer the following questions: (a) What are the underlying or covert issues that shape and are disseminated by the speaker's evaluative language? (b)

How are the authorial voices and textual personas constructed? (c) How does the writer adjust and negotiate the agreeability of his propositions and proposals? (d) What are the different assumptions which the writer makes about the values and belief systems of his respective intended audience?

3. Review of Relevant Literature

Religious discourse refers to "the existence of a specific use of language to express or describe religious experiences, practices, or beliefs..." (Esimaje, 2014, p. 2). It encompasses the language of sermons, prayers, songs and greetings within religious contexts. The discourse exhibits many features that make it interesting for linguistic exploration. According to Akpowowo (2002 cited in Akhimien & Farotimi, 2018), the language of religion has different purposes, ranging from communicating information to asserting religious truth. But one of the most compelling aspects of the genre lies in its power to arouse, evoke and influence emotions and attitudes.

Stiver (1996) discusses the prime focus of the role of language in religion in 20th-century philosophy and argues that there has been a detour from metaphysics to language, what he calls a linguistic turn. He explains that this concern for language is largely due to the conviction that the subject of religion is difficult to express and that the power of words plays a crucial role in creating its realities. Samarin (1976) examines religious discourse from a sociolinguistic perspective and observes that religious communities have distinct linguistic behaviour. He notes that an investigation into the nature of the uniqueness of their use of language is worth the effort. Crystal (1990) also examines liturgical language from a sociolinguistic perspective; and observes the shift in linguistics from the study of language structures to its functions. He notes that a convincing and coherent account of language cannot be provided without focusing on language functions or uses in different contexts.

The interest of discourse analysts in religious discourse analysis has been to investigate the art of linguistic spin in religious speeches to determine the association between linguistic form and function and language manipulation. Explaining the connection between style and purpose of language usage, Adjei, Ewusi-Mensah, and Logogye (2016) posit that in religious circles, speakers manipulate language for purposes such as convincing, persuading, entertaining, educating, informing, etc. They utilise various devices meant primarily to convince the audience to act as well as perform a plethora of functions. The norms and strategies that a speaker applies result from his/her own beliefs, intentions and goals, but at the same time are controlled by the social and cultural values respected by a particular community.

Adam (2008) contextualises religious discourse, following Halliday's systemic understanding of register, as an aspect of the context of situation. Thus, according to Adam, the church setting forms the field for the register of religious texts, the speaker and the audience represent the level of tenor, and the mode is usually spoken (formal, polite). With religious leaders' emerging interest in effecting social change by addressing socio-political issues, their language use changes to reflect such interests. Munson (2012) reinforces the most common way most people view the relationship between religion and social movements. His work crystallises how religion can act as a source of beliefs and justifications within a social movement. He avers that religion is implicated in social movement mobilisation in many more ways than a justification for an ideology. Besides, seemingly secular movements, with secular demands and arguments, are also deeply affected by religion. The movements for women's rights, the environment, peace and immigration reform intersect with religion in important ways, even when this intersection is much less familiar.

Munson (2012) also explains three major relationships between religion and social movement mobilisation. First, movements develop their goals and frame issues in ways that are influenced by religious language and religious beliefs. In most societies, religious vocabulary is widely shared, making it a powerful vehicle for expressing ideas in many movements. Second, religion is also important to many social movements because of its role in shaping people's identities. Religion provides a sense of who "we" are, drawing on the social connections, practices, and habits of thought that many people have developed through religious institutions since childhood. Religion can thus be a powerful source of collective identity and solidarity. Third, the relationship religion often holds with social movements is one of providing resources. Religious institutions like churches are venues for cultivating leadership skills, from the formal leadership of pastors to the informal leadership of congregants at Bible studies, church picnics, ministries, and so on. They are places where large numbers of people regularly gather, thus providing ready audiences for social movements and opening the possibility for efficient "bloc recruitment" of an entire congregation. Given this connection (between religion and social movement), the current study attempts to investigate the representation of social activism through stance construction in the discourse of selected Ehusani writings. To do this, van Dijk's socio-cognition and the appraisal framework are presented as a means of investigating textual identity through analysis of evaluative positioning. The analysis results using Appraisal can offer insights into the nature of the context of situation.

4. Methodology

Data for this study comprise five writings (one public presentation, three posts on Facebook and one open letter to former President Obasanjo). The data were sourced from Rev. Fr. George Ehusani's website and Facebook page, and the purposively sampled texts reflect his vehement reactions to various socio-political maladies ravaging Nigeria. The issues were considered from the religious point of view. The data are reminiscent of Latin America's 1950s and 1960s Liberation Theology, a movement that began within the Roman Catholic Church, combining Christian principles with political activism. The data are most often seen in their attempts to reduce or eliminate social injustice, electoral malpractices, discrimination, leadership recklessness, and ineffectual religiosity. The writer's discussion of theology from the perspective of social change and his interpretation of scriptures as a call to action against greed, corruption and bad leadership put him on the same pedestal as Francis of Assisi, Leo Tolstoy, Martin Luther King Jr., and Desmond Tutu. The provisions of Critical Discourse Analysis, henceforth CDA (with a bias for van Dijk's socio-cognitive approach) and the appraisal framework guide the data analysis. Both theories provide a systematic explanation for the subjective evaluative assessment of the writer's stance on various issues in relation to his pursuit of social change.

5. Theoretical Framework

The theoretical framework comprises Critical Discourse Analysis (CDA) and Appraisal theory. CDA stems from a critical theory of language that sees language as a form of social practice. All social practices are tied to specific historical contexts and are the means by which existing social relations are reproduced or contested and different interests are served. CDA systematically explores often opaque relationships between discursive practices, texts, events and broader social and cultural structures, relations, and processes. van Dijk's (2006) socio-cognitive approach to CDA provides a detailed theory of the actual (cognitive) processes involved in producing or understanding ideological discourse instantiated by group members. His summary of some of the underlying socio-cognitive processes underlying the production and comprehension of ideological discourse reveals the complex and often quite indirect nature of the relation between ideologies and discourse. Such discourse may depend on ideologically biased contexts, on the ideological way participants interpret events as subjective mental models, or, more directly, on general group beliefs that are ideologically controlled.

van Dijk (1996) observes that an understanding of opinion and the function it serves is important because it is by way of opinion that the relation between ideology and discourse can be understood. He believes that an analysis of opinion must incorporate relating society, discourse and cognition. He further explains that opinions are located in our minds and are a type of belief. Beliefs are held to be about what we know to be true or false and what we like or dislike. According to him, opinions are usually regarded as subjective evaluations by which someone thinks something to be true yet might be regarded as false by someone else.

Martin and White's (2005) Appraisal Framework complements CDA in this study to account for discourse resources that convey implicit evaluative meanings. The view of language adopted by the architects of the framework is that of the Systemic Functional Linguistic theory of Halliday and his associates (Halliday, 1994). The approach gives a deep insight into the language of evaluation, which displays a wide variety of meaning-making resources used by a speaker/writer to express personal, evaluative involvement in the text (White, 2015 cited in Ananko, 2017). According to White, the evaluative meanings give some of the mechanisms by which the interpersonal metafunction operates.

The Appraisal theory suggests that the attitudes of the speakers can be expressed with the help of three axes: affect, which conveys positive or negative feelings; judgement, which concerns the attitudes towards behaviour; and appreciation, which involves evaluation of semiotic and natural phenomena (Martin & White, 2005). In addition, other expressions of evaluative meanings are taken into consideration, such as engagement, namely the means of expressing various opinions and graduation, as a source of intensification of evaluation (Ananko, 2017).

6. Analysis and Discussion

As is expected of religious discourse, Ehusani's subjective assessment of the various discursive issues within the selected texts reflects an attempt to challenge various vices that have hitherto hampered the growth and development of Nigeria. The author's review of these imperfections serves two purposes: it eases his pent-up frustration and gives the potential readership something to work on. The broad spectrum of the texts covers four major themes: (a) leadership quagmire and the challenge of governance, (b) a warped electoral process and socio-political instability, (c) quest for social mobilisation and lack of patriotic responsibility, and (d) religious hypocrisy. These overarching themes are conveyed by authorial stances expressed through various engagement strategies by which the selected writings can be construed to reveal their inherent dialogic potentials.

6.1 *Leadership Quagmire and the Challenge of Governance*

An aspect of Ehusani's writings conveys the tragic reality of a lack of enviable leadership in Nigeria. Nwagboso and Duke (2012affirms that credible leadership is the most critical challenge confronting Nigeria since her independence from the British colonialists. Within the sampled data, the author, through his different stances, attempts to emotionally and cognitively construct the concepts of leadership and governance in Nigeria negatively. Such propositions are realised through strategies such as labelling, negative comparison, the use of strong adjectives and authority. Leadership and governance are described with cognitive labels that indicate negative appreciation and judgemental stances towards the phenomena. These labels convey a sense of detestation, disappointment and criticism towards the style of leadership in Nigeria.
Excerpt 1:

> A rogue government, an illegitimate government or a government with a stolen mandate can only hasten, rather than reverse our descent into anarchy, for as Proverbs 29:2 says: "when the righteous are in

authority, the people rejoice, but when the wicked rule, the people groan," and verse 18 says: where there is no vision – where there is no leadership integrity, the people perish (Ehusani, 2007).

The use of strong adjectives such as 'rogue', 'illegitimate', 'stolen' is a judgement of sanction, which challenges the process leading to the emergence of successive democratic regimes in the country. The assertion here is that leadership quality in a country cannot be separated from the process leading to its emergence. This implies that an abuse of the electoral process is construed as indices of failed governance. The incorporation of graduation within the assertion: "can only hasten" expresses force, a means to intensify the relationship between the cause of an action and its effect. This, together with the verb 'hasten' and the noun 'descent', presents an authorial stance that denigrates the capacity of a government to perform if it is a product of a flawed electoral process. To lace his point with a vivid spiritual affirmation, the author engages authority as a strategy: "for as Proverbs 29:2 says...". This strategy is adopted to semantically echo the effect of such bad leadership on the people. Poor leadership quality in Nigeria does not just affect the citizens directly; it also upsets the polity.

Excerpt 2:

> At this conference held in Locuum, one Heinrich Bergstresser, a German participant...observed that Nigerians are an extremely creative and constructive people, but that there is in the country what he called "a destructive undercurrent" that accounts for the fragile balance which has been the fate of the country since its independence from the British (Ehusani, 2007).

Again, the author, through the engagement resource of attribute, expresses positive judgement of esteem on the one hand and negative judgement of sanction on the other. The expression of positive judgement of esteem portends a good attribute for the Nigerian people, while the negative judgement of sanction criticises the Nigerian political landscape. Through such strategy as the use of intense adjectives and adverb ("extremely creative and constructive"), the author projects positive assessment of the Nigerian people by leveraging the strategy of evidentiality: "At this conference held in Locuum...". The authorial stance in this assessment reflects an observation made at the event. With this, the authorial stance serves a distancing function while simultaneously conveying a positive attitude and appreciation by the author towards the Nigerian people since the statement corroborates the author's own point. The positive judgement of esteem semantically constructs some delightsome qualities for the Nigerian people ("creative and constructive"). The assessment infuses the lexeme 'extremely' into the excerpt to intensify scalar meaning in the authorial stance expressed. However, this heteroglossic backdrop infers negative judgement of sanction, which shows that the Nigerian polity is unstable and weak ('fragile') despite the auspicious nature of the people. The reason for such imbalance is coated in vagueness ('a destructive undercurrent'). Though what the author refers to as 'undercurrent' remains elusive, the location of the proposition, given the context, is employed to underscore a scenario that threatens the survival of the nation – assessed to be 'destructive'.

As Excerpt 3 shows, the stench of this supposed decadence is pervasive enough to discourage well-meaning Nigerians in the diaspora from coming down to instigate any positive change.

Excerpt 3:

> Many knowledgeable and principled Nigerians – who in saner climes should assume the responsibility of leadership at all levels – can often not make sense out of the elite madness and corporate death-wish that we witness in our society today, and so they have become cynical, apathetic, despondent and resentful. Our society is today plagued by pathological greed for money and mindless lust for power (Ehusani, 2007).

In the sample above, the author utilises the strategy of negative comparison ('saner') to deepen the assertion of depravity attributed to the leadership in Nigeria. With a judgement of normality, the author posits that Nigerians in the diaspora who have been influenced positively by developmental strides in their domains and who should have offered to contribute positively to nation-building have been frustrated by the intensity of the miseries prevalent in the country as a result of the failure of leadership. The attitudes of these Nigerians towards their country are coated in the use of intense adjectives such as 'cynical', 'apathetic', 'despondent' and 'resentful'. These woes are further projected through the incorporation of graduation with the adjectives 'pathological' and 'mindless'. Both adjectives express force and are suggestive of absoluteness. This dialogistic positioning indicates the author's grouse with leadership breakdown and failure of governance in Nigeria. One vivid example of the author's dialogistic engagement with leadership is the open letter he wrote to former President Olusegun Obasanjo, who attempted to pursue a third term agenda in contravention of the two-term provision in the nation's constitution.

Excerpt 4:

> As a Christian I want you to recognise that even if through the ongoing Process in the Assembly the Constitution is amended to include a third term for the President, it is immoral, unethical, and I dare say gravely sinful, for you, Chief Olusegun Obasanjo as our current (two-term) President, to seek to benefit from this term extension, because there is an elementary principle of justice and an age old wisdom that you cannot change the rules of the game midway in the game and seek to benefit from the change (Ehusani, 2006).

By expressing a judgement of sanction, the author derides the move by former President Olusegun Obasanjo to prolong his stay in power beyond the two terms recognised by the constitution. The writer's authorial stance projects a negative other-representation of the former President. The proposition expressed in this declarative also appears to provoke his target to judge the wisdom in such unconstitutional ambition. The author's negative valuation (appreciation) of such move as 'immoral', 'unethical' is intensified by the use of intense adjective: 'gravely'. This form of valuation is further projected by engagement strategy of evidentiality: "...there is an elementary principle of justice and an age-old wisdom that you cannot change the rules of the game midway in the game and seek to benefit from the change where." Evidentiality as a strategy is deployed here to provide evidence in the discourse of authority figures, institutions and various forms of substantiations that are presentable by claims or points of view. The rhetorical effect of its use in this dialogic positioning will be to question the propriety of the move, as it portends a bad example of leadership qualities.

6.2 *A Warp in the Electoral Process and Socio-Political Instability*

Ehusani, using an engagement stance, construes Nigeria's electoral process and its participants negatively. While expressing negative judgements of capacity towards participants in the electoral process, he projects negative attitudinal meaning of appreciation towards the process itself. The rhetorical effect of this evaluation is that Nigeria's warped electoral process is the creation of its umpires and all stakeholders. The evaluation of the propriety of the electoral process and its participants is presented using the strategies of labelling, intense adjectives and intensification of scalar meanings.

Excerpt 5:

> The ethical and moral imperatives of credible elections is a very crucial topic that is calling for attention in our society today, as indeed many who are engaged in contemporary Nigerian politics do not seem to realise that there are ethical and moral dimensions to political conduct (Ehusani, 2007).

Excerpt 6:

> Many of our country men and women continue to approach politics with a killer's torch. Political party primaries at state and federal levels have often been an exercise in high level brigandage, in which the infrastructures of state are used to intimidate the opposition, and looted resources of state are distributed openly to buy the allegiance of congress delegates, and as could be expected, the results have often gone in favour of the highest bidder (Ehusani, 2007).

The author cognitively represents credible electoral process as a vital component of politics and governance in contemporary Nigeria. Usman (2020) maintains that fairly conducted elections "have the capacity to promote transparency and accountability in governance". Thus, in the above data, the intensification of the meaning of the adjective sequence in the noun phrase "a very crucial topic" foregrounds the weight of credible elections in a democracy. Therefore, the author, expressing a judgement of sanction, criticises political actors in Nigeria who constantly jettison due process in electioneering to promote personal interests. In an instance of a judgement of esteem, the author puts emphasis on normality in describing the severity of the approach of Nigeria's political actors to electioneering: "Many of our countrymen and women continue to approach politics with a killer's torch" (Excerpt 6, Line 1). The authorial stance expressed in this declaration is intended to provoke his audience to instigate necessary reforms to right the wrongs in the political process.

The author further socially represents political players as saboteurs of electoral sanity (using a judgement of esteem). Verbs and adjectives such as 'intimidate', 'buy' and 'looted' are used to express a negative appreciation of the process engineered by the actors. The adjective "high level" is a graduation strategy for stance meaning, as 'brigandage' is up-scaled with additional semantic function to intensify the process being described – that party politics in Nigeria is deformed. The rhetorical effect of this dialogic position is that a credible electoral process cannot be guaranteed where political players fail to preserve the sanctity of 'ethical' and 'moral' issues surrounding elections. Where due diligence is paid to a credible electoral process, however, social stability is guaranteed.

Excerpt 7:

> Free, fair and credible elections are an element of social morality, an ingredient of the rule of law and an imperative of good governance, stability, peace and progress (Ehusani, 2007).

Excerpt 8:

> Failure to execute the remaining stages of our electioneering processes with all civility and justice, and with utmost commitment to peace and the security of lives and property, will result in an increase in the level of anger in the land (Ehusani, 2007).

Within the sampled data above, the author infers the social benefit of a wholesome electoral process through the means of positive appreciation. This positive attributive meaning of appreciation serves as a cognitive means of driving the audience's interest in the pursuit of such a decent phenomenon. In addition to this is a judgement of normality that foregrounds the ruinous effect of an unwholesome electoral process on social stability.

6.3 Quest for Social Mobilization and Lack of Patriotic Responsibility

Through different stances, Ehusani makes attempts to conscientise his readers for possible national transformation. A component of such transformation agenda is the drive for citizens' peaceful co-existence referred to as social mobilisation. This is achievable through commitment to sound moral values.

Excerpt 9:

> See what people do in our society to get the first place: manoeuvering their way to the top, manipulating their way to the front row, wrangling their way to first position, stealing their way to the high table, and even shooting their way to the throne (Ehusani, 2019a).

Within the sampled data, the author, through a subjective assessment of the country's current social reality constructs the Nigerian populace's identities negatively socially, emotionally and cognitively. Such negative valuation is realised through strategies such as strong verbs. The Nigerian populace is described with cognitive referentials that indicate affective and judgemental stances towards them. These descriptions express deep feelings of condemnation and criticism, for instance, 'manoeuvering', 'manipulating', 'stealing', 'shooting'. The evaluation of the esteem of the Nigerian populace is presented using similes and imagery. With these rhetorical devices, the author attempts to inherently woo the cognitive response of readers, increase their affective involvement and heighten their dialogic investment. The ultimate effect is to showcase the endemic decadence being experienced in Nigerian society. Judging from the background of religious discourse, the author tries to propose possible solutions to these social maladies.

Excerpt 10:

The desired change will come about only when the various stakeholders in the Nigerian society, including religious leaders and faith communities, staunchly reject the ignominious status-quo that throws up for leadership positions men and women of base character and dubious wealth (Ehusani, 2007).

Excerpt 11:

> But if today the Nigerian people – including Christian and Muslim politicians experience the much needed conversion and toe the line of sanity and integrity, we may yet pull back from the brink of disaster (Ehusani, 2007).

The authorial stance in the samples above constructs the process that will guarantee the needed progress in the nation. It expresses a judgement of normality realised through strategies such as intensified verb ('staunchly reject'), the use of intense noun modifiers ('base', 'dubious') and intensified adjective ('much needed'). These strategies present a proposition that suggests a way to prevent the collapse of the Nigerian nation. The engagement resources deployed here are means by which the author engages in a dialogue to the extent that he presents himself as reacting to, challenging the status quo and anticipating likely responses from readers.

6.4 *Religious Hypocrisy*

Ehusani's writings are a deep reflection on the charade that characterises the two major religions in the country, especially Christianity. The author specifically bemoans the hypocrisy of the adherents of these faiths and the ineffectiveness of their confessions and beliefs. He traces the malaise in Christianity to the greed and the deceit coming from the leadership of the faith. The authorial stance emotionally and cognitively constructs religious practices and participants (leadership and followership) negatively. Such constructions are realised through the strategies such as the use of intense adjective, noun, verb, authority and intertextuality. Religious activities and leadership are described with cognitive labels that indicate negative affect, appreciation and judgemental stances. These labels express wanton greed and the sheer hypocrisy of religious adherents in Nigeria. Select samples reflect the author's outright frustration over this ugly development.

Excerpt 12:

> In recent times I started becoming discouraged and distressed about this embarrassing reality and asking myself serious questions bordering on the purpose and meaning of my own numerous activities in the face of this sobering reality (Ehusani, 2019b).

Excerpt 13:

> Some of our members perhaps do not appreciate fully the enormity of the problem we are dealing with in the mass movement that we call Christianity in today's Nigeria. And this is the key source of my pain and distress (Ehusani, 2019c).

While expressing negative affect towards the painful reality of an all-pervasive yet ineffective religiosity, the author intensifies scalar meanings in the authorial stance expressed by infusing intense adjectives ('embarrassing', 'serious') to construe a negative appreciation of the phenomenon being described. The location of the negative affect (personal feelings) within the dialogistic exchange is a means by which the author represents himself as challenging and responding to the current reality. The seriousness of this problem seems elusive to his readers, hence, the expression of judgement of sanction ("some of our members perhaps do not appreciate fully..."). Through the strategy of graduation, the author intensifies the scalar meaning in the authorial stance expressed, thereby hoping to make the readers appreciate the "enormity of the problem" that has bedevilled Christianity as practised in Nigeria.

Excerpt 14:

> Nigerians make a lot of noise in the name of religion, but their lives often betray a near-total lack of sense of the fear of God, the sense of right and wrong, the strong desire for and commitment to the virtuous life and hatred for sin, commitment to the common good, care and concern for the poor, discipline or self-control, self-sacrifice, chastity, modesty, frugality and the aversion for violence that are traditionally associated with truly religious people (Ehusani, 2019c).

Excerpt 15:

> Though we claim to be very religious, though our Churches are crowded and we host noisy worship sessions, though some of us can quote passages of the Scripture effortlessly from Genesis to Revelations, and though we host numerous night vigils and deliverance sessions, Nigerian Christians are not being transformed in any significant way, and consequently we are not equipped to transform our society for God (Ehusani, 2019b).

Again, to emphasise the ineffectiveness of Christianity in Nigeria as currently being practised, the author expresses negative judgement of esteem towards the Nigerian Christians to showcase the futility of their numerous church activities that lack any sense of piety. Through the use of intense adjective ('noisy worship sessions'), scalar meaning is intensified. This way, the author attempts to magnify the negative appreciation of the process, thus holding participants culpable of hypocritical identity.

Excerpt 16:

> Jesus says in Matthew 7:20 that "By their fruits, you shall know them." But Christianity as a mass movement in Nigeria is not working. Popular Christianity in Nigeria which features mega Churches and a huge gathering of thousands of people is not working. That religion characterised by the noise-making enterprise which we call prayer; the one that features regular deliverance services, multiple healing miracle crusades, so-called "powerful men of God," dashing celebrity preachers, swaggering motivational speakers, flamboyant Gucci pastors, designer suit evangelists, jerry coil prophets, private jet owning overseers, fashionable Church choirs and trendy Gospel singers, etc., – that religion is not working! (Ehusani, 2019b).

The evaluation of the propriety of the Nigerian church as a component of the entire society is further presented in the above sample using the strategy of authority and the use of intense adjective ('noise-making'). With these discursive strategies, the author construes all of the activities in the Nigerian church as outright shenanigans – lacking absolutely in moral rectitude: "it is not working". This negative attitudinal meaning of appreciation corroborates the intertextual reference presented in the attribute "Jesus says in Matthew 7:20..." The technique also expands the scope for dialogistic negotiation by introducing an additional voice to whom the writer assigns responsibility for the proposition. The rhetorical functionality of this authorially endorsed extra-vocalisation involves both dialogistic and heteroglossic positioning. Here, the author directly introduces a voice (an attribute common with religious discourse), and that voice is evaluated as highly authoritative and convincing. The essence of this attribution is to validate the proposition the author conveys, which he expects his audience (who themselves are victims of the rot) to hold about the phenomenon being addressed.

Excerpt 17:

> Powerful healers and miracle peddlers in our Churches are all cashing in on the desperation of the people to prosper in this world, by any means, foul or fair. This is the enterprise that we call Christianity in today's Nigeria. And it appears that very few people, even among the leaders, recognise that there is a problem here. This is the source of my pain and distress. (Ehusani, 2019c).

The positive self-representation of the author is foregrounded in the authorial stance expressed as a negative affect: "this is the source of my pain and distress". Here, with an engagement stance, the author distances himself from the rot in the religious cycle while indicating his emotional commitment to the realisation of social transformation in the country.

7. Conclusion

The paper maintains that religious discourse has the potential to address cogent issues affecting individuals and society. The study analyses Ehusani's selected writings as discourse that examines societal issues from the religious perspective. Through stance-taking resources, the author emotionally, cognitively and socially engages his intended audience while assessing various issues that hamper the growth and development of Nigeria. The analysis pinpoints four major ideological-based issues disseminated by the speaker's evaluative language, namely, leadership quagmire and the challenge of governance, warp electoral process and socio-political instability, quest for social mobilisation and a lack of patriotic responsibility and religious hypocrisy. These issues were addressed using cognitive labels that indicate negative affect, negative appreciation and negative judgemental stances.

By leveraging the strategy of evidentiality, the author projects a positive assessment of the Nigerian people. He expresses positive judgment of esteem to foreground such latent potentials in them, but which does not translate to positive national development on bad leadership. By expressing a judgement of sanction and negative judgements of esteem and capacity, the author criticises those individuals who steer the ships of religion, politics and leadership in Nigeria. He projects a negative other-representation of them. Where the author expresses a positive appreciation, it is to serve as a cognitive means of driving such desire in the intended audience that will instigate the pursuit of a better society.

The author is able to adjust and negotiate the agreeability of his propositions through negative valuation (appreciation) of various processes of leadership, governance, patriotic engagement and religious responsibility. His stances on these issues are realised through strategies such as labelling, negative comparison, the use of intense/strong adjectives, nouns, verbs and the techniques of authority and intertextuality. For instance, the author utilises the strategy of negative comparison to amplify the assertion of depravity that characterises leadership in Nigeria. The incorporation of graduation amplifies the author's commitment to the pursuit of social transformation. The use of attribute and extra-vocalisation expands the scope of dialogistic negotiation in order to validate those propositions that the author conveys. The rhetorical effect of the author's engagement has the potential to conscientise the intended audience and drive positive change in Nigeria.

References

Adjei, A., Ewusi-Mensah, L. & Logogye, C. (2016). Style in religious discourse: An analysis of the beatitudes. *International Journal of English Language and Linguistics Research*, 4(5), 35-46.

Ajiboye, E. & Abioye, T. (2019). When citizens talk: Stance and representation in online discourse on Biafra agitations. *Discourse & Society*, 30(2), 117-134.

Akhimien, P. & Farotimi, Y. (2018). A study of the conversational features and discourse strategies in select sermons of Pastor E. A. Adeboye. *American Journal of Linguistics*, 6(1), 1-8.

Alsohaibani, A. (2017). Influence of religion on language use: A sociopragmatic study on the influence of religion on speech acts performance. Retrieved 10 August 2020 from www.semanticscholar.org/paper/influence-of-religi on-on-language-use%3A-a-study-on-lsohaibani/fae 08d4b5407e9aee027e7db0618fc559a5bfae5

Ananko, T. (2017). The category of evaluation in political discourse. *Advanced Education*, 8, 128-137. Retrieved 2 June 2020 from https://doi:10.20535/2410-8286.108550.

Crystal, D. (1990). A liturgical language in a socio- linguistic perspective. In D. Jasper & R. C. D. Jasper (Eds.), *Language and the worship of the church* (pp. 120-146). Basingstoke, U.K.: Macmillan.

Ehusani, G. (2007). The ethical and moral imperative of free, credible and peaceful elections: role of religious leaders and faith communities. Retrieved 10 August 2020 from https://www.facebook.com/pages/George-Ehusani/ 1201923313 30679?sk=wall.

Ehusani, G. (2019a). Humility: The most characteristic Christian virtue. Retrieved 10 August 2020 from https://www.facebook.com/pages/George-Ehusani/ 120192331330679?sk=wall.

Ehusani, G. (2019b). Popular Christianity in Nigeria is not working. Retrieved10 August 2020 from https://www.facebook.com/pages/ George-Ehusani/ 120192331330679?sk=wall.

Ehusani, G. (2019c). Infantile religiosity. Retrieved 10 August 2020 from https://www.facebook.com/pages/George-Ehusani/ 1201 92331330679?sk=wall.

Ehusani, G. (2006). An open letter to President Obasanjo. Retrieved 10 August, 2020 from www.nigeriavillagesquare.com

Halliday, M.A.K. (1994). *Introduction to functional grammar*. London: Edward Arnold.

Martin, J. R. & White, P. (2005). *The language of evaluation: Appraisal in English*. New York: Palgrave Macmillan.

Munson, Z. (2012). Finding religion in movement activism. Retrieved 8 August 2020 from https://mobilizingideas.wordpress.com/2012/11 /01/finding-religion-in-movement-activism.

Nwagboso, C. & Duke, O. (2012). Nigeria and the challenges of leadership in the 21st century. *International Journal of Humanities and Social Science*, 2(13), 1-15.

Samarin, W. J. (1976). *Language in religious practice*. Rowley, MA: Newbury House Publishers.

Stiver, D. R. (1996). *The philosophy of religious language: Sign, symbol and story*. Oxford, U.K.: Blackwell.

Usman, M. (2020). The quest for credible elections in Nigeria: a critical evaluation of the 2015 general elections. Retrieved 8th June 2021 from researchgate.net/publication.

van Dijk, T.A. (1996). Opinions and ideologies in editorials. Retrieved 9 August 2020 from https://www.discourse-in- society.org/

editorial.htm.van Dijk, T.A. (2006). Ideology and discourse analysis. *Journal of Political Ideologies*, 11(2), 115-140.

CHAPTER TEN

Psychospiritual Healing as Panacea for the Societal and Psychological Distress in Nigeria

David O. Igbokwe

1. Introduction

Africa is under an enormous burden of societal distress triggered by conflict, insecurity, and poverty.

1.1 *Conflict*

Every part of Africa, from the Central African Region to the West African countries, has some form of armed conflict resulting from several driving factors, including ethnic supremacy and marginalization, as it is in Nigeria, ethnoreligious tension (Salawu, 2010), the so-called "spoils politics' (Bamidele 2020, p. 569), inequality and power play, as evident in South Sudan (Afriyie, Jisong, & Appiah, 2020; Brosché, 2019), as well as the scramble for natural resources, as in the Democratic Republic of Congo (Olaopa & Ojakorotu, 2016). The list is endless, as numerous non-state actors and pressure groups spring up almost on a daily basis. In Nigeria, for instance, the Boko Haram insurgency has claimed thousands of lives since it began in 2009. The fatalities have cascaded into neighboring countries, such as Cameroun, Niger, and Chad (Comolli, 2017; Omenma, 2020). According to Gebremichael *et al.* (2018), some of the causes of incessant conflicts in Nigeria include land ownership, distribution of resources, corruption, ethnic and religious tension, and small and light weapons proliferation. To address the problem of incessant conflict and insurgency in Nigeria, Ukpong-Umo (2016) suggested possible measures like providing quality employment opportunities; improving the worsening political instability; and resolving internal grievances, such as the agitations in the Niger Delta region.

However, violent conflicts have continued either because these measures have not been taken objectively or they have failed to produce the desired results.

1.2 *Insecurity*

The level of insecurity in Africa appears to be second to none. Kidnapping for ransom has become a regular occurrence, especially in Nigeria. Several roads in the country have been rendered impassable because of the activities of bandits. For instance, the Abuja to Kaduna road is almost synonymous with banditry, such that even very high-ranking military personnel, top government officials, and politicians opt for train rides instead of going by that road. If the ruling class cannot ply a road safely even with all their security details, what happens to ordinary citizens? The bandits and insurgents have extended their nefarious activities to the kidnapping of schoolboys and girls. On April 14, 2014, 276 female students aged between 16 to 18 years were kidnapped by Boko Haram from Government Girls Secondary School, Chibok, Borno State, and to date, over a hundred of the students are still missing. While Nigerians were still hoping that all the Chibok girls would be released, another 110 female students were kidnapped on February 19, 2018, from Government Girls Science and Technical College (GGSTC), Dapchi, Yobe State, Nigeria (BBC News, 2018). On December 11, 2020, more than 300 schoolboys were kidnapped in Kankara, Katsina State. In 2021, gunmen kidnapped 27 boys from Government Science College in Kagara, Niger State (BBC News, 2021). On April 20, 2021, armed bandits struck at a private University in Kaduna State, Greenfield University, and kidnapped 23 students and staff, and killed a total of five as of April 26, 2021. They demanded a ransom of N800 Million (HassanWuyo, 2021). The senseless killings in Nigeria, the banditry, and the general insecurity being experienced by citizens are sickening. One wonders how much thinking those in government are doing. The leaders seem clueless and helpless about what is happening in the country they are supposed to be leading.

1.3 *Poverty*

Poverty is now synonymous with Nigeria. With decades of 'hand-downs' from western countries by way of aids, there is nothing much in terms of development to show for the years of help from the advanced economies. In 2018, the World Bank reported that nearly half of Nigeria's population of about 200 million people lived below the international poverty threshold of $2 per day (World Bank, 2020). Interestingly, this report came before the 2020 recession in Nigeria triggered by Covid-19 and the oil price shock, as reported in the World Bank's 2021 *Macro poverty outlook* (MPO) for sub-Saharan Africa. Some authors have linked the Nigerian poverty situation to various reasons, including poor economic growth (Olowa, 2012). Others have, however, argued that poverty in Nigeria has persisted even during periods of economic progress in the nation (Danaan, 2018). In other words, the poverty situation cannot be entirely attributed to the inadequate growth of the economy. The principal challenge with poverty in Nigeria is that it seems intractable, and, according to Dapel (2018), most of the poor people in the country will likely continue to be poor without any hope of escaping poverty all through their lives. He estimates the average age of escaping poverty in Nigeria as 85.46 years. This revelation is very frightening. The scholar further explained that "... the mean age of the poor at their expected time of escaping poverty exceeds the average life expectancy, meaning that some of the poor are not guaranteed to escape poverty in their remaining lifetime" (Dapel, 2018, p.1).

Because the Nigerian poverty situation cuts across all the geopolitical zones in the country (Jaiyeola & Bayat, 2020), concerted efforts should be made to address the increasing rates of income inequality, unemployment, and inflation in Nigeria (Taiga & Ibrahim, 2020). Additionally, the social distress currently experienced in Nigeria and Africa cannot be discussed without highlighting the role of corruption in perpetuating poverty. Corruption and poverty go hand in hand, and scholars have observed that corruption has always affected the economic development of Nigeria negatively (Igiebor, 2019). With over four hundred billion dollars corruptly diverted to private pockets in Nigeria for the past sixty-one years (Ijewereme, 2015), monies that could have gone into infrastructural development and other social amenities, it does not seem that Nigeria's corruption issue is going away soon. While successive governments have continued with the culture of widespread corruption, elements of the judiciary, which ought to uphold the constitution and hold the politicians accountable, have also been adjudged corrupt.

According to Transparency International's most recent Corruption Perception Index (CPI), Nigeria is currently considered the second most corrupt country in West Africa (Uche, 2021). Considering that Nigeria, in 2003, was considered the second most corrupt country in the world by Transparency International, the country's recent West African position seems to indicate that the corruption is reducing. However, judging from the citizens' lived experiences and headline news emanating from Nigeria regarding the massive corruption in the country, it is doubtful that the current CPI adequately captures corruption in Nigeria. It is imperative to note that corruption is not peculiar to Nigeria. Most countries in the African region are considered extremely corrupt (Ajide & Olayiwola, 2021), in such a way that Africa fields most of the countries in the lowest rungs of Transparency International's CPI.

The public sector in Nigeria has been noted to be riddled with the following forms of corruption: Election malpractices, nepotism, favoritism, procurement scam, ghost workers phenomenon, budget padding, and so on. (Ijewereme, 2015). With such a long list of corrupt practices in Nigeria's public sector, David Cameron, the former British Prime Minister, might be right to have labelled Nigeria as a "fantastically corrupt" country (BBC News, 2016). According to Ijewereme (2015), corruption has persisted for too long in Nigeria because of "societal pressure, tribalism, nepotism, 'low risk – high benefits' of involvement in corruption among others" (p. 1). If the public sector laden with the task of regulating activities in the nation is itself riddled with corruption, one can only imagine what happens in the private sector where there is little to no scrutiny. Hence, to win the war against corruption in Nigeria, the citizens who are directly impacted by the corrupt leadership structures must take up their intellectual and moral arms. Nigerians and civil society organizations must rise and demand transparency and accountability from Nigerian leaders (Igiebor, 2019, p. 493).

Akin to the poverty of financial resources among Nigerians is the so-called poverty of the mind, which Ebigbo (2001) describes as not being satisfied with anything. The poverty of the mind has made many Nigerians adopt a defeatist mentality and outlook towards living in Nigeria, making them prefer other climes to their country. However, given the poor economic situation in the country, one may not blame Nigerians for desiring a better life. The recently proposed national minimum wage of 30,000 Naira is only a little over 60 dollars, based on the current (May 2021) exchange rate of 475 Naira per dollar. Thus, given the current economic realities in the country, this proposed take-home pay would hardly take anyone home from their job.

2. Psychological Distress in Nigeria

The increasing rates of conflict, insecurity, and poverty in Nigeria have put an immense amount of psychological stress on Nigerians. Prominent among the results of psychological distress experienced by Nigerians are depression, anxiety, and trauma. Often, these conditions lead to post-traumatic stress disorder (PTSD). According to the global burden of disease authored by Murray *et al.* (1996), "the burden of psychiatric conditions has been heavily underestimated" (p. 21). To a large extent, this underestimation is more obvious in Africa, where Monteiro (2015) considered mental health issues as "…. a silent epidemic throughout Africa due to substantial financial and systemic challenges" (p. 78).

2.1 *Depression*

Depression is pervasive and has been described as the "common cold of mental disorders" (Kandhakatla et al., 2018, p. 1). It has been estimated that one in three Nigerians is at the risk of developing depression (Adeyeye, 2018). Going by the official population estimate of Nigeria, this estimate suggests that about 60 million Nigerians are living with some form of depression. With such a huge part of the population possibly depressed, depression is ubiquitous in Nigeria to state the obvious. Owing to the pervasive and elusive nature of depression, it may be difficult to tell a depressed individual from others. However, to appropriately situate this disorder, the *Diagnostic and statistical manual of mental disorders* (DSM–5), published by the American Psychiatric Association (APA, 2013), defines it as "the presence of sad, empty, or irritable mood, accompanied by somatic and cognitive changes that significantly affect the individual's capacity to function" (p. 155).

What distinguishes a depressed person from others is often the cause, timing, and duration of the condition. Depression in one of its variants has been a prominent feature in the global burden of disease and has contributed significantly to years of life lost to disability (YLDs). Worldwide, non-communicable diseases, such as mental health disorders, including depression and anxiety, are expected to continue contributing to the global burden of disease and disability (Rehm &

Shield, 2019; Mathers, 2020). The report implies that given the increasing psychosocial pressures experienced by many people in modern society, depression and other mental health issues will continue to rise. According to the DSM-5, for someone to be termed depressed, there should be the presence of depressed mood most of the day or almost every day, reduced interest in doing things, weight loss, sleeplessness, low energy level, feelings of irrelevance, or worthlessness, or inappropriate guilt (manifested as low self-esteem), lack of concentration, thoughts of killing oneself, or dying as a result of feelings of hopelessness.

Most disorders in Africa, including somatic disorders, are depressogenic. Ihezue (1989) notes that

> In Nigeria, there is a stigma attached to mental illness and so there may be a tendency for patients to repress their mental symptoms replacing them with somatic ones (p. 220).

This somatisation of emotional distress could be a reason for the erroneous belief that Nigerians do not really get depressed. A better understanding of the situation may be gleaned from Ihezue's description:

> ... the depressive mood can be masked behind a multiplicity of somatic complaints" (p. 220).

In addition to masking depression behind somatic symptoms, the ability to effectively couch depressive symptomatology in words is a principal challenge. Thus, people often somatise emotional distress using culture-specific idioms of distress (Ebigbo, 1982, 1986, 1996; Igbokwe, 2011). According to Ihezue (1989), "Poverty of descriptive nomenclature in several African languages plays a part in making somatization a prominent feature of African depressive symptomatology, for in several of these languages there is no single word for 'depression'" (p. 218). Using the Igbo language as a case in point, depression is implied in phrases such as "*Obi ojo,*" which literally means 'bad mind', '*Iru uju*', which is the same as 'mourning' or 'grief,' and '*Enweghi obi anuri',* which means 'lacking in happiness' or 'unhappiness' (Ihezue, 1989, p. 218). Hence, physical complaints, which feature prominently among those used to mask a depressive profile, include those of ... generalised aches and pains in association with a general feeling of weakness, which the Igbo refer to as '*Osungwodongwo'*. This literally translates as "crushing into smithereens"; and it is an idiom used by the Igbo to explain the enormous mental pain, anguish, and distressing hopelessness, which are the lot of the severely depressed (Ihezue, 1989, p. 221). It is important to note that parallel descriptive phrases for depression exist in all African languages. African readers are therefore challenged to reflect on the word or phrases used to describe depression in their languages. Despite the similarity in the experience of mental health issues such as depression and anxiety, the differences observed in symptoms expression have led to the call for local adaptations of instruments or measures to effectively capture these disorders (Sweetland et al., 2014).

2.2 *Anxiety*

Anxiety is a psychological disorder that comes in different forms. As defined in the DSM-5, "anxiety disorders include disorders that share features of excessive fear and anxiety and related behavioral disturbances" (APA, 2013, p. 189). The most common form of anxiety is generalized anxiety disorder, which is "excessive anxiety and worry (apprehensive expectation) ... about a number of events or activities (such as work or school performance)" (APA, 2013, p. 222). Anxiety and depression tend to comorbid, and this comorbidity has been high in the general population. For instance, Adewuya *et al.* (2018) sampled 11,246 adults from Lagos, Nigeria, and found that, among the sampled participants, "about 20.9% of all cases of depressive symptoms have comorbidity with symptoms of generalised anxiety" (p. 60). The manifestation of this comorbidity between depression and anxiety has also been found to exist among medical students, with as much as 14.3% of a sample of 944 students from a public and a private university in Nigeria manifesting this comorbidity (Falade *et al.*, 2020).

2.3 *Trauma*

Most people in Nigeria have been traumatized either directly or indirectly. The daily experience of trauma really hits home for people living in Nigeria. For instance, it is a common occurrence to be stuck in traffic for hours and miss very important appointments or engagements because many road users take out their frustration on one another while disregarding simple traffic rules. The incessant noise pollution is another exposure that could create such a nuisance that most people have become used to it. In the context of the current discourse, the focus would be on trauma that affects the psyche of most people in Nigeria. This is the trauma of being exposed to situations that create powerlessness, hopelessness and helplessness, and infuse a sense of learned helplessness (Seligman & Maier, 1967; Seligman, 1975) in persons who have been exposed to such traumas which are beyond their control. Incidentally, just as people can learn to be helpless and depressed while experiencing traumatic events, people can also learn to be optimistic in most situations through learned optimism (Seligman, 1991).

According to the Substance Abuse and Mental Health Services Administration (SAMHSA, 2014), "individual trauma results from an event, series of events, or a set of circumstances experienced by an individual as physically or emotionally harmful or life-threatening and has lasting effects on the individual's functioning and mental, physical, social, emotional, or spiritual well-being" (p. 7). Likewise, the APA (2015) defined trauma as,

> … any disturbing experience that results in significant fear, helplessness, dissociation, confusion, or other disruptive feelings intense enough to have a long-lasting negative impact on a person's attitudes, behavior, and other aspects of functioning. Traumatic events include those caused by human behavior (e.g., rape, toxic accidents) as well as by nature (e.g., earthquakes) and often challenge an individual's view of the world as a just, safe, and predictable place… (p. 1104).

The overarching concurrence in all the definitions of trauma given is that it tends to significantly affect different areas of the life of any traumatised person. Scholars have identified several types of trauma that could have a negative impact on an individual's life and functioning. For instance, Gerber and Gerber (2019) describe interpersonal trauma and outline its various forms, including child abuse and neglect, child sexual abuse, intimate partner violence, sexual assault, community violence, human trafficking, historical trauma, and so forth. Researchers have categorised other distressing experiences as social trauma. According to Hamburger (2021),

> Social trauma is a clinical as well as a sociopsychological category: (1) as a clinical category, it defines a group of posttraumatic disorders caused by organized societal violence or genocide where a social group is the

target of planned persecution and therefore not only the individual but also its social environment is afflicted. Therefore, the concept of social trauma also describes (2) the shadowing of the original trauma on long-term social processes, be it on the family, group, or inter-group level (p. 3).

Intergenerational or transgenerational trauma refers to the transmission of trauma between generations. According to (Konig & Reimann, 2018), coming generations who may not have experienced the trauma directly may begin to share the "collective memory of victimhood, loss, and despair" (p. 20). There is also the concept of collective trauma, which Hirschberger (2018) succinctly defined as follows:

> The term *collective trauma* refers to the psychological reactions to a traumatic event that affects an entire society; it does not merely reflect a historical fact, the recollection of a terrible event that happened to a group of people. It suggests that the tragedy is represented in the collective memory of the group, and like all forms of memory, it comprises not only a reproduction of the events but also an ongoing reconstruction of the trauma in an attempt to make sense of it (p. 1).

Based on the above categories and definitions of trauma, and with the increasing poverty and psychological distress experienced by many people in Nigeria, it is beyond doubt that the prevailing conditions in the country expose the citizens to trauma. Indeed, the preponderance of road traffic deaths, armed robbery, terrorist insurgency, widespread banditry, kidnapping for ransom, intimate partner violence, non-partner sexual violence, violent communal clashes, many of which have been ongoing for years, do expose individuals and whole populations to trauma. This increased exposure to trauma in Nigeria seems further compounded by the limited access to mental health resources and the societal stigma associated with psychotherapy. Such lack of mental health resources, or the disdain for psychological treatment, may result in a huge population living with posttraumatic stress disorder (PTSD), given that exposure to violence, armed conflict, and mass-casualty events experienced in Nigeria are often recurrent and prolonged.

2.4 *Post-traumatic Stress Disorder*

PTSD is a psychological disorder that may occur in individuals who have experienced or witnessed a traumatic or life-threatening event. According to the DSM-5 (APA, 2013, p. 271), "Exposure to actual or threatened death, serious injury, or sexual violence" could lead to the manifestation of PTSD. In other words, PTSD refers to the negative aftermath effect of experiencing the traumatic event directly, seeing it happen to others, hearing that it happened to a close relative or friend, or being repeatedly exposed to details of traumatic events. After such exposure to trauma, the individual may experience psychosomatic symptoms, such as intrusive memories about the event, distressing dreams, flashbacks, intense or prolonged distress, and avoiding internal or external cues of the traumatic events. Other symptoms include changes in thinking and mood relating to the traumatic event, arousal and reaction due to the event, such as being irritable, reckless, lacking concentration, hypervigilance, and sleep disturbance (APA, 2013).

3. Ehusani's Practice of Psychospiritual Healing

The best way forward in salvaging Nigerians from the effects of social and psychological distress is through psychospiritual healing. Psychospiritual is a term used for the integration of psychological and spiritual principles and techniques. Thus, psychospiritual healing would involve the use of a combination of psychological tools and religious approaches to facilitate healing from mental illness. The psychospiritual approach to healing springs from the belief that an individual's spiritual beliefs and cultural practices constitute a critical factor in his or her emotional and psychological wellbeing, healing and development. Given that this approach to healing considers the more subtle spiritual and cultural aspects of the human person, the first task would be to consider the African culture and identify where Africans lost it as a people. The question is, what suddenly made Africans less human? When did they lose their acclaimed humanism and communalism, such that violent conflicts, widespread insecurity, widespread poverty, and high-level corruption seem to be synonymous with Africa? In his 1987 album, *Slave*, the legendary South African reggae musician, Lucky Philip Dube, sang a song with the lyrics, "*I am going back to my roots....*" It is time for Africans to go back to their roots and begin to draw wisdom from previously neglected sources. It is time to draw wisdom from African humanism to have a more humanized world (Ehusani, 2019), and psychospiritual healing can pave the way for this return to humanism.

Part of this journey towards psychospiritual healing of the Nigerian psyche battered by societal and psychological distress is to develop a mindset about the human person that is different from what currently prevails. In this regard, Ehusani's (2019) concept of '*Ozovehe*', which means "the human person is life," can be a ready tool for reorienting the Nigerian mind toward the desired change. While all Nigerians must be involved in these reorientation efforts, politicians and those in the leadership positions must be at the forefront of working for the desired change by ensuring that all political and leadership activities are conducted with deep-seated concern for the human person. With such reorientation and the eventual appreciation of the human person, Nigeria may begin to experience a significant reduction in cases of insecurity, conflict, poverty, and corruption, and with time, these evils may be eradicated.

Being very passionate about helping people deal with trauma and as part of his efforts to enhance positive social change, Ehusani provides the platform for addressing the negative impacts of traumatic experiences through psychospiritual healing. His brainchild, the Basic Course in Psycho-trauma Healing, which is a week-long course offered by the Psychospiritual Institute of Lux Terra Leadership Foundation, is a course that every leader should undertake as part of their induction to understand the reality of trauma and how traumatic events could trigger certain behavioural patterns in them and those they lead. This course has the potential to dissuade leaders from using unsuspecting citizens, especially miscreants, to foment trouble and perpetuate conflict, insecurity, poverty, and corruption. Interestingly, since the course started in 2016, hundreds of laypersons and professionals, including academics, doctors, psychologists, social workers, religious leaders, functionaries of emergency services, non-governmental organisations and volunteers who work with trauma victims and suicide prevention groups have been trained. Interaction with some of these participants reveal that many of them benefitted immensely, both personally and professionally, from participating in the programme. Given the importance of the trauma healing training program and the positive feedback it has generated from the trainees, extending the scope to capture national and political leaders could be a way to help break the cycle of social and psychological distress in Nigeria.

4. A Psychospiritual Healing Tool: Harmony Restoration Theory and Therapy

Professor Peter Onyekwere Ebigbo propounded the Harmony Restoration Theory (HRT) and developed the Harmony Restoration Therapy (Ebigbo, 1989, 1994, 1995a, 1995b, 2001). The HRT can be an effective tool in psychospiritual healing. Drawing insights from oral literature, such as folklore imbued with insightful proverbs, the theory focuses majorly on the African cosmocentrism, which determines the state of health or ill-health of the African. A principal tenet of the theory and its therapy is drawn from an Igbo proverb that says, *"Onye ya na uwa ya di na nma anaghi aria ahu"* (i.e., The person who is at peace with their world does not fall sick). Parallels of thoughts and proverbs along this line can be found in other Nigerian and African folklore and even names. Ebigbo (2001) notes that:

> According to the native African and, of course, Nigerian, a person is healthy if he/she is at peace with his/her world. Health here implies a state of harmony with his/her world or cosmos ... the sum total of the animate and inanimate beings with whom he/she entertains relationship (p. 20).

Igbokwe and Ndom (2008), in concurrence with comparable thoughts relating to harmony restoration existing in other cultures, notes:

> In Africa, the individual is inextricably tied to society, and everything is done in unison. Proverbs like *"Igwe bu ike,"* and *"onye aghala nwanne ya"* (i.e., unity is strength, and let no one forsake his sibling) are two Igbo proverbs that illustrate this. The equivalents of such proverbs exist in other cultures. For instance, the Xhosas of South Africa have a proverb which says: *"umuntu ngumuntu ngabantu"* (i.e., a person is a person through persons). (pp.69-70)

Understanding and consciously exhibiting the Igbo proverb, "The person who is at peace with their world does not fall sick," '*Ozovehe*' (i.e., the human person is life, Ehusani, 2019, p. 3), and the Xhosa proverb, "a person is a person through persons," would be important in the quest towards making Nigeria a better place for all citizens to thrive and become better versions of themselves. As John Mbiti, the Kenyan-born Christian Philosopher and Anglican priest once noted, "the individual is conscious of himself in terms of "I am because we are, and because we are, therefore I am" (Mbiti, 1970, p. 279). There is a strong possibility that this social collectivism, as seen in proverbs, folklore, religions, and myths will, once again, be one of the tripods upon which the success of Nigeria will stand instead of the retrogressive tripod of insecurity, conflict, and poverty. The collectivistic ideology of the African depicts the need for personal and societal harmony. Whenever societal harmony is disrupted, disharmony sets in, and "... disharmony is the major source of conflict, in the home, office, everywhere" (Igbokwe & Ndom, 2008, p. 72). Ebigbo (2001) brings to the fore the fact that the structure of the African personality has three dimensions or components, namely: The endocosmos, the mesocosmos and the exocosmos. Cosmos represents a sum total of the individual's world which, according to the HR Theory, is tripartite in nature (Igbokwe *et al.*, 2015). Given the interconnectedness of religion and culture for the African, psychospiritual healing will involve maintaining harmony in all the three components which make up the African personality or cosmos. Ebigbo (2017) describes the HRT as "a psychotherapeutic framework or rubric that takes into consideration the evolving world of the African" (p.20). A brief description of the three components of the cosmos or the African personality now follows. Ebigbo (2017, p. 22) describes the endocosmos as

> the aspect of this world that relates to the person, one's mind [and] one's body. The *endocosmos* has to do with someone's personality, the person's disposition and therefore the person's preparedness to relate with others outside of oneself.

Also, according to the author, the mesocosmos refers to,

> the world of relationship of the individual, that is, the individual and one's immediate and extended families, mother, father, brothers, sisters, grandparents, cousins, uncles, aunts, etc. The relationships that are important to the individual outside the family also belong to the *mesocosmos*" (Ebigbo, 2017, p. 22).

"The exocosmos represents a very important world of relationship to the ancestors, to spirits, deities, gods, and indeed, all forces outside of one but which are outside the concrete world of relationships. The *African* believes strongly in spirits and is very religious." (Ebigbo, 2017, p. 22).

As soon as there is a disruption in any of the components of the individual's cosmos, there is disharmony, and "the overall effect of disharmony is either psychological or physiological ill-health" (Igbokwe *et al.*, 2015, p. 34). Once disharmony is detected, such as seen in the societal and psychological distress being experienced by Africans, the therapist draws up or plots a cosmogram (i.e., a pictorial representation of the endocosmic, mesocosmic and exocosmic relationships of the client) to detect the particular source of the disharmony, and psychotherapy in the form of harmony restoration therapy (HRT) is used to mend the relationship (Ebigbo, 2017). There have been successful efforts toward developing a measuring scale to assist the therapist in drawing up the area or source of any disharmony a client might be going through. Such efforts include the development and initial factorial validation of the Harmony-Disharmony Scale (HD Scale) by Igbokwe *et al* (2015). The HD-Scale is a 59-item screening tool with four response Likert format. The scale has 3 subscales or factors, namely: the endocosmos, mesocosmos and exocosmos. A 15-item short form of the HD-Scale is currently being finalized to serve as a rapid tool for discovering discordant relationships within an individual's cosmos. It is important to note that after administering the scale and drawing the cosmogram, further information is then obtained through in-depth interviews. Another measurement scale exists for use in HRT. The scale which is referred to as the Harmony Restoration Measurement Scale (HRMS), is also a validated instrument (Ebigbo, 2017; See also Ebigbo, Elekwachi, Eze, Nweze & Innocent, 2010).

5. Conclusion

From the quest of the sages of Africa's independence to the desires and pursuits of the newer generations, such as the millennials (Generation Y), Generation Z, and Generation Alpha (McCrindle, 2019), the Africa we envisage is a place of peace, harmony, tranquility and impressive development - a humanized Africa with every perk that makes for the good life. However, this Africa has constantly eluded both sages and newborns to date. Despite the enormous thoughts being invested into making the African continent a better place and the incalculable amount of funds that have been invested, the continent seems to be doing more rhetoric with little matching action. However, the desired change can begin with the healing of the African peoples from a psychospiritual perspective.

Specifically, the social and psychological distress experienced for decades by many Nigerians can best be addressed by a psychospiritual healing that integrates and uses harmony restoration as a tool to ensure complete harmony and wholesomeness in the individual citizens. While professionals, the clergy, humanitarian organisations and well-meaning individuals may follow the example of Father Ehusani and the Psychospiritual Institute of the Lux Terra Leadership Foundation to encourage the psychospiritual healing of depressed and traumatized Nigerians, the government must also assist in this regard by ensuring the psychological and general well-being of all Nigerians, towards meeting Goal Three of the United Nations (2015) sustainable development goals, namely, good health and well-being. If hay is not made while the sun shines and psychospiritual healing is ignored, the coming generation may meet Nigeria in its current unimpressive state.

References

Adewuya, A. O., Atilola, O., Ola, B. A., Coker, O. A. Zachariah. M. P., Olugbile O, Fasawe, A. & Idris, O. (2018). Current prevalence, comorbidity and associated factors for symptoms of depression and generalised anxiety in the Lagos State Mental Health Survey (LSMHS), Nigeria. *Comprehensive Psychiatry*, 81, 60-65. Doi: 10.1016/j.comppsych.2017.11.010.

Adeyeye, S. (2018, October 12). 60 million Nigerians are at risk of depression – NOIPolls/Joy, Inc. National Report reveals. Retrieved April 14, 2021, from https://www.pulse.ng/news/metro/60-million-nigerians-are-at-risk-of-depression-noipollsjoy-inc-national-report/tz4c1dj

Afriyie, F. A., Jisong, J., & Appiah, K. Y. (2020). Comprehensive analysis of South Sudan conflict: Determinants and repercussions. *Journal of Liberty and International Affairs*, 6 (1), 33-47.

Ajide, F. M. & Olayiwola, J. A. (2021). Remittances and corruption in Nigeria. *Journal of Economics and Development*, 23 (1), 19-33. Retrieved April 14, 2021, from https://doi.org/10.1108/JED-04-2020-0046

American Psychiatric Association. (2013). *Diagnostic and statistical manual of mental disorders (5th ed.)*. Washington, D C: Author.

American Psychological Association. (2015). *APA dictionary of psychology*. Washington, DC: Author.

Bamidele, S. (2020). Ethnic conflict and the politics of spoils in Nigeria. *Social Change, 50*(4), 569-583. Retrieved April 14, 2021, from https://doi.org/10.1177/0049085720964280

BBC News. (2021 February 17). Nigeria gunmen raid Kagara school and abduct boys. Retrieved April 14, 2021, from https://www.bbc.com/news/world-africa-56095731

BBC News (2018, February 26). Nigeria Dapchi school kidnappings: What we know. Retrieved April 14, 2021, from https://www.bbc.com/news/world-africa-43197694

BBC News (2016, May 10). David Cameron calls Nigeria and Afghanistan 'fantastically corrupt.' Retrieved April 14, 2021, from https://www.bbc.com/news/uk-politics-36260193

Brosché J. (2019) Ethno-communal conflict in Sudan and South Sudan. In S, Ratuva (Ed.), *The Palgrave handbook of ethnicity*. Palgrave Macmillan, Singapore. Retrieved April 14, 2021, from https://doi.org/10.1007/978-981-13-2898-5_49

Comolli, V. (2017). The evolution and impact of Boko Haram in the Lake Chad Basin. Retrieved April 14, 2021, from https://odihpn.org/magazine/the-evolution-and-impact-of-boko-haram-in-the-lake-chad-basin/

Danaan, V. V. (2018). Analysing poverty in Nigeria through theoretical lenses. *Journal of Sustainable Development, 11*(1), 20-31. DOI: 10.5539/jsd.v11n1p20

Dapel, Z. (2018). Will the poor in Nigeria escape poverty in their lifetime? Center for Global Development Working Paper No. 483. Retrieved April 14, 2021, from https://ssrn.com/abstract=3208860 or http://dx.doi.org/10.2139/ssrn.3208860

Ebigbo, P. O. (1982). The development of a culture-specific (Nigeria) screening scale of somatic complaints indicating psychiatric disturbance. *Culture, Medicine & Psychiatry, 6*, 29-43.

Ebigbo, P. O. (1986). A cross sectional study of Nigerian females using the Enugu Somatization Scale. *Culture, Medicine & Psychiatry, 10*, 167-185.

Ebigbo, P. O. (1989). The mind, the body and society: An African perspective. In K. Pertzer & P. O. Ebigbo (Eds.), *Clinical psychology in Africa* (pp. 233-250). Enugu: Chuka Printing Company Ltd.

Ebigbo, P. O. (1994). Psychotherapy in Africa: Quo Vadis? An invited paper delivered at the 16th international congress of psychotherapy held in Seoul, Korea, August 21-25, 1994.

Ebigbo, P. O. (1995a). Emergence of psychotherapy in Africa presidential address at the 1st IFP Conference in Nigeria at the NIIA, Victoria Island, Lagos, 6th-9th November, 1995.

Ebigbo, P. O. (1995b). Harmony Restoration Therapy: An African contribution to psychotherapy. A Paper presented at the Annual Meeting of the Royal College of Psychiatrists held in Torquay, England, 4th -7th July, 1995.

Ebigbo, P. O. (1996). Somatic complaints of Nigerians. *Journal of Psychology in Africa* (South of the Sahara, the Caribbean & Afro- Latin America), 1 (6), 28 -49.

Ebigbo, P. O. (2001). In search of the Nigerian psyche: A contribution to nation building. Nigerian National Merit Award Winners Lecture, September 26, 2001.

Ebigbo, P. O., Elekwachi, C. L., Eze, J. C., Nweze, F. C. & Innocent, C. U. (2010). Development of Harmony Restoration Measurement Scale. *Nigerian Journal of Clinical Psychology*, 8, 25–49.

Ebigbo, P.O. (2017). Harmony restoration therapy: Theory and practice. *International Journal for Psychotherapy in Africa*, 2(1), 20-35.

Ehusani, G. O. (2019). *An Afro-Christian vision, Ozovehe: Towards a more humanized world* (25th Anniversary ed.), Abuja: Lux Terra Leadership Foundation.

Falade, J., Oyebanji, H. A., Babatola, A. O., Falade, O. O. & Ojo, T. O. (2020). Prevalence and correlates of psychiatric morbidity, comorbid anxiety and depression among medical students in public and private tertiary institutions in a Nigerian state: A cross-sectional analytical study. *Pan African Medical Journal*, 37 (53), 1-15. Doi: 10.11604/pamj.2020.37.53.24994

Gebremichael, M., Kifle, A. A., Kidane, A., Wendyam, H., Fitiwi, M. & Shariff, Z. S. (2018). Nigeria conflict insight. Addis Ababa: Institute for Peace and Security Studies, Ababa University. Retrieved April 14, 2021, from: https://www.africaportal.org/publications/nigeria-conflict-insight/

Gerber, M. R. & Gerber, E. B. (2019). An introduction to trauma and health. In M. R. Gerber (Ed.), *Trauma-Informed healthcare approaches: A guide for primary care.* pp. 3-23. Springer Nature, Switzerland AG. Retrieved April 14, 2021, from https://doi.org/10.1007/978-3-030-04342-1_1

Hamburger, A. (2021). Social trauma: A bridging concept. In A. Hamburger, C. Hancheva & V. D. Volkan (Eds.), *Social trauma: An interdisciplinary handbook.* Springer International Publishing Switzerland. Retrieved April 14, 2021, from https://doi.org/10.1007/978-3-030-47817-9_1

HassanWuyo, I. (2021, April 26). Breaking: Two more Greenfield University students killed in Kaduna. *Vanguard Newspaper.* Retrieved April 14, 2021, from https://www.vanguardngr.com/2021/04/breaking-two-more-greenfield-university-students-killed-in-kaduna/

Hirschberger G. (2018). Collective trauma and the social construction of meaning. *Frontiers in psychology,* 9, 1441. Retrieved April 14, 2021, from https://doi.org/10.3389/fpsyg.2018.01441

Igbokwe, D. O. & Ndom, R. J. E. (2008). Harmony Restoration Therapy: A treatment method of African origin. *Nigerian Journal of Clinical Psychology, 6* (1 & 2), 61-77.

Igbokwe, D. O. (2011). Confirmatory factor analysis on the Enugu Somatization Scale. *Ife Psychologia.* 19 (1), 195-225.

Igbokwe, D. O., Adeusi, S. O., Elegbeleye, A. & Agoha. B. C. E. (2015). Harmony-Disharmony Scale: Development and initial factorial validation. *Covenant International Journal of Psychology,* 1 (1), 33-49.

Igiebor, G. O. (2019). Political corruption in Nigeria: Implications for economic development in the Fourth Republic. *Journal of Developing Societies,* 35 (4), 493-513. Doi:10.1177/0169796X19890745

Ihezue, U. H. (1989). The influence of sociocultural factors on symptoms of depressive illness. In K. Pertzer & P. O. Ebigbo (Eds.), *Clinical Psychology in Africa* (pp. 217-223). Enugu: Chuka Printing Company Ltd.

Ijewereme, O. B. (2015). Anatomy of corruption in the Nigerian public sector: Theoretical perspectives and some empirical explanations. *SAGE Open,* 1-16. Retrieved April 14, 2021, https://doi.org/10.1177/2158244015581188

Jaiyeola, A. O. & Bayat, A. (2020). Assessment of trends in income poverty in Nigeria from 2010–2013: An analysis based on the Nigeria

General Household Survey. *Journal of Poverty*, 24 (3), 185-202. DOI: 10.1080/10875549.2019.1668900

Kandhakatla, R., Yarra, R., Pallepati, A & Patra, S. (2018). Depression: A common cold of mental disorders. *Alzheimers Dement Cognitive Neurology*, 2(2), 1-3. Doi: 10.15761/ADCN.1000124

Konig, U. & Reimann, C. (2018). Closing a gap in conflict transformation: Understanding collective and transgenerational trauma. Retrieved April 14, 2021, from https://www.ximpulse.ch › 1806CollectiveTrauma

Mathers, C. D. (2020). History of global burden of disease assessment at the World Health Organization. *Archives of Public Health*, 78, 77. Retrieved April 14, 2021, from https://doi.org/10.1186/s13690-020-00458-3

Mbiti, J. (1970). *African traditional religion and philosophy*. London: Longman.

McCrindle, M. (2019). Generation Alpha: Mark McCrindle Q & A with the New York Times. Retrieved April 14, 2021, from https://mccrindle.com.au/insights/blog/generation-alpha-mark-mccrindle-q-new-york-times/

Monteiro, N. M. (2015). Addressing mental illness in Africa: Global health challenges and local opportunities. *Community Psychology in Global Perspective*, 1 (2), 78-95.

Murray, C. J. L., Lopez, A. D., World Health Organization, World Bank, & Harvard School of Public Health (1996). *The global burden of disease: A comprehensive assessment of mortality and disability from diseases, injuries, and risk factors in 1990 and projected to 2020*. World Health Organization, Harvard School of Public Health, World Bank. Retrieved April 14, 2021, from https://apps.who.int/iris/handle/10665/41864

Olaopa, O. R. & Ojakorotu, V. (2016) Conflict about natural resources and the prospect of development in the Democratic Republic of Congo. *Journal of Social Sciences*, 49 (3-1), 244-256. Doi: 10.1080/09718923.2016.11893618.

Olowa, O. (2012). Concept, measurement and causes of poverty: Nigeria in perspective. *American Journal of Economics*, 2 (1), 25-36. 10.5923/j.economics.20120201.04.

Omenma, J. (2020). Untold story of Boko Haram insurgency: The Lake Chad oil and gas connection. *Politics and Religion*, 13 (1), 180-213. Doi:10.1017/S1755048319000166.

Rehm, J. & Shield, K. D. (2019). Global burden of disease and the impact of mental and addictive disorders. *Current Psychiatry Reports*, 21 (2), 10. Doi: 10.1007/s11920-019-0997-0.

Salawu, B. (2010). Ethno-religious Conflicts in Nigeria: Causal analysis and proposals for new management strategies. *European Journal of Social Sciences*, 13 (3), 345-353.

Seligman, M. E. P. & Maier, S. F. (1967). Failure to escape traumatic shock. *Journal of Experimental Psychology*, 74, 1-9. Retrieved April 14, 2021, from http://dx.doi.org/10.1037/h0024514.

Seligman, M. E. P. (1975). *Helplessness: On depression, development and death*. San Francisco, CA: Freeman.

Seligman, M. E. P. (1991). *Learned optimism: How to change your mind and your life*. New York, NY: Pocket Books.

Substance Abuse and Mental Health Services Administration (SAMHSA, 2014). *SAMHSA's concept of trauma and guidance for a trauma-informed approach*. HHS Publication No. (SMA) 14-4884. Rockville, MD: Substance Abuse and Mental Health Services Administration.

Sweetland, A. C., Belkin, G. & Verdeli, H. (2014). Measuring depression and anxiety in sub-saharan Africa. *Depression and Anxiety*, 31 (3), 223-232. Retrieved April 14, 2021, from http://dx.doi.org/10.1002/da.22142

Taiga, U. U. & Ibrahim, V. H. (2020). Income inequality and poverty in Nigeria: An empirical analysis. *IOSR Journal of Economics and Finance*, 11 (3), 7-14.

Uche, J. (2021). Nigeria, now 2nd most corrupt country in West Africa – Transparency International. Retrieved April 14, 2021, from https://nairametrics.com/2021/01/28/nigeria-now-2nd-most-corrupt-country-in-west-africa-transparency-international/

Ukpong-Umo, R. E. (2016). Insurgency in Nigeria and the challenge of nationhood. *Nigerian Journal of Rural Sociology*, 16 (3), 64-69.

United Nations. (2015). Transforming our world: The 2030 Agenda for Sustainable Development. Retrieved April 14, 2021, from https://www.un.org/sustainabledevelopment/sustainable-development-goals/

World Bank (2020). Macro-poverty outlook for Sub-Saharan Africa: Country-by-country analysis and projections for the developing world. Retrieved April 14, 2021, from https://www.worldbank.org/en/publication/macro-poverty-outlook/mpo_ssa.

CHAPTER ELEVEN

A Digital Priest in a Digital Society: Exploring the Persona of Rev. Fr. George Ehusani

Justine John Dyikuk

Every society has its excitements and challenges. Since the Catholic priest is a product of his society, he has to navigate both faith and culture. The modern culture, with its trappings of advances in Information and Communications Technology (ICT) and irresistible smartphones' Internet-based communication, has made ministry challenging. It is within this popular culture that the priest is called to ministry. This makes steering between media and ministry more challenging. It is within this atmosphere that Rev. Fr. George Ehusani, the convener of *Lux Terra* Foundation, Abuja, has held the fort as a priest for four decades. To investigate his adventures in combining his vocation as a priest with his engagement with the print and electronic media, this chapter, "A Digital Priest in a Digital Society: Exploring the Persona of Father Ehusani," x-rays extant literature about Ehusani's activities and finds his commitment to celebrating the Word and the Sacraments, being media savvy, and willingness to be relevant digitally as factors that keep him afloat in our digital society. It recommends mentoring the young in media and ministry, creating a robust media outfit for *Lux Terra*, and further documentation of useful resources as helpful tips for remaining relevant to contemporary times. The chapter concludes by describing Fr. Ehusani as a colossus and an e-priest who has paid his dues to Church and society in Nigeria and beyond.

1. Introduction

Before now, the general conception about Catholic priests was that they were protected from any secular engagements. Therefore, they were only to be seen praying. Many people believed that priests were not to leave their constituencies as ministers of the Word and the sacraments. It meant that the society expected priests to only celebrate the Holy Mass and administer the other sacraments. Any priest who attempted to befriend the media was courting trouble as he could be described as the son of a king who decided to dance naked in the market square. Conservatives were often not comfortable with priests who thought outside the box. It is crucial to note that although there are various documents of the Church on the use of means of communication, the Pre-Vatican II Church was slow in relating with the secular media. As such, clerics blatantly familiarising themselves with the secular media and making headlines were looked upon with some suspicion. As time went on, this view was further heightened by the alleged sex scandals of some priests in America and Europe, which rocked the Church (Donadio, 2019).

However, with successive church documents addressing social communications, such as *Inter Mirifica* (1963), Communio *et Progressio* (1971) (Mirus, 2010), and World Communication Day Messages of various Pontiffs, perspectives began to change. The emergence of the modern means of communication began to create a desire for the Church to use them to organise mass movements among the faithful (Arx, 2015). The emergence of the Pontifical Council for Social Communications as an image-maker of the Vatican and the Universal Church helped improve priests' involvement with the secular media. Progressives have argued that it is high time the "hood" was removed from the "Priest." In other words, given the dynamic nature of society plus its advances in digital technology, Bishops and superiors should permit and encourage priests to use traditional and social media to purge the secular society of its ills.

It is against this backdrop that Fr. George Omaku Ehusani broke with an erstwhile resistance to the use of media, thus becoming a seasoned communicator and friend of the media in Nigeria. In a conservative society that does not celebrate being in the news, Fr. Ehusani broke with the past to become a communicator par excellence. This chapter explores his persona in terms of early beginnings, service to God and humanity as an e-priest in an e-world, navigating media and ministry, *Lux Terra* style of strategic communication, and recommendations towards better years for this dogged pastor who has held the fort for four decades as a priest of God.

2. The Persona of Father Ehusani: Exploring Family, Education, and Vocation

Fr. George Ehusani was born on December 6, 1957, in the present-day Kogi State. After his primary education at a Catholic school in Okene (1964-70), he began discerning The Call to become a priest. His entry into Ministry was also influenced by his wise grandmother, who taught him to love God. She had an African Traditional Religious background but was converted to Christianity and became part of the first generation of Christians in Karaworo, Kogi State (Ojeifo, 2016; Osso, 2017).

During his secondary school days at Abdul Aziz Atta Memorial College (1971-75), Ehusani distinguished himself as a brilliant and spiritually upright young man. He became the president of Young Catholic Students (YCS) in the Diocese of Lokoja at the age of 16 years. During the Christmas vigil of 1974, the young George had a transforming spiritual experience which led him to accept the call to the priesthood. Between 1975 and 1978, he had his philosophical studies at the Saints Peter and Paul Major Seminary, Ibadan, and thereafter proceeded to Saint Augustine's Major Seminary, Jos, for his theological studies. After graduating in May 1981, he was ordained a Catholic priest for Lokoja Diocese on August 15, 1981 (Ojeifo, 2016; Osso, 2017).

Ehusani bagged a doctorate degree in Ministry from the Howard University School of Divinity Washington DC in 1990. His doctoral essay won the most distinguished dissertation award of the year. The multi-talented priest has served his spiritual and secular community in several ways. For instance, he was the editor of *The Light Catholic Newspaper* in Lokoja Diocese, he worked as a teacher and a supervisor of Religious Education at the Kogi State Education Board, and in 1994, he was a theological expert at the first Synod of Bishops for Africa in Rome. From 1994 to 2007, he served the Church in Nigeria as Deputy Secretary-General and Secretary-General of the Catholic Secretariat of Nigeria (CSN). Between 2007 and 2008, Fr. George undertook his sabbatical year at the Development Agency of the German Catholic Bishops Conference in Germany (Ojeifo, 2016; Osso, 2017). On his return to Nigeria, he founded the Lux Terra Leadership Foundation, an initiative to train purposeful and transformational leaders in the Church and society in Nigeria. Currently, he serves as the Executive Director of the Foundation.

3. Fr. Ehusani: A Digital Priest in a Digital Society?

Fr. Ehusani has courted the media with ease in his forty-year journey as a priest and scholar. Prompted by Fr. Ehusani's ample use of the media through his Lux Terra Foundation, a veteran Nigerian journalist, Eugenia Abu, noted that:

> Religious leaders get to hear how media influencers and the messages they propagate can affect their congregation negatively, how social media is weaponising corruption, and how using the same media tools they use can affect their congregations positively (Abu, 2018).

Such social pulpit interventions can lead to knowledge-sharing on the impact of corruption on national development and the positive ways leaders can fight corruption in the social space. They can further provide powerful insights into how to address national problems through purposeful strategies. During these interventions, participants learn how they can be role models who would identify methods of curbing all forms of corruption in churches and mosques (Abu, 2018).

Fr. Ehusani understands the value of the print media. He is widely published and read. His works include *An Afro-Christian vision:*

> Ọzọvẹhẹ!": Toward a more Humanized World (1991), The Social Gospel: An Outline of the Church's Current Teaching on Human Development (1992), The Politics of Population Control (1994), A Prophetic Church (1996), Fragments of Truth (1997), Petals of Truth (1998), Challenges of the Church in the 21st Century (2000), Nigeria: Years Eaten by the Locusts (2002a), Witness and Role of Priests and Religious in Nigeria (2002b), Flames of Truth (2006a) and Gospel Reflections for Our Time (2006b).

These works are filled with poetic, theological, and philosophical expositions on a diverse range of subject matter (People Pill, 2020; Abu, 2018). Among his works are three poetry anthologies, 22 music CDs, and scores of both audio and video-recorded homilies. He has preached several retreats and published articles covering various issues, including social anthropology, social justice, Christian humanism, and Christian spirituality (National Impact, 2009).

As an ardent user of the internet, Fr. Ehusani employs traditional and social media to advance the truth of the gospel without fear or favour. A large selection of his works is found on various websites and aims to make his thoughts more readily available to a wider public. Recently, his sermon on the wickedness and deception of the Nigerian leadership went viral on Facebook, WhatsApp, and other social media handles. For many scholars, Fr. George Ehusani is easily grouped with Bishop Matthew Hassan Kukah, the late Fr. Munachi Ezeogu, and a few others who have paid their dues as far as using the media in service of the gospel is concerned (Dyikuk, 2019).

4. Ehusani: Between Media and Ministry

Here, we shall explore Fr. Ehusani as an orator, a skilled communicator, an internet-savvy priest, and an expert Church communicator. This would help us better appreciate his engagement with the media as a priest.

4.1 *Ehusani the Orator*

Fr. Ehusani is an orator that everyone would love to listen to at any time. He takes advantage of the three principles of every communicative act – that is, being novel, evoking a sense of emotion, and employing catchphrases to sweep his audience off their feet. Those who have heard him talk through traditional or social media platforms would have realised that there is always something new to learn and that he speaks passionately. His homilies often leave the faithful with some catchphrases to reflect on throughout the week. For instance, after listening to him deliver a lecture at the Intervention Academy on October 31, 2018, Adagbo Onoja, a lecturer in the Department of Political Science and Diplomacy at Veritas University, Abuja, and member of the Editorial Committee of *Intervention*, disclosed that listening to Fr. Ehusani was like experiencing a trance (Onoja, 2018). This statement acknowledges that the clergyman is blessed with the power of oratory.

4.2 *Ehusani the Skilled Communicator*

Fr. Ehusani believes that collaboration and communication are at the heart of the tensions and conflicts in Nigeria. In his essays, he canvasses for opening the lines of communication and establishing what he describes as a "dialogue of civilisation" between Christian and Islamic groups. Thus, these two faiths can jointly initiate and run human and community development projects or programmes that promote and defend human rights and dignity. This is in addition to Christian and Islamic groups mutually owning and funding community health centres, orphanages, vocational schools, and special institutions for handicapped persons and problem children in various towns or villages (Ehusani, 2002).

Fr. Ehusani is convinced that the society would be the better for it if individual Christians and Muslims can collaborate to establish NGOs and/or pressure groups aimed at promoting and defending the rights of women and children. This will further enhance interpersonal and group communication in a society that has a penchant for stigmatisation based on ethnicity, religious, and political beliefs, as well as educating the populace on the advantages of mutual tolerance and respect among people of various religious and political persuasions. He further argues that these groups could offer legal support to poor people and minority groups whose rights are often violated by the elite in the society (Ehusani, 2002). He surmised that if Christians and Muslims in Nigeria follow the tenets of their religion and prevent selfish individuals from manipulating them, the society would be a better place to live in (Ehusani, 2002).

4.3 *Ehusani the Internet-Savvy Priest*

The late Archbishop Gabriel Gonsum Ganaka of Jos was fond of saying that "The priest should be a gentleman, a scholar, and a saint." Despite this rich assertion, many priests are not media literate. Although the digital age requires that the contemporary Catholic priest have the Bible in his left hand and a newspaper in his right, like Archbishop Ganaka would insist, many priests still lag behind. On the contrary, through his website, Fr. Ehusani is able to use his works to engage the wider public. This way, he is able to fulfil the Great Commission of Christ and project the Church to others in good light.

4.4 *Ehusani the Expert Church Communicator*

Although his area of specialisation is not communication, Fr. Ehusani is not only familiar with the media, but he is also in touch with the mind of the Church concerning the use of the means of communication. For example, in his 2018 World Communications Day Reflection, Ehusani emphasised that God is the source and culmination of all communication and stressed that all communications media should ultimately lead us back to Him. Going down memory lane, he noted that such celebrations which guide the communication apostolate of the Church with powerful messages of the Roman Pontiffs from Saint John Paul II to Francis, help us to recognise the truth, isolate it, and sort it out from the tangle of affirmations and contradictions. In the reflection, he clarified other areas like the consciousness of media recipients who are also responsible for what they consume from the media, the need to defend ourselves from fake news, the need to ensure media education, and the need to promote relationships and solidarity (Catholic Bishops Conference of Nigeria, 2020).

Fr. Ehusani also dwelt on other areas such as celebrating heroes in the media, fostering peace journalism, overcoming copyist mentality, overcoming the culture of mediocrity and indolence, the "Brown Envelopes" phenomenon, and greed. He cautioned against indiscipline and unmitigated curiosity and urged all and sundry to overcome media illiteracy in order to mitigate the destructive effects of fake news. Fr. Ehusani warned the public about using social media to perpetuate fake news under cover of anonymity while calling on information technologists "to work hard to overcome the present challenge of anonymity, such that before long those who disseminate hate speeches through the internet could be easily fished out and punished according to the laws of the land" (Catholic Bishops Conference of Nigeria, 2020).

5. Strategic Communication: The Lux Terra Style

Fr. Ehusani, through the Lux Terra Foundation, engages in strategic communication. In particular, he engages traditional and social media in disseminating information, delivers public lectures, trains professioals and volunteers for psycho-spiritual therapy, conducts sundry workshops, and advocates for the poor:

5.1 *Human Capacity through Lux Terra Foundation*

The inspiration of what is known today as Lux Terra Leadership Foundation started between 2008 and 2013 when Fr. Ehusani served as the parish priest of the Catholic Church of the Assumption, Asokoro,

Abuja. It was during this time that he established the Centre. To be sure, Lux Terra is a not-for-profit organisation aimed at training and mentoring future leaders for both the Church and Nigerian society (Ojeifo, 2016; Abu, 2018). Also, "The Lux Terra Leadership Foundation is a multiple resource outfit and training facility whose purpose is to expose leaders and potential leaders to the dynamics of purposeful, visionary, transformative, and inspiring servant leadership" (LT-Leadership, 2020). Built on the principles of Catholic Social Teaching (CST), this Foundation believes that building human capacity is the driver of religious, socio-economic and political development. With people-oriented programmes targeted at various segments of the society, the Centre aspires to be Nigeria's cradle for excellence in terms of the development of children, youth, and women.

5.2 *Initiating Psycho-Spiritual Therapy*

To further enlarge the organisation, the prolific priest set up what is known today as the Psycho-Spiritual Institute (PSI) in 2012. The institute has its first study centre in Nairobi, Kenya. The Institute, which is affiliated with the Catholic University of Eastern Africa, awards Master's degrees in Psycho-Spiritual Therapy. Since its inception, PSI has been training and graduating professionals in psycho-spiritual therapy for English-speaking African countries (Ojeifo, 2016). In the quest for human capacity building and raising mature leaders who are concerned about the health of their nation, graduates from PSI are currently involved in giving professional counselling and therapy sessions to victims of Boko Haram insurgency and others who are suffering from depression and addiction.

5.3 *Engagement with Traditional and Social Media*

Those who are conversant with the media activities of Fr. Ehusani know that he hosts a programme on various television stations like AIT, Lumen Christi TV, NTA, and other TV and radio stations in Nigeria. People are amazed at the depth of divine wisdom the multi-talented preacher displays on the programme and from the pulpit (Ojeifo, 2016). He is also a good singer and guitarist. Fr. Ehusani has a penchant for shared homilies, which entails a thematic presentation of the readings through a thorough analysis, asking questions for feedback, and elaborating on the text with vivid examples from day-to-day experiences of the people. With features like broadcasting on AIT and live-streaming on Facebook and other social media platforms, he is able to reach millions of people across the globe. With this, Fr. George can have a digital encounter with those whom Prensky refers to as *digital emigrants* and *digital natives* (Prensky, 2001). While *digital emigrants* watch his homilies on television, *digital natives* surf the internet to access the celebration of Holy Mass.

5.4 *Public Lectures, Workshops, and Passion for the Poor*

As a social critic, Fr. Ehusani has never shied away from public debates on national development. He uses the Lux Terra platform for delivering public lectures, conducting workshops, and engaging in public enlightenment campaigns. He is counted among the likes of Martin Luther King Jr. in the civil rights movement, Mahatma Gandhi in India, and Nelson Mandela in South Africa, who stood up with courage to bring about needed changes in the society through non-violence means. For instance, in one of his sermons titled "The Revenge of the Poor," he asserted that the revenge of the poor is at the corner. It is difficult to escape it:

> You can have your jeep, you can have your generators, you can even have bulletproof cars, but the revenge of the poor as it happened in France, in Russia and also in Sudan will happen here. Unless we change our direction, we will end up where we are heading and where we are heading now is, unfortunately, a violent revolution" (National Impact, 2009).

6. A Digital Priest in a Digital Society: Recommendations Towards Better Years

In order to advance the Centre and push its activities to greater heights, it is crucial to pursue the following: Mentoring the young in media and ministry, establishing a robust media outfit for Lux Terra, undertaking research towards memory and documentation of resources, remaining relevant to digital culture, and enlarging psycho-spiritual therapy and reporting activities related to it:

6.1. Mentoring the Young in Media and Ministry

Although Fr. Ehusani has done a lot to advance the course of the gospel through various engagements with the media, the Centre can further push the frontiers of new evangelisation by establishing a unit for programmes on youth in media ministry. This entails the production of Catholic movies, music, and flyers, as well as initiating drama or choreography that has rich content (Dyikuk, 2019). Such efforts would further help the Centre achieve one of its cardinal objectives of youth empowerment.

6.2. Debuting a robust Media Outfit for Lux Terra

Since the Centre enjoys large followership, it needs to establish a robust media outfit with the capacity to introduce non-Catholics to the basics of the faith, including the Seven Sacraments. Besides, the outfit can deploy platforms like Facebook, WhatsApp, Instagram, and Twitter to target the youth population, and somewhat establish a virtual congregation. Such virtual congregation could be constituted into a forum where Sunday and weekday reflections, rich Christian photo-enhanced messages, caller tunes, hymns, and videos can be transmitted not only in English, but also in French, Hausa, Igbo and Yoruba (Dyikuk 2017, 2019).

6.3. Research, Memory and Documentation of Resources

As someone who is widely published, Fr. Ehusani should think of establishing both actual and virtual libraries. This would make his works perpetually alive. In furtherance of research, memory, and documentation, video and audio messages should be kept for posterity. Like the shrine of Archbishop Fulton Sheen, the cleric should plan for the future so that his efforts might not be in vain. This requires planning and huge investments, and no amount spent on a timeless project such as this should be considered a waste.

6.4. Remaining Relevant to Digital Culture

As a digital priest in a digital society, Fr. Ehusani has decided to whet the appetites of readers and audiences who have been following him. This is aside a legion of youths across various divides in Nigeria who consider him a mentor, confidant, life coach, luminary, and friend. While these qualities are accolades in the right direction, they require consistency and commitment. Therefore, as someone who has always stung society to consciousness, Fr. Ehusani should remain relevant to the digital culture he is called to minister in by constantly updating himself and being in touch with current realities.

6.5. *Enlarging and Reporting Activities of Psycho-Spiritual Therapy*

Although Fr. Ehusani has done well through his Center, the contributions of the PSI in Kenya and the activities of the graduates are not well known to the public. One would have expected that a programme that has run for eight years and produced many professionals in psycho-spiritual therapy from English-speaking African countries should have filled the airwaves beyond Church circles. It is, therefore, crucial for the Centre to saturate the media with the activities of the PSI and report the impact graduates of the Institute are making in society. This would likely attract more funding to enlarge the current scope of the PSI degree.

7. Conclusion

In this article, we have seen that Fr. Ehusani's work as a priest, public intellectual, Executive Director of Lux Terra Foundation, and his engagement with the media has exposed him to heterogeneous audiences at home and abroad. This exposure came at the high price of diligence and commitment. At a time when many priests prefer to be off-camera, Fr. Ehusani seizes the slightest opportunity to preach, teach and sing to a broken world in search of hope. The darling host on Lumen Christi TV is passionate about what he does as he is determined to make society a better place. No doubt, his enduring legacies as a life coach for the youth opens up avenues for this cleric to remain young at heart and relevant to changing times. The pages of his life are replete with the story of a digital priest in a digital society who comes across as an orator, a dyadic communicator, a web guru, and a communication expert.

Because strategic communication is key to the services of Lux Terra Leadership Foundation, the Centre engages in human capacity building through psycho-spiritual therapy, uses both traditional and social media, and delivers public lectures/workshops. Mentoring the young in media and ministry, creating a robust media outfit for Lux Terra, undertaking research towards memory and documentation of resources, remaining relevant to digital culture and enlarging activities of the Psycho-Spiritual Institute as well as putting it out in the news are critical to enhancing the work of this digital priest in a fast-changing society.

Fr. Ehusani comes from a humble background, but with the influence of his mother, he pursued education and sought the truth. As a result, fate led him to become a Catholic priest who is not always in the news but has a platform that makes news and empowers others. Wherever his story is told, it would be said that he is both a colossus and an e-priest who has paid his dues to the Church and society in Nigeria and beyond.

References

Abioye, T. (2011). Language and ideology in George Ehusani's writings. Ibadan: Kraft Books.

Abu, E. (2018). Five books in celebration of Rev. Fr. George Ehusani. https://dailytrust.com/five-books-in-celebration-of-rev-fr-george-ehusani. Accessed 8/28/2020.

Arx, J. V. (2015). How did Vatican I change the church?www.america magazine.org/issue/post-traumatic-church. Accessed 9/30/2020.

Catholic Bishops Conference of Nigeria. (2018). Nigerian journalists urged to protect the society from menace of social media. www.cbcn-ng.org/newsdetail.php?tab=805. Accessed 9/29/2020.

Donadio, R. (2019). The spotlight effect: This Church scandal was revealed by outsiders. www.theatlantic.com/international/archive/2019/02/catholic-churchs-sex-abuse-scandal-was-driven-outsiders/583489/Accessed 9/30/2020.

Dyikuk, J. J. (2019). Media and Ministry: Examining the role of priests in Nigeria in new evangelisation. *Annals of Journalism and Mass Communication*. Vol. 1, Is. 2, [15-22].

Dyikuk, J. J. (2017b). Christianity and the digital age: Sustaining the online church. *International Journal of Journalism and Mass Communication*. 3(1): 043-049.

Ehusani, G. (2002). Theologians Christian-Islamic cooperation in the building of a just and peaceful society. *Bulletin of Ecumenical Theology*. The Ecumenical Association of Nigeria. Vol.14. [27-38].

Ehusani, G. (2020). *Reflections*: George Ehusani. www.georgeehusani.org/. Accessed 9/29/2020.

Ehusani, G. O. (1991). *An Afro-Christian vision: "Ọzọvẹhẹ!": Toward a more Humanized World*. California: University Press of America.

Ehusani, G. O. (1992). *The Social Gospel: An Outline of the Church's Current Teaching on Human Development*. Ibadan: Kraft Books.

Ehusani, G. O. (1994). *The Politics of Population Control*. Zaria: Ahmadu Bello University Press.

Ehusani, G. O. (1996). *A Prophetic Church*. Ede: Provincial Pastoral Institute Publications/

Ehusani, G. O. (1998). *Petals of Truth*. Ibadan: Kraft Books.

Ehusani, G. O. (2002a). *Nigeria: Years Eaten by the Locust*. Ibadan: Kraft Books.

Ehusani, G. O. (2002b). *Witness and Role of Priests and Religious in Nigeria*. Abuja: Gaudium et Spes Institute.

Ehusani, G. O. (2006a). *Flames of Truth*. Ibadan: Kraft Books.

Ehusani, G. O. (2006b). *Gospel Reflections For Our Time*. Ibadan: Better Yourself Books.

Ehusani, G. O. (1997). *Fragments of Truth*: Ibadan: Kraft Books.

Ehusani, G. O. (2000). Challenges for the Church in the 21st Century: A Memorandum to the Leaders of the Nigerian Church. Lagos: Sovereign Ventures.

LT-Leadership. (2020). Lux Terra Leadership Foundation. www.ltleadership.org/index_our-staff.html. Accessed 8/28/2020.

Mirus, J. (2010). Vatican II on social Communication. www.catholicculture.org/commentary/vatican-ii-on-social-communication/Accessed 9/30/2020.

National Impact. (2009). Rev Fr George Ehusani blows hot on national television. https://nationalimpact.com.ng/2019/07/15/rev-fr-george-ehusani-blows-hot-on-national-television/. Accessed 8/28/2020.

Ojeifo, E. (2016). Ehusani: Priest, gentleman and scholar at 35. https://guardian.ng/opinion/ehusani-priest-gentleman-and-scholar-at-35/. Accessed 8/28/2020.

Onoja, A. (2018). George Ehusani and the universe called the university. https://intervention.ng/13615/. Accessed 9/29/2020.

Osso, N. (2017). Blerf's WHO is WHO in Nigeria: Ehusani, Rev. Fr. George Omaku. https://blerf.org/index.php/biography/ehusani-rev-fr-george-omaku/. Accessed 8/28/2020.

People Pill. (2020). George Ehusani: Nigerian catholic priest. https://peoplepill.com/people/george-ehusani/.Accessed 8/28/2020.

Prensky, M. (2001). "Digital Natives, Digital Immigrants." *On the Horizon*. 9.5 [1-6].

CHAPTER TWELVE

Truth in the Lens of Trilogy: George Ehusani's Poesies

Rex Emmanuel Odoemenam

1. Introduction

Truth is not metaphor; truth is truth. It is not bitter, contrary to popular assumptions. Truth is acceptable to those with truth in them. Wherever the inference is made of truth as a bitter pill, those who make bold such claims have no truth in them. Truth responds to truth, and when found wanting, acknowledges, makes amends and proceeds forth. This is the evident undertone that pervades the meditations of Rev. Fr. George Ehusani in the trilogy: *Fragments of truth (Fragments)* (1997*), Petals of truth (Petals)* (1998*)* and *Flames of truth (Flames)* (2006*).*

The medieval writer, Dante Alighieri found inspiration for his trilogy in Beatrice, his angel of light, who guided him through the abysmal depths of the inferno, to the tortuous chains and chambers of purgatory and finally into paradise in the *Divine comedy* (1472/1555). For Ehusani's trilogy, the underlying inspiration is the search for and meditation on *Truth* - Christ the light, the way and the *Truth*. Evidently, like the daily experiences of life and existence, there are themes of trouble and despair scattered, deliberately perhaps, all over this meditative trilogy. This is possibly to reflect the uncertainties rocking the boat of the poet's journey as he moves through existence. This fragile uncertainty of existence is exemplified in multiple texts dealing, tangentially, with the subject matter of existence in Nigeria and other related subjects. Worthy of mention in this regard are Chinua Achebe's *There was a country* (2013), *The trouble with Nigeria* (1984), "The education of a British protected child" (2009), among others. Similar themes are found in some of the works of Rev. Fr. George Ehusani: *'Nigeria: Years eaten by the locust' (2002), The social gospel: An outline of the Church's current teaching on human development'*

(1992) and *'An Afro-Christian vision, 'Ozovene': Toward a more humanised world (1991).* In offering visions for a better world, in his writings, Fr. Ehusani reflects on the social-political and economic imbalances in Nigeria and proffers solutions to counter them.

Many scholars, Abioye *(2011)* Ojeifo *(2011),* Okeregbe *(2011) and* Chukwu's *(2013),* for example, have also examined various aspects of Fr. Ehusani's writings. Especially with respect to his trilogy, these scholarly presentations support Fr. Ehusani's conception of *truth* as the redeeming force. Find truth, acknowledge it and there would certainly be some rays of hope at the end of the tunnel.

2. Fragments of Truth

Observably, Ehusani's meditations travelled through many years of constant continuous, productive, metamorphous incubation. Anyone familiar with James Joyce's *A portrait of the artist as a young man* (1916) would recognize in the first of Ehusani's trilogy – *Fragments of truth*, the powerful voice of a militantly-charging youthful zealot agitated by the ugly social-political and economic circumstances that he justifiably feels aggrieved about - situations that ought not to be, given indications of multiple abundance. How could a youth, reasonable in thought and attitude, ignore and not be fired-up by hunger and deliberate deprivations?

In *Fragments,* Fr. Ehusani responds to *Power* on behalf of aggrieved youths by predicting a revolution if the youth's anger is not doused. If his message in the text is not understood, here is a summary of the salient points. One, that the worse of people come with the worse of uprisings. In other words, if people have been oppressed for too long, when they eventually revolt, the pent up anger bursts without control. Two, most violent uprisings should be expected of most docile populations that are victims of oppressive and unjust systems. Fr. Ehusani argues in the poem *'Madness' (p. 11)* that in such systems *"only mad people can be well" (p. 11).* The recent Arab spring revolution lends credence to this. During the period, a common, ordinary man, fed up with a relentless oppressive regime, seemingly unable to do anything about it, set himself ablaze. This incident triggered a violent revolution that toppled governments, systems, and dictatorships.

One could rightly say that socio-political and economic intrigue dominates the poet's ambiance in *Fragments.* This collection with yellow paperback cover and an artistic frontal display of red breaking sparsely on white background is made up of sixty nine poems individually titled according to their inspiration. *The Dedication (p .5)* whets the appetite of a ready reader with the following lines:

> To all who burn inside
> with passion
> for love
> for life
> for truth
> for justice
> for peace (p. 5).

This dedication is repeated for all books of the trilogy.
Titles such as *'Wipe your tears' (p. 44)* is set in historic Nigeria's pre-1999 military dictatorships that damaged much of Nigeria's thriving social-political and economic structures and provided the disruptive bases upon which all other ills set in. The opening lines of the poem *'Wipe your tears' (p. 44)* – *"weep not child"*- borrowed from the consoling tone of Ngugi wa Thiong'o's *(1964)* famous first novel -*Weep not child (1964)* is very instructive of the disruptive situations the poem confronts. It further says *"...for all is not lost..." (line 2)* to demonstrate the vision of hope that the poem brings to a society evidently in distress. The poem *'Power' (p .9)* argues that

> of causes and effects
> Absolute power
> And violent uprising
> Are supreme...

In *'Madness' (p. 11)*, the poet argues that he knows

> ... a land
> where the worst
> is not bad enough" (p. 11)

to show the extent to which things had gone awry. In *'I am Angry' (p. 13)*, one need not search beyond the evidently self-proclaiming title. The poet speaks of "prolonged nightmare ... the crime is beyond pardon ... My people have been abused...they have suffered for too long ..."

Furthermore, titles of poems such as 'History is Recording' (p.17), 'National Lament' (p. 22), 'Monstrosity' (p. 25), 'Stillborn' (p. 27), 'R I P' (p. 30), 'The Dreamer's Lament' (p. 55), 'We Want Bread' (p. 96), among others, heighten the impact of the social-political and economic instability in the poet's locale. Equally insightful are the poems with repeated appeals to truth such as 'Truth Must Be Told' (p.98), 'Truth' (p. 122) and 'Truth and Light' (p. 128).

There are, however, some questions that the young militant voice of the poet persona provokes in a critical mind given the realities of Nigeria which is the geographic focal point of the poet. The following are some of them:

- Will the judgment day predicted in 'Visitation' (p. 20) ever come?
- Will there ever be "an outbreak of fire as the young visit swords of vengeance on the old who are wolves in shepherds' clothing...?" ('National Lament', p. 22).
- Do the present realities negate the assertion that the young might visit vengeance on duplicitous leaders and those who have caused them anguish?
- Have the *Old* not already succeeded in turning the young against each other?
- Have they – the Old, not already sown seeds of discord and forced down the throat of the young lies of ethno-religious divisiveness?
- Are the youths not already dejected, confused, inflicting upon themselves escapist horrors of drug addiction, crime and other self-debasing afflictions?

Despite the implications of these weighty questions, the oppressor remains unshaken and unmoved. The poet saw no hope in the then "shackled transition that was doomed from the seed to crash into perdition..." as he wrote in 'Stillborn' (p. 27). The 'Freedom' (p.47) that the poet spoke of can only be seen as prophetic. It is not as that which already is nor near to come, and, definitely, not as that which ended military dictatorships and ushered in civilian criminals, but as that which in an undated future must come – "I can see freedom conceived for this land and this time it will come to light..." (p. 47).

3. Petals of Truth

The remarkable artistic growth of the poet is evident with the publication of *Petals of truth*, the second phase of the trilogy. The major preoccupation in *Petals* is a further definition and refinement of the notion of truth. Accordingly, this phase provokes profound thoughts. Truth is freedom; freedom is truth. Truth is God; God is Love; and love is freedom. But are truth, love and freedom an escapist's flight from their realities? Is the peace that love brings, freedom? Is loving an excuse for not confronting one's realities?

The poet here brings to the table of truth, a petal called *Love*. The deepening voice of the poet's maturity is apparent and his artistic age evident, as he opens *Petals* with the voice of ripening. Like 'petals'- the hitherto hidden part of a blooming flower coming to light, the poet's hidden qualities of artistic maturation and spiritual meditation also come vividly in contact with the light of *Truth*. At this stage, the light of *Truth* has shone upon this *petal* called *love* and opened it up to that *Truth*. It, like the bees, has tasted the nectar and is now proclaiming that *Truth* can be reached through *Love*.

While it would be said that literary artistry is present in all parts of the trilogy, so is social-political intrigues and spiritual insights. The maturation of the poet could be felt in the surefootedness and exhibited confidence of the poetic voice in *Petals*. This second of the trilogy covered in red paperback with green flowery artworks adorning the front page began with the first poem in the collection titled *'These Forty Years'* (p. 11), a poem which remarkably underscores the impact of years on the growth and maturation of the poetic voice. As the poet persona ruminates:

> These forty years
> Have taken me
> Across the raging rivers
> of juvenile idealism
> And the volatile mountains
> Of self-righteous perfectionism... (p. 11)

Titles such as: 'Friendship' (p.13), 'I Can Love' (p.17), 'Beauty' (p.19), 'Listen Father' (p.135), 'Serenity' (p.119) and many others highlight the impact of years on the poet's outlook towards life as evidenced in the self-explanatory titles of the poems.

With the grace of years comes wisdom found in love at the threshold of truth as evidenced in the voice of the poet persona. Naturally, there is a reduced militancy of tone as the poet adopts an inward search for meaning in his much more self-reflective meditations. The poet, however, does not relent in his critical view of his society, as he says in his reverie that "people suffer who are silent" ('Protestation', pp. 35-41). This collection numbering more than sixty poems culminates fittingly in the poem titled *Disarm Our Hearts' (p. 77)*. It sums up the poet's fundamental disposition and worldview, the prevalent harsh realities around him notwithstanding. The poet reveals a deeper self-realization in spirituality and life's outlook with these moving lines: "Disarm our hearts mighty God and impress it upon us that we cannot shake hands with clenched fists…" ('Disarm our Hearts', p. 77).

4. Flames of Truth

The poet's essence, having taken form, erupts in pruning *Flames* embodying *Truth* in *Flames of Truth*. Things are here, viewed through the prism of flames as this last of the trilogy takes *self* and all other things through the crucible. Evidently, the many years of Nigeria under military dictatorships provided the bulk of the historical background, inspiration and theme for the two previous parts of the trilogy. There is no time-frame given for the material events that provided the inspiration that collectively shaped this part of the trilogy. They are all embodied in a crucible called 'history' in 'Mysterious Desire' (p.11). Beyond a deep concentration on the eternal and complete de-emphasis on the mundane, the poet's powerful use of the evocative and invocative tones captures and captivates the reader. In 'Mysterious Desire' (p.11), the poet persona draws on the reflective invocative and says:

> Amidst history's dark night
> Of loveless toil
> My soul thirsts and my flesh pines
> Like parched soil awaiting the rain…
>
> Hush my heart
> Still my soul… (p. 11)

In my view, the spiritual awakening in the collection - *Fragments* took form in *Petals* and erupted into full dynamism in *Flames*. and fully formed consciousness in recognition of the ephemeral nature of things in *Flames*, the last collection of the trilogy.

One would not neglect the role of allusions in this trilogy more like in Geoffrey Chaucer's 'Canterbury Tales' (1952). Just as Chaucer referenced many authors and authorities he knew, the poet persona in this trilogy leaned very much on Biblical allusions. The poem 'Disarm Our Hearts' (p. 47) repeated in *Petals* has the tone of the Sermon on the Mount in the Biblical gospel of Mathew (Chapter 5-7). The use of powerful idioms and vivid images is also a significant part of Ehusani's artistry:

> "…we cannot shake hands with clenched fists … war begins in the heart … darkness cannot drive away darkness" (p. 47). And the poem titled *'Home'* is a fitting example of the use of proverb (p. 73):

When the hair gets bushy

> In the course of one's sojourn
> Through life
> My people say
> Home is the place
> To go for a shave… (p. 73).

Constantly, as the poet takes both his life and the events that shape it through the crucible, *Flames* gives life and being to the poet's truth. There is a clear departure from the mundane with detailed focus on more enduring aspects of *being* and existence, as could be conceived by only a spiritually condensed personage. It is in this part of the trilogy that the existential edifice, which the poet debates, is painted more vividly. 'Come Holy Spirit' (p. 15) is the title of eleven poems in the collection dealing with a profound interior desire for transcendence. The poem 'Materialism' (p. 71) presents a sharp contrast to such desire for transcendence. Many more of such titles that promote the spiritual against the purely mundane, are in this part of the trilogy.

5. Conclusion

In conclusion, a one-directional view of the poet's trilogy would render a deeply reflective work such as this trilogy undeserving limitations. Therefore, a trifocal approach that considers its spiritual ambrosia, social-political and economic intrigues and literary artistry, all of which have been briefly dealt with here, is recommended. In other words, although the trilogy is not physically arranged in a trifocal pattern of specific themes and subject matters, a discerning reader would, however, readily identify the dominant influence of spirituality, artistic growth and socio-political themes in all the texts. From the examination of the texts, it does not appear like the idea of a trilogy was originally conceived as the foundational framework of its three collections. However, the poet penned ideas clogging his mind and the ideas manifested as they are in three objectively linked architectonics.

References

Abioye, T. (2011). *Language and ideology in George Ehusani's writings*. Ibadan: Kraft Books Limited.
Achebe, C. (1984). *The trouble with Nigeria*. Enugu: Fourth Dimension.
Achebe, C. (2013). *There was a country*. London: Penguin Books.
Achebe, C. (2013). *The education of a British-protected child*. London: Penguin Books.
Alighieri, D. (1472/1555). *Divine comedy*. Venice: Gabriel Giolito.
Chaucer, G. (1952). *Canterbury tales*. Maryland: Penguin Books.
Chukwu, C. O. (2013). *Footprints of a mentor: Living legacies of Rev. Father George Ehusani in the eyes of a young mentee*. Abuja: Lux Terra Leadership Foundation.
Ehusani, Omaku George. (1991). *An Afro-Christian vision: "OZOVEHE!" Towards a more humanized world*. Boston: University Press of America Inc.
Ehusani, G. (1992). *The social gospel: An outline of the church's current teaching on human development*. Ibadan: Kraft Books Limited.
Ehusani, G. (1997). *Fragments of truth*. Ibadan: Kraft Books Limited.
Ehusani, G. (1998). *Petals of truth*. Ibadan: Kraft Books Limited.
Ehusani, G. (2002). *Nigeria: Years eaten by the locust*. Ibadan: Kraft Books Limited.

Ehusani, G. (2003) *A prophetic church*. Ibadan: Kraft Books Limited.

Ehusani, G. (2006). *Flames of truth*. Ibadan: Kraft Books Limited.

Joyce, J. (1916). *A portrait of the artiste as a young man*. Dublin: B.W. Huebsch.

Ojeifo, E. (Ed). (2011). *Young people and the hunger for meaning: Rev Fr. George Ehusani in conversation Vol 1*. Abuja: Lux Terra Leadership Foundation.

Okeregbe, T. (Ed). (2011) *Engaging the world with passion: Rev. Fr. George Ehusani in conversation Vol 2*. Abuja: Lux Terra Leadership Foundation.

Wa Thiong'o, N. (1964). *Weep not child*. London: Heineman.

CHAPTER THIRTEEN

Rev. Fr. George Ehusani: The Torch Bearer

Andrew E. Zamani

1. Introduction

One does not know which portion of the Holy Scriptures guides the Ministry of Fr. George Ehusani; the part that may be the appropriate frame of reference may be *Luke 4:18-19:* The Spirit of the LORD is on me, because he has anointed me to proclaim good news to the poor. He has sent me to proclaim freedom for the prisoners and recovery of sight for the blind, to set the oppressed free, [19] to proclaim the year of the LORD's favor.

Priesthood is a calling. My lay understanding of it is that the call is a first step, other steps include counsel for clarity of the experience, formal training and deployment to supervised ministry for exposure, supervision and mentoring. It does not matter whether he is Catholic, Evangelical, Pentecostal or Apostolic. One believes very strongly that in addition to acquiring biblical knowledge, the priest socialized to mature in his understanding of life and develop personal discipline in the service of God and humanity.

Meeting Fr. George Ehusani for the first time gives you the impression of a controversial social critic and advocate. One who is radically self-opinionated and too stubborn to be persuaded against his views and principles. No doubt, he has views, he has principles; it is important for him in his personal and official capacities to have them.

This was the impression I had of him about a decade ago when we shared an interview desk at the Africa Independent Television to discuss poverty and social justice issues in Nigeria. He expressed strong views on these issues and called out our leaders as being responsible for perpetrating poverty and injustice. At the same time, he was mindful of what was required to correct their predicament, and two of the suggestions he proffered were the imperatives for mind-set change and provision of mental health services for the casualties of these conditions.

One was not surprised to discover later that he was the Director of Lux Terra Leadership Foundation. One found out that it is the medium through which he trains leaders, shapes professional behavior, influences ethical re-orientation, facilitates behavior change and promotes inter-faith dialogue. He has facilitated these through strategic partnerships and "Reflections", a program of the Media Unit of the Foundation that is produced, directed and anchored by him. Through these, Fr George has been able to address the malaise of society in a multi-faceted way. I see this as a profound approach to Christian evangelism where his advocacy for behavior change on secular issues is similar to his call for repentance through his pedagogical homilies.

2. Exemplary Leadership

Fr. Ehusani is one who is irritated by prosperity sermons and the "mass-appeal hypnotic evangelism" by new generation, untrained and self-acclaimed "men of God". He believes that these so called "men of God" mis-present the Gospel and by so doing misrepresent Christianity. According to him, whoever is called by God must be trained and supervised, for genuine "men of God" are those who have passed the test of obedience – to the scriptures and the leadership of the Church. Therefore humans should not ascribe to themselves "ownership of the church or its denominations," because such amounts to fraud. He believes the Christian, as the "salt" and "Light" of the world, must lead by example.

To lead a world that is impeccably corrupt and sinful, Christians must be upright, above board and truthful, otherwise their claim to being a godly breed remains wishful thinking and a clause of perpetual ridicule. One area in which Fr. Ehusani has impacted many spiritually is by sharing his experiences of personal life struggles and the challenges. By so doing, it has been very easy for Fr Ehusani to earn the trust of parish members and friends. The genuineness he conveys in his interpersonal relationships has enabled him to access the depth of the experiences of his troubled parish members and to assist them to find solutions.

An area in which many Christians have the most difficulty, is in verbal witnessing. They often prefer to substitute the biblical injunction for them to win souls with prayers or financial support for missions, mainly because of lack of confidence or compelling social demands for religious neutrality among other considerations. This difficulty melts away, however, when one meets Fr. Ehusani, because he exudes uncommon pride in being a Christian anytime and everywhere. Therefore, one is convinced meeting him for the first time that he is a Christian, not a "priest-apologist" to Christianity.

There are priests who treat the priesthood as a career and not a calling. They are often stereotyped in their relationships with people, preferring to be served rather than serving. With Fr. Ehusani, the confidence gained by associating with him inadvertently becomes the inspiration to respond to his challenge to become a Christian witness. Therefore, a significant percentage of the Christian laity in the country, across denominations has committed to active, person-to-person witnessing through his profound influence. The results have been tremendous in terms of their conversion indices, discipleship appeals and spiritual edification.

3. Social Advocacy

Fr. Ehusani is a strikingly fearless social advocate on many national issues. Over time, he has led campaigns against corruption, environmental degradation and injustice. He has also led strong advocacy for the expansion of existing health care facilities, improvement of social security and good governance programmes.

By these, he illustrates the fact that he serves the purposes of God by being involved in the affairs of society. We are all affected by the environment in which we live and should be concerned about the happenings around us. He is one of the most informed clergymen I have ever met. His knowledge and understanding of the world around him have enabled him to preach against social vices, to organize positive social action for development and to give a voice to the voiceless.

Two years ago, he warned the elite and politicians that a time would come when "poor and unemployed angry Abuja youths will march in protest to "demand" what "rightfully" belongs to them or simply take over the streets of the city. This was prophetic, as youth restiveness, urban crime and massive civil protests have increased in Abuja. All these developments have been attributed to poverty, unemployment, social exclusion and injustice.

Since the advent of COVID-19, he has led several aggressive sensitization activities to educate the public on the disease and methods of prevention and remediation. Similar campaigns against drug abuse, child molestation, sexual and gender based violence have been made through his weekly television program called "Reflections", with tangible behavior change outcomes. Corporate and political leaderships in Nigeria have been greatly impacted by the issues raised during these media conversations, resulting in the reversal of poorly conceived policies or programs and adoption of the eloquent propositions of discussants.

4. Psycho-Spiritual Outreach

In an era where pastors use miracles to mobilize membership, doing the contrary is a high risk for losing membership or not attracting any at all. The vogue in Nigeria and indeed most of Africa is for pastors to claim omnipotence in order to have perpetual control of their congregants, especially over money and their private lives. The phenomenon is such that overseers of large churches in Nigeria have amassed wealth and acquired property at the expense of their parishioners. Through proclaimed visions and prophecies such clergymen continue to perfect hypnotic practices to perfect their schemes and scams.

Media reports are replete with stories of people who have been defrauded of huge sums of monies and of women or young impressionable youths that have been sexually abused based on their precarious family circumstances. The exploitation of their vulnerabilities and/or weaknesses keeps them perpetually poor, powerless and helpless. Fr. Ehusani is against this and assumes a completely different position.

He believes in the power of science and the invincibility of the spirit. For him there is no conflict between spirituality and science. According to him, science is the elaboration of the spirit with no possibilities of conflict between them except between their practitioners. He therefore uses science to complement his philosophical and biblical understanding of pain and suffering on one hand and to help on the other.

Persons who have approached him for help to resolve family conflicts, deal with addiction problems, process grief and or cope with trauma have received holistic treatment from him, either through personal pastoral psycho-spiritual care or through shared caregiving with professional counsellors, psychologists, mental health specialists and social workers. At the behest of Boko Haram insurgency in the North-

East for instance, he saw the need for the training of a critical mass of trauma counsellors, to meet the mental health needs of victims of insurgency, especially those in the internally displaced persons' camps. He believes that the psycho-spiritual approach is one that guarantees complete healing, as one without the other heightens the possibility of a vicious cycle of suffering.

Participating in these training sessions has been a rare privilege, as one has observed many trainees come to terms with their repressed traumatic experiences for the first time. One has observed persons who would otherwise be described as emotionally protected and stable, break down as they disclose their repressed experiences with co-participants for the first time. Training curricula have always been drawn by Lux Terra Foundation and the Department of Psychology, Nasarawa State University, Keffi. Following the pedagogy, extended periods of supervised internships are provided to enable trainees gain practical experience before they are issued a joint certificate to attest to their completion of training and competences to provide mental health and psychosocial support. Elsewhere in Nairobi, priests are being trained at postgraduate level at the Psycho-Spiritual Institute run by the Lux Terra Foundation to fill the vacuum in psycho-spiritual therapy.

Some testimonies from trainees are that the training enabled them confront their repressed conflicts or traumatic experiences for the first time; and that for the first time they were experiencing complete release and relief. The same approach has made people to confront their anger and un-expressed grudges against family members and friends.

The most profound outcome of this exercise is that it has afforded Christian and Muslim practitioners the opportunity to understand the scriptural bases for their common humanity and the value of neutrality, empathy, and love in trauma healing. A lot has been achieved in promoting inter-faith solidarity for providing mental health and psycho-social support for traumatized victims of violence and insurgency.

5. Facilitating Change

The state of the nation has been a major concern to most Nigerians. Apart from the moral decay that has permeated every fabric of society, the nation appears to be in a state of lawlessness. Governors who have served their terms in office with pending corruption charges are recycled whether as board members of parastatals, Senators or Ministers of the

Federal Republic. It is unthinkable that in a corrective regime, ethnic militias are emerging with unhindered propensity for violence. The state of healthcare has degenerated such that our secondary and tertiary health facilities are now mere consultation clinics. Here in Nigeria Governors prefer to negotiate ransoms with bandits and kidnappers rather than negotiate wages with their workers. This is a nation where what defines national interest is driven either by religion or ethnicity. Right now, Nigeria's industrial capacity utilization is at its lowest ebb. Our correctional centers are replete with hunger-driven "thieves" while pen-robbers glide our streets in posh cars and inhabit magnificent mansions. It is no longer clear to most of us what patriotism is. Who will bell the cat? The Church? Or Who?

Anybody could. Any socially organized group could, but the Church is the place where Fr. Ehusani belongs. He is a catholic priest and so we must consider the Church as the bastion of hope for Nigeria. But this is what he has to say about the challenge before the Church on this matter in an interview granted Opinion Nigeria in 2019:

The truth is that I have been going through some crisis on account of which I have been asking myself whether all my teaching, preaching, writing and social advocacy engagements amount to anything at all in the Nigerian setting. I observe that the Nigerian society is not changing for the better, and people are not being radically transformed in our Churches. Though we claim to be very religious, though our Churches are crowded, and we host noisy worship sessions, though some of us can quote passages of the Scripture effortlessly from Genesis to Revelation, and though we host numerous night vigils and deliverance sessions, Nigerian Christians are not being transformed in any significant way, and consequently we are not equipped to transform our society for God. The spiritual formation of most of us Christians has often left large areas of our lives more or less untouched and unredeemed. Like the iceberg which has only about 10% of its dimensions above the waters, and the remaining 90% underneath the surface, there are layers and layers of the life of the average Nigerian Christian that seems unreached by the Gospel of Christ. Like other Nigerians out there, who have never encountered Jesus Christ, and who have never benefited from the grace of baptism and confirmation, or the sustaining power of the Sacraments, Nigerian Christians live with anger and bitterness, fear and anxiety, wickedness and hatred, resentment and un-forgiveness, self-indulgence and addiction to the pleasures of the flesh, selfishness and greed, vanity and vainglory, and we are stuck in fetishism, occultism, and primitive superstition.

How then is the Church prepared to take up this challenge? Fr. Ehusani in the same interview does a deep reflection and comments thus: But Christianity as a mass movement in Nigeria is not working. Popular Christianity in Nigeria which features mega Churches and a huge gathering of thousands of people, is not working. That religion characterized by the noise-making enterprise which we call prayer; the one that features regular deliverance services, multiple healing miracle crusades, so-called "powerful men of God," dashing celebrity preachers, swaggering motivational speakers, flamboyant Gucci pastors, designer suit evangelists, jerry coil prophets, private jet owning overseers, fashionable Church choirs and trendy Gospel singers, and so on – that religion is not working! Let us be honest with ourselves: Nigerians are not being transformed for Christ in any significant way. We Nigerian Christians cannot show that we are better than our forebears who never heard about Jesus Christ. With all our feverish activism and massive Churches everywhere, we cannot demonstrate that we are better than people of other religions in godliness and holiness, in love and unity, in mercy and forgiveness, in gentleness and patience, in civic discipline and social morality, and in the practice of justice and the promotion of peace. Our marriage and family lives are often not better than the marriage and family lives of others in our environment who have never heard about Jesus Christ. There is nothing to show that the rate of marital infidelity and general promiscuity among Christians is any less than what obtains in the secular society. The young people in our Churches often do not behave better than other young people in their towns and villages or in their schools and colleges. Though we profess Christianity and are sometimes ready to go to war in "defense" of our religion, we have often remained greedy, avaricious, corrupt, undisciplined, fraudulent, adulterous, fetish, superstitious, exploitative and oppressive of the poor in our midst.

These views may appear to be a critical assessment of Christianity and the Church in Nigeria from one who is a major stake holder and should be a defender of same. Some might even suggest that this potentially jettisons the unity of the Church in Nigeria and presents her to the public for ridicule. People are entitled to their opinions. Those who know Rev. Father George Ehusani also know that he is fearless, realistic and truthful. He bears the marks of the prophets of old whose major preoccupation was to deliver the message to whom it was ordered. Nathan told David, "Thou art the man (the guilty adulterer and murderer)". He did not beg the issue. He passed the message and indicted David's hypocrisy. These comments are products of deep reflections and inward search both of self and the in-group. He admits shortly in the ensuing quote that these realities became so distressing and confusing at a point that he took time out to re-examine himself as well as appraise his ministry. He says:

> In recent times I started becoming discouraged and distressed about this embarrassing reality and asking myself serious questions bordering on the purpose and meaning of my own numerous activities in the face of this sobering reality. And this is one reason why I went away on a 21-day retreat. And in the course of the retreat, I sought the face of God, trying to discern his will in my confusion. I came back from the retreat determined not to spend the rest of my active life simply oiling the wheel or servicing structures that may not deliver any goods. Yes, I came back determined not to spend the rest of my life along the path of such shallow, hollow and mediocre religiosity.

But he is undeterred and determined to make a difference. He is a pathological optimist. Fr. Ehusani is a possibility thinker, one who has an alternative positive definition for failure. He sees solutions in virtually every debilitating challenge and raises a strong voice all the time for the brighter side. After all, this is the essence of the priesthood. As we all reflect on his forty years of priesthood, we are helping him in a way to increase the depth of his reflections on the journey so far but above all we are committing to supporting him as equal yoke partners to succeed in his stewardship. This man has godly indignation with the current vices in the land and the spiritual decadence that grow them. While he does posit as a self-righteous person, he is determined to serve; to play a role and make a difference. The starting point is Him. He is poised to be the change that he wishes to see. He expresses it this way:

> I have taken a close look at the Acts of Apostles, and seen once again how the early Christians gave loud, courageous and radical witness to the life of Jesus Christ, and I am convinced that (even in the Nigerian environment of today) with the power of the Holy Spirit poured out to the Church on Pentecost day, we can submit ourselves wholeheartedly to the Lord, and He will set us on the path of authentic Christian discipleship. We must start thinking of doing a few things differently. It

was Albert Einstein who said that you cannot solve a problem with the same level of consciousness that created the problem. And in education, I learned that if one has been teaching a class for a long time and they keep failing, it is either that all the students are idiots, or the teacher needs to re-examine his methodology. So we need to stop for a moment and ask ourselves what this whole enterprise of going to Church in Nigeria is all about.

In the context of his priestly calling, Fr. Ehusani feels empathy for the myriad societal problems that beguile Nigeria and feels an obligation to facilitate change. Whereas many of his colleagues with equally brilliant minds would solicit government patronage to make a contribution, he deploys the whole of himself to cause the change that he hopes to see. His rich sense of empathy easily endears him to the "erring, defective and importunate" who gladly oblige information about their predicaments and weaknesses for the psycho-spiritual help that they need. In addition to providing godly help, he is quick to refer those who need professional psychological, medical and social service interventions to trusted colleagues within the network of trusted friends nationwide.

Talking about his trusted friends nationwide, it should be of interest to readers that Fr. George is one who has conquered his human nature. His network of friends extends beyond the religious to the secular and diverse professions. In this context he has managed inter-faith relationships excellently, including hosting Islamic Scholars for extended periods of time at the foundation to examine controversial religious and social challenges such as insurgency, bigotry and corruption among others. By his disposition and conduct, Fr. George has in his forty years of priesthood proven his mettle as a faithful servant of God not by self-serving claims but by deeds. The testimony that I have written of him is an agreement with the commendation of Jesus Christ to his disciples that through their godly services, "men shall see your good works and glorify your father who is in heaven." My prayer is for God to enlarge his coast, increase his anointing to meet the complicated demands of ministry and finish strong.

Afterword

Fr. George Ehusani: A Tribute

On behalf of the Management staff and students of Veritas University, Abuja, it is my pleasure to pen this tribute to the indefatigable Founder and Executive Director of Lux Terra Leadership Foundation, Rev. Fr. George Ehusani, on the occasion of his 40th priestly anniversary in the vineyard of the Lord.

Fr. George, as he is fondly called, was ordained a priest of the Catholic Diocese of Lokoja on the 15th of August 1981. Over the years he has built a reputation for himself as a sound theologian, teacher, poet, musician, human rights activist, social commentator, and dedicated priest of the Catholic Church. In fact, Fr. George is not just your regular priest, rather he is a well-rounded individual and academic scholar par excellence. As a matter of fact, it is on record that he earned his doctorate degree in Ministry from the prestigious Howard University School of Divinity, Washington DC, in 1990, and his doctoral essay won the award of the most distinguished dissertation of the year. This achievement was no mean feat for a young Nigerian priest developing an Afrocentric Christian anthropology.

Since his ordination, Rev. Fr. George Ehusani has served the Church in so many capacities, some of which include: Theology expert at the first Synod of Bishops for Africa in Rome in 1994; Deputy Secretary-General and later Secretary-General of the Catholic Secretariat of Nigeria from 1994-2007; Parish Priest of the Catholic Church of Assumption, Asokoro, Abuja, from 2008 to 2013, during which period he established Lux Terra Leadership Foundation - an institute committed to the training of present and future leaders of the Church and Society in Nigeria. He worked as the Editor of *the Light* Catholic newspaper in Lokoja Diocese, a role he played for many years. He also has worked with the Kogi State Education Board where he worked as teacher and supervisor of Religious Education. In 2012, Rev. Fr. George set up the Psycho-Spiritual Institute (PSI) in Nairobi, Kenya, which is affiliated to the Catholic University of East Africa, Nairobi and awards Master of Arts degree in Psycho-Spiritual Therapy, for candidates from English speaking African countries. He is also a member of the Faculty in the

Institute which has its first campus in Nairobi, Kenya. The Abuja campus of the institute offers short training programmes in Basic Skills for Psycho-Trauma Healing for a wide range of professionals and volunteers. Fr. George has also served as Faculty Member of the Haggai Institute for Advanced Leadership Training, whose leading campuses are located in Hawaii and Singapore. Fr. George is a Fellow of the Nigerian Psychological Association and continues to serve on the Board of a number of local and international organizations including the Editorial Board of The Guardian Newspapers and the Board of Trustees of the Centre for Values in Leadership, just to mention a few.

He has published many Christian books and poetry anthologies. Some of his works have also touched on the socio-political circumstances of Nigeria which give readers a new perspective into the socio-political dynamics of the country. Some of his widely read books and anthologies include:

> Language and Ideology in George Ehusani's Writings" (2011) "An Afro-Christian Vision: "Ozovehe": Toward a More Humanized World" (1991), "Nigeria: Years Eaten by the Locust," (2002), "Witness and Role of Priests and Religious in Nigeria" (2002), "Fragments of Truth: Poems," (1997), "A Prophetic Church," with three editions published between 1996 and 2003, "Petals of Truth: Poems" (1998), "Flames of Truth" (2006) "Gospel Reflections for Our Time,"(2003) and "A Word for the Day" (2020).

Since the relocation of Veritas University to its main campus in Abuja in 2014, Fr. George has been a good friend and supporter of our noble institution. Through his Lux Terra Leadership Foundation, Fr. George has assisted the Management of Veritas University to anchor leadership training programmes for members of the University's Senate. He has always heeded our call to grace us with his presence in providing leadership trainings to our academic and non-Teaching staff during our annual staff retreat programmes. He has also been a source of joy and inspiration to our students as he has always taken time out of his busy schedule to mentor our students during student orientation week at different times. His lectures and moral instructions have impacted positively on their lives, and we remain beholden to Fr. George for his dedication to service in the training and mentoring of staff and students of Veritas University, Abuja.

Indeed, Fr. George has mentored so many young people in Nigeria and across Africa. He is well respected by his fellow priests and loved by so many across the boundaries of Nigeria and beyond. No doubt, his calm, gentle and simple ways have endeared him to so many. His contributions to leadership training in Nigeria and Africa for the future generation is remarkable and indeed worthy of emulation. Millions of people to date continue to watch his TV programmes on African Independent Television and Lumen Christi Television, as well as via his online platforms.

Fr. George remains an asset to the Church, and we are lucky to live in the same time as such a man of honour and truth. He has and shall always be a scholar of repute, a wonderful man of God, a preacher of peace, an advocate of truth and good governance through spirit led leadership, a messenger of love and compassion and most of all an inspiration to us all to always love and serve God in truth and with sincerity of heart. We are therefore happy to be associated with Fr. George Ehusani and felicitate with him on the joyous occasion of his 40th priestly ordination. As a faith-based organisation, we shall continue to always pray for Fr. George as we wish him more years of fruitful service in health of mind and body.

Fr. George, you are truly appreciated and loved, and we the Veritas University community look forward to more memorable interactions and engagement with you and the Lux Terra Leadership Foundation.

Rev. Fr. Prof. Hyacinth E. ICHOKU
Vice-Chancellor, Veritas University, Abuja

Index

A

Abiola, M.K.O, 128
Abioye, Taiwo, 9, 24, 25, 33, 38, 42, 128, 129, 134, 140, 181, 198, 232, 236, 242
African Christian humanism, 10, 47, 89, 100
African worldview, 124
AIT, 228
Alighieri, Dante, 235, 242
Almajiri, 33, 42, 44
American Psychiatric Association, 113, 119, 205, 215
Anglican Holy Communion service, 71
Anglo-Irish Agreement, 1985, 170
Anxiety, 207, 220
Aristotle, 49, 64, 65, 90, 91, 166, 177
Asante, Molefi, 58, 64, 103
Auswitz Concentration Camp, 80
Azuwike, Anthony, 11

B

Baal, 136
Baba Ahmed, Hakeem, 152
Baroque music, 68
Biblical allusions, 241
British colonialists, 187
British Crown, 175
Brueggemann, Walter, 123, 128, 129, 137, 140
Buhari, Muhammadu, 128

C

Calvary, 75
Cameron, David, 204, 216
Catholic Diocese of Lokoja, 144
Catholic Party, 167
Catholic priests, 112, 113, 114, 115, 120, 221
Catholic Social Teaching, 228
Catholic University of Eastern Africa, 23, 228
Celibacy, 115
Central African Region, 201
Centre for Values in Leadership, vii, 20, 25, 150, 256
Chaucer, Dante, 241, 242
Christian theological anthropology., 124
Civic engagement, 29, 30, 31
CNN, 145
Collier, Paul, 153
Confident pluralism, 164
Corruption Perception Index, 204
Covey, Stephen R, 145, 149, 150, 155
COVID-19 pandemic, 77
Critical Discourse Analysis, 185

D

Darby, John, 168, 178
Davies, Steve, 64, 69, 85
Democratic Republic of Congo, 201, 219
Democratic Republic of Congo (DRC), 152
Depression, 205, 218, 220
Didacticism, 28, 29, 43
Digital society, 13, 221, 230, 231
Diocese of Lokoja, 20, 23, 223, 255
Drucker, Peter, 151
Dufford, Bob, 68
Dunlop, John, 169, 178
Dyikuk, Justine John, 12, 225, 230, 232
Dylan, Bob, 67, 107, 109

E

Ebigbo, Peter Onyekwere, 204, 206, 212, 213, 214, 216, 217, 218
Economism, 98
Edema, Philip, 10, 89, 92, 94, 97, 109

258

Ehusani, Richard, 9, 10, 11, 12, 13, 19, 20, 23, 24, 25, 26, 23, 24, 25, 27, 29, 31, 32, 33, 34, 35, 36, 37, 38, 39, 40, 41, 42, 43, 44, 45, 47, 51, 53, 54, 55, 56, 57, 58, 59, 60, 61, 62, 63, 64, 67, 68, 69, 73, 74, 75, 76, 77, 79, 80, 81, 82, 83, 84, 85, 86, 89, 95, 96,97, 98, 99, 100, 101, 102, 103, 104, 105, 106, 107, 108, 133, 136, 140
Ethnic supremacy, 201
Evidentiality, 188, 190, 197

F

Fanon, Franz, 32, 152
Foley, John, 68
Francis of Assisi, 185

G

Galtung, Johan, 159
Gelineau psalmody, 68
Gelineau, Joseph, 68
Generation Y, 214
Generation Z, 214
Genocidal war, 168
Ghouse, Mike, 172, 178
Girls Science and Technical College (GGSTC), Dapchi, Yobe State, 202
Goleman, Daniel, 151, 156
Government Girls Secondary School, Chibok, Borno State, 202
Government Science College in Kagara, Niger State, 202
Gowon, Yakubu, 168
Green, Abner, 165, 177
Greenfield University, 202, 218
Gregorian Pontifical Urban University in Rome, 154
Grudin, Robert, 48, 49, 64
Gülen movement, 166
Gulen, Fethullah, 166

H

Haggai Institute for Advanced Leadership Training, 25, 256
Harmony Restoration Theory, 212
Heteroglossic positioning, 196
Holy Apostles' College, Cromwell, Connecticut, USA, vi, 24
Holy Spirit, 76, 78, 241, 252
Howard University School of Divinity, Washington DC, USA, vii, 24, 255
Humanism, 9, 10, 48, 51, 52, 53, 56, 57, 64, 65, 89, 94, 95, 100, 109
Hylomorphism, 90

I

Ichoku, Hyacinth E, 257
Igbokwe, David O., 12, 56, 201, 206, 212, 213, 214, 218, 221, 245
Inazu, John, 164, 165, 166, 178
Intertextuality, 194, 198
Irish Republican Army (IRA), 167

J

Jihadism, 175
John Paul II, 83, 85, 86, 92, 99, 227
Jombadi, Abiodun, 12, 181
Judeo-Christian convictions, 136

K

Kankara, Katsina State, 202
Kant, Immanuel, 91, 107, 109
Katongole, Emmanuel, 138, 140
Kierkegaard, Soren, 83, 84, 86
King Jr., Martin Luther, 85, 185
Kole, JIMOH Anselm, 9, 19
Konrad Adenauer Stiftung Prize for International Development, 25

L

Landry, Carey, 68
Lekki Tollgate Massacre, 145
Logotherapy, 10, 80, 81, 84
Lumen Christi TV, 228, 231

Lux Terra Leadership Foundation, 9, 12, 19, 20, 23, 24, 26, 23, 44, 86, 140, 211, 215, 217, 223, 227, 231, 233, 242, 243, 246, 255, 256, 257

M

Madinah Treaty, 172
Makozi, Fr. Alexius, 23
Marginalization, 201
Mbiti, John, 101, 127, 140, 212, 213, 219
Mental wellbeing, 11, 80, 116, 118
Militancy, 176, 240
Mozambique, 117

N

Nairobi, 20, 23, 110, 228, 249, 255
Nasarawa State University, Keffi, 22, 23, 249
National Democratic Coalition (NADECO), 128
Neo-Platonists, 91
New Testament, 126, 136
Nietzsche, Friedrich, 68
Nigerian civil war, 168
Noogenic neuroses, 80
Northern Ireland, 166, 167, 168, 169, 170, 177, 178
NTA, 228
Nwaoduah, Ifeoma, 77
Nyerere, Julius, 147, 153

O

Obasanjo, Olusegun, 190
Odoemenam, Emmanuel, 13, 235
Odozor, Paulinus, 126, 141
Ojukwu, Odumegwu, 173, 178
Okene, vi, 23, 223

P

Pan-African scholars, 100
Parishioners, 116
Pastoral caregiving, 114

Patito's Gang, 152
Peacebuilding, 159, 160, 161, 166, 170, 171, 175
Pluralism, 164, 178
Pontifical Council for Social Communications, 222
Pope John Paul II, 147
Prophet Elijah, 136
Prophetic imagination, 11, 123, 124, 127, 133, 134, 135, 136, 137, 138, 139
Protestants, 83, 95, 167
Psychospiritual healing, 12, 210, 211, 212, 213, 215
Psycho-Spiritual Institute, 20, 23, 228, 232, 249, 255
Putin, Vladimir, 147
Pythagoras of Samos, 68

Q

Qur'an, 166, 171, 172, 179

R

Reggae, 74, 75, 76, 77, 78, 210
Religious discourse, 181, 182, 183
Renaissance scholars, 48
Ricoeur, Paul, 171, 179
Roman empire, 136
Roosevelt, Franklin Delano, 147
Rousseau, Jean Jacques, 165
Rusk, Tom, 174

S

Saint Augustine's Major Seminary, Jos, 23, 223
Saints Peter and Paul Catholic Major Seminary Bodija, Ibadan,, 23
Sanusi, Lamido, 164, 172, 173, 178
Schopenhauer, Arthur, 68, 86
Schumpeter, Joseph, 147, 156
Seal of confession, 115
Self-Affirmation theory, 79
Sheen, Archbishop Fulton, 149, 230
Sinn Fein, 167

Sociolinguistics, 182
Socrates, 90
South Sudan, 173, 201, 215, 216
St Augustine, 68, 70
St Thomas Aquinas, 68, 91
Stephen, OGBEIYE, 10, 19, 74
Substance Abuse and Mental Health Services Administration, 208, 220

T

Terrorism, 96, 106, 176
Textlinguistics, 182
Tolstoy, Leo, 185
Transparency International, 204, 220
Trauma, 23, 113, 119, 121, 122, 207, 217, 256
Tutu, Desmond, 185

U

United States of America, 23, 68

V

Veritas University, Abuja, 225, 255
Vietnam War, 149

W

Wallace, Paul, 119, 171, 179
West African countries, 201
World Bank, 203, 219

Y

Yom Kippur Arab-Israeli war, 143

www.ingramcontent.com/pod-product-compliance
Lightning Source LLC
Chambersburg PA
CBHW021139230426
43667CB00005B/183